Sunspot Literary Journal

2019

Writing a New World

Sunspot Literary Journal 2019
Volume 1 Issue 4
Writing a New World

Published by Sun Dogs Creations
Changing the World One Book at a Time
Print ISBN: 978-1-951389-00-0
eBook ISBN: 978-1-951389-01-7

Cover Image by Kit Alloway
Cover Design by Angel Leya
Sunspot Logo by Timothy Boardman

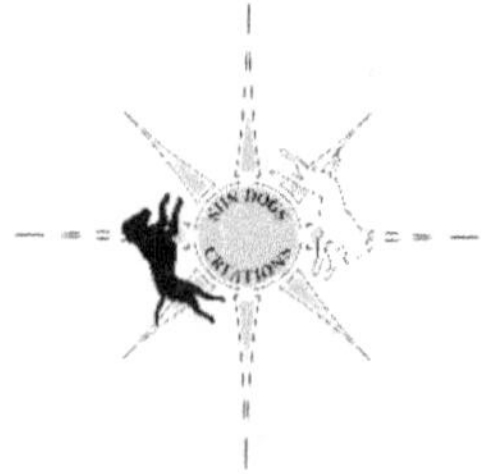

Congratulations to *Sunspot's* Pushcart Prize Nominees

Nina Wilson	"Feeding on Men"
Max Carp	"The First Epistle to Carmelo DeAndre Jones A.K.A. Notorious"
Kayo Chang Black	"The Nikah"
Ron Pullins	"Dada's Home"
Tiffany Promise	"Saint Magpie of Loserville"
Claudine Jacques, Author & Patricia Worth, Translator	"Other People's Land"

SUNSPOT LITERARY JOURNAL
WRITING A NEW WORLD

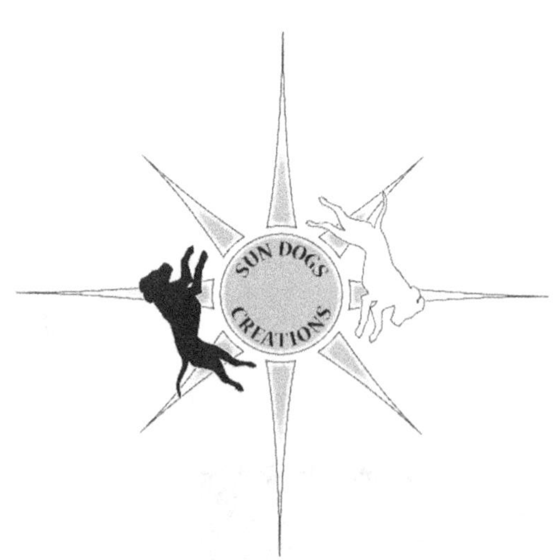

SUN DOGS CREATIONS
CHANGING THE WORLD ONE BOOK AT A TIME

TABLE OF CONTENTS

FEEDING ON MEN

PUSHCART PRIZE NOMINEE

NINA WILSON

Dark calls to Darkness.[1]
Like calls to like.[2]
I who have died a thousand times[3]
am a creature of flickering hope.[4]
Must I tell again the words I know for the ears of men?[5]
Theirs are the voices moving night to morning
Their voices are denials of all dying.[6]
Sometimes words are not enough.[7]

In my blood I heard the world's weeping.[8]
My soul is enslaved so many ways with bolts and bones.[9]
Must I really become dust?[10]
You mocked me, the master of my image.[11]
I do not choose to dream.[12]

For our old Lord lives all alone.[13]
Wherever I wander, wherever I roam.

---

[1] Deirdre Wilson
[2] Edgar Guest
[3] Grace Mansfield
[4] Edgar Guest
[5] Louise Bogan
[6] Alastair Reid
[7] Lemony Snicket
[8] Rachel Korn
[9] H. Marvell
[10] Melech Ravitch
[11] Chaim Grade
[12] Ezra Pound
[13] Ezra Pound

My heart is not here.[14]
I gave you innocence, I gave you hope.
Return you me guilt and despair?[15]
I am tired of kings.[16]
Our priest is the muttering wind.[17]

Why was I forged as a link in this chain?[18]
If I can hear a symphony where tree tops blow[19]
While living beyond the river valley
So quiet green and still[20]
I'll find my place in space as big as a fly[21]
To kiss as winds kiss.[22]

The most dangerous creation of society
Is the man who has nothing to lose.[23]
If you win, you need not explain.
If you lose, you should not be there to explain.[24]

We come from one mind of human kind.[25]
We children are formless—slow to wake.[26]
Our words are flame and ash[27]
Hatred which could destroy so much
Never failed to destroy the man who hated.[28]
So man cried, but with God's voice
And God bled, but with man's blood.[29]

---

[14] Robert Burns
[15] Shelley
[16] Emerson
[17] Shelley
[18] Edith M Roberts
[19] Marian Killroy
[20] Mary Ann Cassiday
[21] Jacob Goldstein
[22] Ezra Pound
[23] James Baldwin
[24] Adolf Hitler
[25] Shelley
[26] Abbie Austan Evans
[27] Grace Mansfield
[28] James Baldwin
[29] Ted Hughes

Black, immortal ink[30]
I ask "what if the wind turned against the rain?"[31]
The wind fills our mouths with strange words.[32]
Great words, you frighten me.[33]
Words, they will tear you limb from limb
In the name of love.[34]
We don't see things as they are
We see them as we are.[35]
Where white is black
And blank is white.[36]

When God, was dying[37]
We listened
We have watched him die a thousand times.[38]
Death times death is being.[39]

The earth has music for those who listen.[40]
We grow never weary for we are old.[41]
Say not 'good night' but in
Some brighter time, bid me 'good morning.'[42]

We are the songs that were never sung.[43]
I, I am a salvaged half star
That managed not to be killed.[44]
But now I feed on men.[45]

---

[30] Silet
[31] Silet
[32] Ezra Pound
[33] Gerard de Nerval
[34] James Baldwin
[35] Anais Nin
[36] Ted Hughes
[37] WS Merwin
[38] Ezra Pound
[39] H. Lievick
[40] George Santayana
[41] Ezra Pound
[42] Anna L. Barbarid
[43] Viola Perty Wange
[44] Jacob Goldstein
[45] Edmund Spenser

THE SHOVELERS

$100 FOR 100 WORDS CONTEST FINALIST

BOB THURBER

The shovelers arrive early, dragging their shadows across the snow. Most are thick-bodied old men with wide shoulders and short beards, but there are a few scraggy, pasty-faced youths among them. Long coats conceal their overalls. Most wear wool caps. All wear boots. The group huddles beside the gravesite to share cigarettes. Soon a truck will arrive, bringing tools. The foreman will hand out pickaxes and shovels then stand back and watch. The foreman is not a shoveler, though he used to be, but so long ago only the fathers of the shovelers remember. Those fathers who were themselves shovelers.

The Power of Freedom

Shaun Haugen

Dear Brittney,

It has been a while since I have written you. In fact it has been since you were in prison that I last wrote. We have texted and talked but nothing endeared like the letters we exchanged then. I believe letters are more adorned than any other form of communication. Letter writing is the most sincere form of writing, and it is only with this sincerity that I can talk about the following events. And it is with honest intentions that I write to you in hopes of easing your apprehensions of what society thinks of you now that you are out. We first met many years ago at a mental health program and since then our paths have crossed an unduly amount. Your presence is with me now as I write; I feel you close to my heart and I address your spirit and character written through words that I hope will touch you. Letters are more real, more genuine, more authentic. They allow me to contemplate and to search for true meaning. This is why I write, to get a sense of you in my mind's eye and to share a piece of my heart that evokes feelings on subject matters that need processing. I want to recall these events, so you know you were and are now, not alone.

I was overcome with joy to see you at the volunteer event It's My Park Day. You looked older since the last time I saw you. That's how you know time has passed. The time I had seen you before was in the Travis County jail, you had recently been booked and were probably waiting to see a judge. I was being transferred. I saw you from across the room as the males were lined up and leaving. I raised my fist in a sign of power but was too afraid to call out your name. I tried then to make a psychic connection with you, but you were staring straight ahead. I knew at that time I had missed you. Your dark brown hair was long, very long, you looked strong, you looked hard, and yet you looked defeated of power. What were you thinking about when you were looking into space? You looked perplexed and angry. These two emotions go together well in jail. There is a lot of time to contemplate for the things we have done, to judge oneself and evaluate one's conscience in order to understand what got us caught up in the first place. It is never the initial act that is the cause for our being put in jail, but a series of events and problems beforehand that cause us to lose our composure and commit a serious offense of power.

I remember your pose, your stature, your sternness. They say prison makes you harder. I know that was the truth for me. You get beaten down by cell blocks and iron doors. The locks are a high-power machine under the force of an apathetically abusive prison guard who has nearly all the power over you. Sometimes the guard would not let us out because they call in a lock down. Sometimes they lock us up from being out of our cells because they call a lock down. Lock downs are only supposed to occur when there is a fight, but this is not always the case, sometimes the guards just like to exercise their power, sometimes they are just trying to control and limit the amount of power an inmate has.

Guard power is supposed to keep us in line. Literally keep us single file when we walk, keep us controlled when we eat, keep us down when we look at them, keep us contraband free when they strip search us to the naked skin. Their faces show helplessness, a nonchalant type of oppression. They are not there to answer questions or be spoken to. There is a form to fill out for that. They are not there to hand out food plates, there is another inmate to do that. Their power is in the uniforms they wear and in the keys that jingle at their hip. Their power is in that key that opens a trap door within the cell door. I used to suck the air's life force in when the current would flow through, after all the miniature traps of each cell were opened. Anything to get on the other side of that cell block. Do you feel me?

They say prison makes you harder, maybe because living on cement surrounded by concrete masonry blocks is a form of cell torture. They use solitary confinement too. Solitary confinement is literally a method of punishment that prunes the synapses in your brain. I had been there too. Only once, I do not know why, I do not remember, I think I flipped off a prison guard and yelled at him up in his face. I was not the violent type, just angry, pissed off. Without self-composure I lacked tolerance power.

I remember walking in line with three other inmates. Walking anywhere out of the cellblock was a form of power. To get to go to the nurses station (where you would be able to see a female inmate), or visit your lawyer (the only person you could see in the flesh from the outside) was a glimpse of life beyond. Going outside the cell and into the halls was power. But an inmate once got ahead of himself by a couple steps and the prison guard tased him from five feet away and he dropped to the floor and convulsed. This was an exercise of power against power. I knew that this was a form of control, prison abuse. Another time a guard told me to behave because I was painting on the window of my cell door with jelly, mustard, and ketchup packets that I had saved up. The guard said the goon squad was going to come in and rough me up. This is a place where power goes unchecked.

Then there were jail visits. Inmates used to be able to see visitors through a window with a phone connecting each side of the window. But they got rid of this method because seeing a visitor through the glass was too much power. Love is power and human heat is power. You could touch your hand to your visitor's hand through the glass and feel their power, the warmth of love. Whoever enforces the rules wanted to stop that and so visitors were now only allowed to visit through a cheap computer screen that came in all pixelated.

I remember once writing to you saying that good people go to jail all the time. It is true, inmates, and nurses, and social workers, and visitors... My letters gave you power, I could see it in your response. I had been there and know what gave me power and I knew what it would take to get you through. Letters helped get me through. Letters with pictures of the outside and words of love. The guards would boast saying, "This is your home now!" But I knew this was not my home, this was a jail and this was not my home. I taped some of my favorite letters to the wall so that I knew where my home was. But I did not decorate, because I knew that this was not my home.

There were four forms of technology that gave me power. The visitors' computer screened monitor, the television, the radio, and the phone. The television was a constant distraction (sometimes you would see an interesting clip or commercial). We were never let out long enough to watch a complete program. Sometimes you would get a cell where you could see the television through the window. But in order to listen to the television you would have to tune in to a special broadcasting station on the radio. The television gave me power under times of extreme duress and desperation. But I would rather use the battery on the radio for music and sports. The radio was my most comforting form of power. I would listen to music, Dodger's baseball games that came on at night and the Catholic station.

These things gave me extreme power over the depression and sorrow I experienced. I would have to count the days that the battery would last in the radio so that I could buy new ones on commissary in order not to waste any commissary money. They would only give you two batteries at a time and you could not store any extra replacements.

Commissary too was a major source of power in the form of energy and relief. You could buy something but only people from outside of prison could put money on your account. This would allow you to buy a calling card. Calls were not free and they charged by the minute (power of the outside influence). This economic source of power was what got me through from day to day. I could buy soda pop and candies and chips and thermal clothes and socks and a phone card and paper and a pen and use them when I felt so sad that I wanted to cut my wrists but didn't have anything sharp enough. So, when I felt so feeble and hopeless I would sustain myself with an item off of commissary. I would eat a Milky Way, or Cheetos and soda, or draw a picture, or warm myself, something, anything to activate the power of dopamine receptors. I would write letters to family and one friend that kept in touch with me. I would write my dreams on paper, I would write my delusions on paper.

Besides books from the library–which caused me extreme gloom because the protagonists were always in a better position than my own, releasing in me power struggle/power dichotomy/power balance/power of comparison where I wanted to be right there with the main character–were the delusions. Delusions are the last form of power that kept me alive. The delusions saved my life and the insanity made it easier to cope because the fantasies were real in my head. I would auditorily hear the voice of Julia, a girl who spoke to me about her time in prison and how she got out. All I really remember was that she was desperately suicidal when she was incarcerated and she would speak to me and tell me there is a better life waiting on the other side. I would hear the voice of India every time the sun beamed through the window in the mornings as I watched its golden light move across the wall. The voice of India called on me to come to this foreign land and I could hear the sounds of a bohemian culture ripe with beauty and imagined it to be some sort of massive holy shrine, a place to go to waiting on the outside.

When you have been ostracized by society you are stripped of all your power as a contributing citizen. You forever look on the outside in, you are labeled, you are indefinitely going to lack the power of exactitude and certainty with an assertiveness that you are doing the right thing. Going through the pen makes you question most of your future decisions for some time. Going through the pen makes you doubt, makes you fearful because you know what punishment is possible and what realities exist away from the confines of a blissfully ignorant community. Societal position will always weigh on you with an informal balance of power. In their eyes you have been rehabilitated or been restored power. But it is not the same. Now you have a more powerful conscience than most others because you have been forever changed by this event of succumbing all your freedoms of power. Now out, you can see the reckless acts and deeds in everyday society, committing both harm and virtue, you see how choice affects others not just oneself. Pain is evident all over the world, but the hardness makes the infliction of pain more tolerable.

I will say that incarceration has made me more pure than I ever thought I would be and I see it in you. Purity is boring though, the sin has been conscientiously cut out not because it is necessarily fire and brimstone, but because it feels better not to feel the guilt and carry that weight. I think most people just want to feel better about themselves and that takes self-discipline, or empowerment. What I'm talking about is purity at heart, what Dali Lama practices. Because purity isn't a constant feeling of bliss, I still get upset sometimes, it is a feeling of steadiness, persistence, and self-control, especially when impure things fall upon you. This is not my philosophy it is simply a way of living. I don't really feel up or down, because emotions should be used sparingly in the moments of most poignant of times or those of tender joyous arousal. Your memory bank is a powerful vault of who you are and I pray that we crack the code upon death and see the beauty and make sense of the shame. I want to know you forever dear friend–infinite power!

When I saw you the first time from being released, at the volunteer event in the Austin park, I saw the soft you, I saw the born again you, I saw the hesitant you, I saw the reformed you. But I also saw the vulnerable you. You looked strong but bewildered, testing the waters, making sure not to upset or disturb the equilibrium of the state of affairs. You fully contributed to societal interaction, not because you wanted to but because you knew it was right. 100%.

Do you think there is some error in love that causes people to break the law? Love might be harder to understand than power. We love for the good and the bad. When we love and don't receive love back this alters our perception of what love is and maybe we find love in the bad, the drugs, the money, the lust, the violence, the hate; we all struggle over our own powers.

Powerless gets tangled up in all that self-destruction, because there are different types of power as I have mentioned, just like there are different types of love. You have learned to love yourself. I see it in you. I don't mean vanity though. See how convoluted love and power can be? All this life seems rooted in pleasure. When you don't feel anything what are you to do? Go back to the habits that make you feel? I want you to remember the past, as difficult as that may be, so you never get lost in that darkness again. And now I ask, what are you going to do with all your newfound power?

When I got out I felt a lot like a disease of society, like I shouldn't be there. Most inmates eventually get cut loose though. The power that society holds over others' past experiences and others' future choices either positioning them or limiting them towards opportunity, that's rank power. But now it has been three years since I was let out (upon understanding that I am now mentally fit) and I have been reminded that this is still the beginning of the rest of my life. Knowing that you have been stripped of almost all power and now have regained your will, you must realize your potential. You are more powerful than most to have survived such administering of incarceration. And, remember too, this is still the beginning of the rest of your life.

All power to you!

With love,

Shaun

No Regrets

Epiphany Ferrell

The Bridesmaid

We've said careless things to each other like "I need you" and "soon" and "together." We've gotten good at pretending.

I could confide in my roommate over honey chamomile tea, but she won't be my roommate much longer. Busy little bee, she is, planning her wedding. She can make almost anything. I helped her decorate some of the dried gourds, which I called "squash" until she corrected me, laughing at my inability to identify objects which to her are common.

She's so sure of her love. She imagines I want what she has. I smile for her and congratulate her decisions. She's adept at planning. Even the color of our bridesmaids' dresses is perfect—shrimp, a weird name for a color, but it brings out the blue of my eyes.

He won't be at her wedding. He isn't in our circle of friends. His wife, though, is the photographer. Who knows what she sees through filters and lenses? I feel his fingers on the soft skin of my back when his wife, the photographer, shooting the wedding-dress-selection party, focuses on me.

I lean toward my roommate, breathing in the lavender of the soap she uses, and look over her seating chart as though where one ought to be placed matters more than where one is.

The Bride

Everyone is excited, my maid of honor most of all. I hope she catches the bouquet. Misery loves company.

He's letting me have my way in everything. It's my big day, he said–and everything should be right, goddamn it, beyond reproach.

How does a woman know the difference between doubt and doom? Doubt is normal. How couldn't it be? Didn't I have doubts when I went off to college? Can't you see the tremor in my passport photo? Didn't I hesitate when I signed my first lease? And that all worked out ok. This will, too. In ten years, I'll look back and think what a silly girl I was.

We will have bright and attractive children, and I will drive a Lexus to soccer practice. It's a life many would envy. I'm an ungrateful woman.

I drove the long way home again today and lingered in the cemetery, reading long-dead names.

I was supposed to finalize my flower selection today. I don't care about the flowers. Rosemary for remembrance, pansies for thoughts, and rue. I forget the others.

The Bridesmaid

Maybe he does mean those words, maybe he does.

The Bride

I had my chance to be an artist, he's right—that year I went to Italy. That year was my opportunity to produce something memorable. He says there are artists and there are people who make pictures. Pictures are nice, it's no shame to make pictures, he says. I took the restoration job he helped me find, and he's right, I was lucky to get it.

Safety, what is wrong with wanting safety? And quality sheets?

The Bridesmaid

I could never tell her this, but I don't like her future husband very much. If I told her I didn't like him, she'd think I was jealous. I wonder what it's like, to be as sure as she is.

She says she admires his strength of will, she says it takes a strong-willed man to hold her interest. She says she is flighty and impractical. These are not things I would say about her. These are not things I have known about her. These are not things I believe about her.

I'm helping her box up her life here, ready for her new life. Her oil paints have gone dry.

The First Epistle to Carmelo DeAndre Jones A.K.A. Notorious

Pushcart Prize Nominee

Single Word Contest Finalist

Max Carp

The First Epistle To
Carmelo DeAndre Jones A.K.A. Notorious

Author: Donny B. *Theme*: Christian Experience *Date of Writing*: c. A.D. 2019

Introduction:
Salutation, 1:1-2

1 DONNY B. BULGER, of Hoboken, New Jersey, a servant of Jesus Christ, to ye who has obtained like precious faith through the righteousness of God and our Savior.
2 Grace be unto ye, bro, and peace be multiplied through the knowledge of God, and of Jesus, Our Lord,

I. Great Christian Virtues, 1:3-8

3 For our gospel came unto ye not in word alone, but also in power and in the Holy Spirit, as ye have full knowledge of the manner of men you and I were back in the day in Atlantic City, wanting of nothing but to get a whoop whoop.
4 And it was written that from faith springeth virtue, and from virtue knowledge, and likewise knowledge giveth birth to self-control and brotherly love.

5 But he that lacketh these latter things, especially as particular to my predicament, of which I am compelled to write to ye, is blind and hath forgotten that his old sins had been purged.
6 Wherefore, I will not be negligent to put ye in remembrance of these things, though ye know some of them and ye may be suspecting of others.
7 Yea, I think it fitting as long as I am in this tabernacle, to stir you up by means of an apology,
8 Knowing that it should serve as instruction to ye, that ye may continue to have faith in our Lord and that your faith be increased in abundance.

II. Conflict of the Spirit with the Old Nature, 2:1-7

2 Now, then, when ye are after the flesh ye do mind the things of the flesh, but when ye are after the Spirit ye mind the things of the Spirit.
2 For to be carnally minded is death, where to be spiritually minded is life and peace.
3 And I know that in my flesh dwelleth no good thing, for the good that I would, I do not, but the evil which I would not, *that* I do.
4 It is no more I that do it, but sin that dwelleth in me that doeth it.
5 And I speak unto ye as unto carnal, even as unto babes in Christ.
6 For whereas there is between us strife and division, are ye not carnal? Am I not likewise carnal? Do we not walk as *men*? Ye tell me, bro.
7 For while one saith, I owe ye nothing; and another, Ye are in my debt; are we not carnal?

III. Donny's willing descent into depravity, 3:1-15

3 Wherefore, I will not be negligent in paying my debts to ye, as I willingly walked after the flesh in the lust of uncleanness and did not settle my accounts.
2 One would be in his right to surmise that ye have tempted me so, not unlike the Serpent, but the sin is mine to bear alone.
3 I was indeed struck by the large gold cross ye carried round your neck, showing ye in that light as a brother in spirit, even though I be a man of the cloth and ye be a lowly pimp of the streets and a cavorter.
4 And that comely c*unt whom ye called by the name of Chocolate Thunder, with the skin that the sun hath looked upon, she did tempt me so with her carnal ways.
5 Verily, I said to her, Thy hair is as a flock of goats, that appear on Mount Tammany,
6 Thy neck is like the Tower of Pisa builded for the motion of thy head, that bringeth to mind a

beloved bird of my youth, the three-toed woodpecker,
7 Thy breasts are like chocolate ice cream cones melting on the Turnpike in mid-July,
8 Ye are indeed a supreme c*unt, no false advertisements, for there is no blemish in thee.
9 And then God gave us up to uncleanness through the lusts of our own hearts, and we did dishonor our bodies between ourselves.
10 And we did serve the creature more than the Creator, and that we did more than once, nay, even more than thrice over.
11 And God gave us up unto vile affections, for Chocolate Thunder did exchange the natural use for that which goes against nature,
12 If ye shall catch my drift.
13 And after our lust organs gave us a baptism of delight, the harlot did make me promise to further remunerate ye in jewels or silver in exchange for working that which is unseemly,
14 But I found myself in the throes of my reprobate mind, and I did make light of that promise whilst I absconded to the nearest parish under the cover of dark and shame.
15 And thus I have remained indebted to ye, my brother in spirit and partner in the carnal, all of these years, even as I forgot not my trespassing.

IV. Progress towards maturity thanks to Alcoholics Anonymous, 4:1-28

4 Yea, it is indeed possible for those who have tasted of the heavenly gifts, and yet have fallen away, to renew them again unto repentance.
2 Although perhaps we are meant to cut to the bone ere the light of redemption illuminates the dark night of the soul.
3 And as surely as the happy hour is long I did hit rock bottom, for whilst wearing my priestly garb I did proceed to retch all over the counter at The Drawn & Quartered Pub (yea, bro, the one downtown).
4 Oh, the depths of my depravity knoweth no bounds! And I looked round me and saw the scorning faces, and thought, why dost thou judge thy brother? Why dost though set at nought thy brother?
5 Brethren, do ye not see, an orphan I was and a plaything for my earthly fathers, and father figures likewise, and my heart was broken long ere I was to attain the stature of a man. Do ye not see that I groan within myself, waiting for the redemption of my body? Do ye not see that my heart's desire is that I might be saved?
6 Verily, soon as the thought entered my mind a mighty man arose from the barstool adjacent to mine and stoodeth there like

a fir tree, nay, like an angel, at my side.
7 He wipedeth the foul fluids off my chin, and his likewise, and suddenly there came a sound from above like a mighty wind and he saith to me, Lookit here, ye ignorant sonofabitch. I cannot promise to fix ye, but I shall help ye be more loving of yourself. I cannot grow for ye, but I shall help ye know a new freedom.
8 Verily, verily, it appeared unto me like cloven tongues as of fire, and I fell to the damp floor and asked "Who art thou, Man?"
9 And the Man saith, I am what I shall be unto ye. In the name of Alcoholics Anonymous I hereby grant ye sponsorship.
10 And I, trembling and astounded, said, "Sponsor, what wilt thou have me to do now?" And He saith unto me, Before the Moon is full in the sky ye shall see me again. And I shall take ye with me then and it shall be told thee what thou must to do.
11 And all the drunks and sundry derelicts at The Drawn & Quartered stood there speechless, seeing the Man but hearing no voice.
12 And for seven days afterward I did lose the function of mine ears, as all I could hear was like the swarming of bees. And neither did I eat nor drink any spirits, bro.
13 That I have recollection of.
14 And on the seventh day Sponsor found me curled up naked like a babe onto the floor of the clergy house, clutching my lust organs, and he laid his hands on me that I might receive back my hearing, and saith to me, Arise and cleanse yourself, ye filthy lout. The AA gang awaits ye.
15 And as I stood bereft of a cutting rejoinder, the Spirit made me go with Him, nothing doubting.
16 Thus began my instruction, and I took fast hold of her and kept her, for she is my life.
17 Day upon day and step upon step I toil on this road, wishing my heart not to fail for fear, and for looking after those vile things which are come upon the earth, but lifting my head up to see redemption draweth nigh.
18 And Sponsor's wise words carry me through. "Keep coming back," He saith unto me, "It works if you work it." And that I do, one day at a time, even as I may bleed out for Him.
19 And it hath come to pass that a year later I find myself at the ninth step, whereby I am to make amends to people I have brought harm to. All but ye I have not been able to reach, for they, as I, are surely keen on covering the shame, so rejoice in receiving this gift of atonement in the name of all whom I have injured.
20 I shall not ask ye for forgiveness, though if forgiveness is

granted me, I shall be pleased and grateful.
21 I only ask that ye accept this jar that ye shall find inside the package along with this epistle, and which requires no explanation other than, yea, it doth indeed contain my lust organs, now forever separated from the corruption of c*unt through lust.
22 For was it not written that if one of thy members offend thee, ye should cast it from thee, lest thy whole body should be cast into hell? Verily, I have made myself eunuch for the kingdom of heaven's sake.
23 Even as I writhe in pain I feel the infection spreading through my body yet I am at peace with my soul and only wish I had made use of a sharper instrument. Be that as it may, I do hope that by the graciousness of yer heart ye might present the family jewels, haha, to Chocolate Thunder for safe-keeping and eternal reminder that salvation is always at hand.
24 Indeed I do now hear the ambulance sirens drawing near, or is it just the bells ringing the end of the world, as the whole creation groaneth and travaileth in pain together with God's children.

Benediction
25 Whilst ye receive this tithe of fleshly mint, I pray ye not omit the weightier matters of the law, mercy and faith.
26 And should ye feel a cry for help arise within ye I shall not be far away to lend a hand, nor would I face ye in judgment.
27 I shall now leave ye with this piece of wisdom, as the infection spreads within my body and yet cleanses my soul, in knowledge that I shall escape the bondage of corruption that is in the world through c*unt and c*untiness likewise.
28 As Sponsor saith, Who art thou that judgest another person without knowing the whole story? Ye may think ye understand, but ye don't. May the grace of our Lord and Sponsor be with ye, bro. Amen.

As a God

$100 for 100 Words Contest Finalist

Mary-Chris Hines

Her son, the monk, black vestments;
In his cell the voices, organ,
Moaning, chanting. He prays to lords
She never read or heard before.
The religious day starts each sunrise,
Services run all night,
His face white beneath the hood,
Eyes focused beyond her.
Mourning, she enters the kitchen,
Pours more coffee, awaits his reckoning.
She loves him as a God
And bows before him, crying.

USETAH' BE PEOPLE

ROEETHYL LUNN

We were familiar with the Chitlin Strut entertainers. They came to town and did their shows in tuxedos and evening gowns which mirrored the air of success. We saw the way they lived and were not envious of them—hobos living out of their own cars. We had Black preachers, teachers and successful farmers—the local Black aristocracy—who separated themselves from us and look down on us with disdain. But we never had access to Blacks at higher levels of success and accomplishment. We didn't have those images to imitate.

We didn't start seeing storied Black people in print until after desegregation happened. The now defunct Dixiecrats was the political party of choice in our state then, and it had instructed local officials to censor any material which promoted integration or otherwise posed a threat to the *Southern way of life.* So when I first started researching Black-owned publications such as *Ebony, Hue,* or *Jet* magazines and saw archived black-and-white, glossed-over images of Eartha Kitts and Josephine Baker being celebrated in France, and Martin Luther King and his wife dressed so elegantly and dancing at his Nobel Peace Prize gala in Sweden, I was astonished. I was surprised to see Black people back in those days living their lives like affluent people do today. I still cannot get myself to believe that even back then some Black people were well educated, lived in nice homes, own their own companies, and actually lived in foreign countries. I was astounded at the great chasm that existed between their lives and the way we had to live our lives in the South. Every time I saw these images, I always found myself thinking or saying out aloud in a dumbfounded stupor, "So *this* is what some Black people were doing while we were picking cotton." How were those people notified? How were they and not us alerted to the fact that the opportunities which they involved themselves in were available to them? How did they know that they could involve themselves in these kinds of endeavors? What gave them privy to do this, and why wasn't all of us, granted such an insight?

Living under the sponsorship of a segregated South and being regulated in every aspect by belittling Jim Crow laws was not only taxing, it was often perilous for a Black person during the early to mid-1900s and before. Members of my family considered ourselves blessed because we had a history of just being mistreated and dismissed, and not counted among the ones that were hanged or executed innocently.

For me personally, I knew that racially based atrocities were out there. I heard when they were publicly recognized or reported in newspapers, but as a child and then as a teenage girl growing up in the 1950s and '60s, the only harsh realities of Jim Crow in which I could be recognized were centered primarily around my family's finances. We were sharecroppers, and my father was basically illiterate. He could write his name and spell out words to read them, but he couldn't count very well. At the end of the year and time for accounts to be settled, he could only trust that the landowner was not taking advantage of him. When my mother suspected that the calculations were wrong, my father didn't have the nerve to confront the landowner, or he didn't trust himself enough to be able to get a job as a day laborer or as a janitor at one of the mills downtown.

I was ashamed and did not want my classmates or teachers in the modern and sanitary school that I attended to know how poorly my family lived. My parents could not afford the twenty cents a day it cost to have my school's hot cafeteria lunch, so I spent the lunch hour in the library reading books and periodicals. Except for electric lights, an electric stove if you were lucky, and an old car or truck, most of the people in my area lived as if we were in the last part of the eighteen century instead of the mid-nineteen hundreds. We had no running water or bathroom in our house. We washed ourselves in tin tubs and used a smelly outhouse, hid ourselves in the woods, or sought out overgrown weeds in fields when we needed to relieve ourselves. There was no money to purchase toilet tissue, sanitary napkins, toothpaste, or hair rollers. We used leaves and corn cobs when we defecated, used tightly wrapped old rags to keep menstrual blood from seeping out of our confined area, rubbed Ivory soap or baking soda on the corner of a wet towel to clean our teeth, and used brown paper bags, torn apart and twisted into individual spiral strips, to roll our hair.

We were grateful to God when desegregation came and lifted Jim Crow's ties.

Factories began hiring Black men and women as full-scale employees, and with these new wages, families were now able to purchase fully constructed, three-bedroom brick homes or partially completed wooden shell ones. We were given a chance to live a better quality of life. We saw ourselves as different people, a people of hope and opportunity. It took decades before we began to see that desegregation, even with its influx of new advantages, was only a pyrrhic victory. For those of us who lived lives before it came, saw and suffered through the costs required to bring it into being, and are still living after it has happened in this "New Day," reflection will help us confess that underneath are elements that should have been hurled away: poverty, ignorance, and social injustice. Thrown out also were elements of Black life that are now needed and much desired. Black people have forgotten how to love and care for each other's wellbeing, have colorful personalities yet sturdy ways, and having the faith-girded, incomprehensibly resourceful, and rebounding character of Black folks that used to be.

Snoot

Our favorite visitation from my mother's people was not a brother of hers, in particular, but a first cousin of hers who everyone called Snoot. Snoot was a football player sized middle-age man. He was tall, dirty red in color, and wild, just like the rest of his family. Everyone loved him because he was quick-witted and knew how to stir up fun. He would always bring my mother some homemade wine when he came, and winked at her when he laughingly told her to "Keep dis to use when ya cook yo' Christmas cakes...Here, let dem chillum taste some...ain't gon hurt 'em." When he would open one of the jars, my parents would allow him to let us taste a little of it. Snoot loved drinking and rabblerousing at all the juke joints he could find, and in the wee hours of the morning when he apparently couldn't find anyone else in Chesterfield, South Carolina to amuse him, he would "suddenly git a hankerin'" to come visit us. We could always hear him coming because every car he seemed to have found always had a loud and ticking sound. No matter what time of night, we would hear his old car, and someone would shout loudly, "Dat's Snoot." We would always wake up grinning. When he was ready to leave, and we were saying goodbye to him, he could make us fall out laughing when he would begin talking to his car. After he got it cranked, and got it running good, he'd ask it, "Where you goin', car? Listen at it, ya'll. That thing talk'n. Listen what it say'n."

Even though Snoot would mouth what the car was supposedly saying, we could hear it ourselves as the motor said, "Ches..ter..field, Ches.. ter..field." We never saw Snoot in the daytime. And the very first boyfriend I ever had looked and acted just like him.

Idel and Her Sisters

The women in my mother's family believed strongly in being caretakers. In that way, they were similar, but in other ways, they were so diverse.

My mother was tall and heavy, but to our puzzlement, my father always called her Slim. When one of her friends discovered she still had a picture of my mother when they were young and showed it to us, I could see that she was beautiful and had been very slim. By the time I came to know her, she was in her middle forties and had suffered through years of taking care of ten living children, burying the children that had aborted themselves before their time was due, performing labor-demanding farm chores, preparing thousands of meals, and having to take the authoritative position in every major decision our father ever made. She was still a handsome woman; but over the years, she had disregarded her physical beauty. The hair that hung to her mid-back on the picture had changed into a mixed gray and black curly fuzz, like Albert Einstein's, and her long bout with asthma and type 2 diabetes left her eyes looking weak on some days.

On the other hand, Lela Mae kept herself up and was always a beautiful woman. She had delicate features, beautiful and well-fitting sundresses and coats, beautifully polished nails, and black silky hair—like a lighter complexion version of Lena Horn. She eventually moved to Maryland and married a man with a well-paying job. Lela Mae always considered my mother as her mother, and in gratitude for my mother's earlier efforts, she alone or she and her husband Bubber were forever taking yearly trips down South to see us in the summer, driving long and spring-colored cars that had rear ends that look like small whales. Lela Mae and her husband never had children, so she scattered her motherly affections on her sisters' children. She sent us clothes regularly and always sent my mother train tickets in late fall—after the summer crops were harvested—for her to come visit her and harvest more clothes or anything else in Lela Mae's house she could bring back home in her large suitcases.

Nellie, my mother's other sister, had a wider face than my mother or Lela Mae. She and all her children look as if they had within their bloodline a Native American or an Asian. She married a widower who had children that was nearly as old as she, and my mother said Nelly addressed her husband, Brooks, as *sir* while they were dating. Nellie wore an apron over her dress every day, and even though she and her husband raised both his children and her and his children, she was a better housekeeper. Her house stayed cleaner and more organized than my mother's. Nellie kept her house dark in summer with shades drawn and screen doors closed. We kept our house wide open in summer, so our house had flytraps and Nellie's didn't. Brooks sheltered her. He insisted on being the only authority figure in their house, and when he died, she had difficulty adjusting. After Brooks died, they had to leave the farm and move into a house near town. Even with the move, she still lived within the same seven-mile radius in the same small, Southern county all of her life. I cannot remember whether she ever even visited other states as my mother did. I know she never went to a doctor until the ambulance attendants took her to one shortly after she died. I know she was a great cook, and the preacher was always at their house for meals, especially in the summer on Sundays because she collected her menus from the fruit trees and the vegetable garden in which she took pride in. I know the children Nellie gave birth to always called her *Miss* all of their lives, as her stepchildren called her. They answered her when she summoned them by saying, "Miss, M'am?" as if they were questioning whether or not she'd even called them. I know Nellie's children also had, back then (and still have now), a habit of holding their syllables longer than others. They always "sang," as the locals call it, when they pronounced their words—which ended up sounding like they were saying, "Mis-ish, Mah-am." Singing some words while speaking is a habit that I sometimes have, along with a lot of my mother's people.

Baltimore

One of the earliest and most confusing memories I can recall from that time period (and the way my people used to be) is getting off a train in Baltimore, and seeing rain mixed with cylinder-shaped pods of ice coming down from the sky. I must have been about five years old at that time. I believe this to be so because I am two years older than my youngest sister, Betty Jean. Betty Jean could not come with us on that trip because my mother had a habit of taking only two of her sturdier-walking younger children with her on her annual trip to visit with Lela Mae.

As we were coming off the train's steps in Baltimore with my mother, I remember her holding my hand tightly and then instructing my next-older sister Lela and me, sternly, not to move an inch. She had to release our hands for a moment to claim and struggle with our large suitcases and then show our tickets to the white man with a cold-looking face. He was dressed in a splendid maroon and black uniform with gold trimmings.

The man frightened me. I stumbled and had a hard time convincing my mother later that I was not being disobedient. I had to let my mother's hand go because the things I was noticing were different up here in Baltimore and frightening. But most of all, the voice—that usually comes from within me and from within other very small children to calm us and reassure us and to help explain the things we could not understand—was being silent. It didn't tell me to not be afraid of cold-face man. It wasn't coming to me to tell me also why the raindrops up North had ice in them, and how the wooden toy soldiers that could only stand in a storefront window during Christmas time back home had somehow in this city managed to come alive enough to step and move his large arms up and down.

Winter, 2019

Except for my cousin, Monk, my sisters Eva, Mildred, and Betty Jean, my baby brother, and the City of Baltimore, everyone and everything else in this narrative is either dead or otherwise gone. The only memories left are always preceded by the caption *How it used to be in the South* or *How Black people used to be* before desegregation came and restructured everything.

Eric Is

Randall Weber-Levine

Eric is a man with unrestricted will. He awakes. He sits in bed struggling to get his mind ready for the day, checks his phone to see a text from Emily, contemplates what to respond, mills about in his underwear. He heads downstairs, puts a cup of coffee on the stove, takes a glance at the morning news on his phone, reaches for a mug. He looks at the cereal selection above his cupboards. He considers the Special K first and then the Cheerios. He thinks for a second. He decides Cheerios.

Eric is a man with restricted will. He goes to work. He checks emails, sits in on a meeting, chats with Greg in the cafeteria, drafts a memo. He walks down the same corridor he walks down every day letting his fingers graze the bumpy wallpaper, ambles into the bathroom taking in the scent of fresh urinal cake, takes a piss, looks up to the heavens as he gets to the end. He stares at his eyes in the mirror questioning whether he actually enjoys his job. He thinks for a second. Without realizing the hands of capitalism that have molded him, he decides he does.

Eric is a simulation yet he doesn't know it. He leaves work. He gets in his green Volvo, turns on the radio, rolls the windows down, listens to "Shattered" by the Rolling Stones. He sings along "laughter, joy, and loneliness and sex and sex and sex and sexxxxxx," feels the summer breeze swinging through the window, bobs his head to the tune, drums on the steering wheel with his right hand slightly off beat. He contemplates changing the radio station. He thinks for a second. The program decides to keep the radio station, and he feels content with what he believes was his decision.

Eric is a simulation and he knows it. He arrives home. He smells the warm scent of his wife's chicken potpie, hugs his children, helps with homework, watches *60 Minutes* with his wife. He gets in bed, feels the satin of his wife's nightgown, rubs his fingertips up and down her spine gently, rests his chin on her head. He deliberates whether he should try to have sex with her or get as much sleep as possible. He thinks for a second. The program decides to have him kiss her passionately, and he accepts the decisions as his own even though he knows it's not.

Eric is both everything and nothing. He smiles. He lies back sated, smells his wife's lavender-scented hair, looks out the window to the stars sitting heavy on the black sky, reflects. He thinks for a second. It doesn't matter who is making the decisions. They are part of him no matter what. Life is short and sweet. And the beauty of it all is not in the decisions.

Eric is happy.

I AM TRYING TO FORGIVE YOU

ZACHARIAH CLAYPOLE WHITE

i am trying to
    forgive you

hope creeps
    hurricane slow
across my hands
    overwhelms
the rivers and levies
of my palms
settles along my wrist

i carry storm
    waters to you
scatter them
    in honey jars
along your window

in every dream
    you throw open the door
smile as thunder enters

/

our fathers speak
in lightning strikes
you tell me of the
    first woman

who
    weighted prayers along her tongue

    and lined your teeth with fireflies

    in the dew-damp grass

//

we test LSD
with inexperience
wrap our hands in sap and wire
plant
        an apple tree
in the crossroads

        i pick the sour fruit
with knives and matchsticks

        you press   a hammer
like weary lips
to my forehead

        yes

        i have seen the angel

        beneath my chair

        she does not speak

        and i do not listen

///

would you understand
greet me
in the cemetery
where our ghosts
have grown haphazard
beneath the honeysuckle

i am trying to forgive you
and yet...
and yet...
and yet...

Cuntaminated

Single Word Contest Finalist

Sharmin Mirman

In a workplace infested with backstabbers and bitches, slime balls and snake oil salesmen–phonies, enablers, liars and cheaters-I was a misfit. This was no place for a woman like me–an introverted introvert empath–Brooklyn transplant–direct, loyal, honest, adaptive. I could be a chameleon and fit in with them–observing the callous-the devious-the wretched imposters-the shrewd-the underhanded manipulators-the planners that got away with all that their power allowed–the actors on the public stage–a cast of villains and opportunists-smiling and playing such sincere characters–so believable–if you only knew! If you saw behind the scenes–if you read their murky auras–if you saw who they were when the cameras weren't on–when the masks came off–when their treacherous malignant hearts beat away their morality–beat away their consciences–beat down whoever got in their way–beat down the truth–the rules-the right way–the decency–the noble–the traditions. They slithered around the halls-cloaked in the rotting husks of decency turned to dust—the facade sloughed off like empty snakeskin-crumbling and scattered like brittle dry leaves at their feet-honor eviscerated from their very souls. The inconsolable ghosts-watch and weep silently-bereft. The halls need sweeping-the halls need sweeping.

They made their plans behind closed doors-a cohort of cunts-consorting, colluding. They hurt good people-stabbed them in the back when nobody was looking-when they could get away with it–and they could-and they did-because of their power–because of their lies-because they had two faces–so much taken! Dispensable disposable employees-discarded like bloody tampons-flushed away with no concern-out of sight–out of mind-forgotten–moving on with no accountability–lacking a true north–a moral compass and the right to ever say my name again.

Dada's Home

Pushcart Prize Nominee

Ron Pullins

Man enters door.

"Hello, dear. I'm home," he says. He sets his briefcase on a table that isn't there and it drops to the floor.

She reads the paper. Not today's, but a paper from some other day, because they don't take the paper anymore. They bought it once. No more. She reads in light from a lamp with tassels. The light shines on her lap filled with news and knitting.

"Pick that up," she says. "You're a pig."

She is not angry. No. She takes up knitting once again. Something red, and narrow, and not too long. The project barely reaches over the basket. A scarf, perhaps, or some part of a scarf. At least part of something red.

He takes off his hat and hangs it on a hook that doesn't exist in a closet that isn't there. "Hard day at the office, let me tell you."

She doesn't acknowledge his unremarkable hat or coat as they drop to the floor. Likewise, he knows how things should be. Gravity, after all, is life.

"This time I'm going to leave your crap on the floor," she says. "Your wrinkled, dirty crap. People will laugh when they see your dirty crap. But I don't care."

Like some red woolen worm, the scarf, or some part of a scarf, or some part of something red, wiggles off her lap and hangs in the air. She knits at the other end.

"I hope they laugh. I'm laughing," she says. But she's not. Not really. She folds her wool, buries her needles and her unfinished scarf, or some part of a scarf, or some part of something red, in a basket and stashes it to the back corner of the chair in which she has been sitting. She stands. She goes to the window, pulls back flimsy curtains that have been waving in the heat that rises from the radiator. She looks out the window for something that isn't there. It has never been. She sighs.

"I say," he says. "The sun is under the yardarm. Time I'd say for a drinky poo. Fix me something, dear," he says as he sits.

"A martini, I suppose," she says.

"Now that is a drink," he says. It always has been.

The ice is there, the shaker, the gin, the glass, and the condiments. She begins to mix and shake.

"You always say that."

"Say what, my dear?" he asks. He finds the paper in her chair, takes it, and shakes it open.

"The yardarm bit. It makes me sick."

"Yes. Join me dear, dear pumpkin doodle, for a drinky poo." By yardarm he earlier implies some geometry of sun and sky, earth and time, light and falling shadow that gives meaning both to time and place.

She understands.

"You drink too much," she says. "Every night you drink, and drink, and drink."

"Yes," he says. "One olive, if you please."

"You say that, too. Night after night. You come home, strip your soul of hat and coat, and say, 'Fix me a drink, one olive.' It makes me sick."

"Yes." The sports pages are buried deep within the print. They are often hard to find. And worn away as old sports are.

"Just one time I'd like to think I'd dare to put in something more than an olive," she says. "An onion, perhaps."

"Yes," he says, and turns to page 3B where a story that has been terminated on 1B is set to resume. "I love our time together, night after night, as you do, dear. Family. Ah, I just say, 'family,' and I feel the bliss."

"One olive, you lush," she says. "I've heard those same things, 'love' and 'family,' a million times."

The martini is ready in its wide brimmed glass with gin filled almost to the flaring brim, one olive, red toothpick, fog on the cool glass. She serves him, then pours one for herself. Sips. Pours.

"Thank you, dear. Come sit with me. Relax. We'll read the news now each to each," he says.

"Where were you all day?" she says. She sits, carefully, so the waves of her martini do not wash over the flare of the glass.

"At work, of course," he says. He sips. His eyelids narrow, but his eyes turn up to heaven. "As I am every day all day as I have been all year for all the years of my life. Doing the same thing. Taking pieces of paper from one pile over here and putting them in another pile over there." He sets his martini down on a table that isn't there and the glass drops to the floor and shatters.

"Your office is closed," she says. She picks up her knitting buried between her and the arm of her chair. She knits. "You were fired. Weeks ago. But you come and go from home, every day, and then come and go from work, like some skunk who comes out at night to dig up worms."

"A skunk?"

"A skunk."

"You've said that before, dear," he says. "The old skunk piece. Many, many times. I long for a new metaphor. 'Skunk' is funny. I don't mean otherwise. Very funny. But it's grubs."

"Grubs?"

"Grubs, not worms," he says. "Skunks dig for grubs. They always have. They always do. Every night. You've told me that story a hundred, hundred times, and every time you're wrong. Every time. 'Worms.' Ha. No, grubs. Now, that's funny."

"Grubs. Worms. Like a skunk, every day, the same thing. You come home. Take off your hat. Take off your coat. Sit in your chair. Say sweet nothings. Then drink, and drink, and read a paper so old it's yellow. You were fired, dear. You have no job, no place to go, except in and out of here. You make me sick." She sips her drink.

He sips his drink. But his glass is gone as well as the martini it once held.

"Yes. Join me, dear, in reading the news. We will endure together this celestial hour when the sun dips beneath the yardarm. Yes, yardarm. You always do. Every night. Can tonight be any different?"

She sets her martini on a table beside her chair which isn't there, and it drops and shatters on the floor. She acknowledges nothing. She knits. The long red scarf, or some part of a scarf, or some part of something red, edges away across the floor.

"Nothing ever changes," she says.

"Your scarf is lovely and grows lovelier."

"Is that this then?"

"And it grows longer."

"And later longer still," she says.

"And what is there to change? And why? Once you know a thing, I say, get comfortable and enjoy it."

"Out there," she says. "Every night...."

"What?"

"I wonder," she says.

"You wonder. Then, that's your curse."

"Here it is so much the same. Hat. Coat. Chairs. Martinis. You. Hat. Coat. Chairs. Martinis. You....."

"Newspaper."

"Newspaper. That might have been interesting for a while. But now I am afraid of it," she says.

"Of out there?"

"Yes. That, too."

"It's pretty much the same. Rise. Go. Paper, paper, paper, paper. Come. Lie. Rise. Go."

"Put on hat," she says.

"Yes."

"Put on coat."

"Yes."

"It makes me wonder," she says.

"I hope I don't sound like a Marxist." He shakes the paper and reads.

"Sometimes, dear. But I don't care." She reaches for her martini which isn't there and sips from a glass she doesn't have. "Thinking. It drags me back to the way things are."

He drops a corner of the paper just a bit and looks at her, with his broad smile and loving eyes. "Now you sound like a Marxist, too." He gently laughs.

The red scarf, or some piece of a scarf, or some piece of something bumps into a wall.

"Did I say they let poor Mattie go?" he says.

"Mattie, indeed," she says. "You say that every day. Poor Mattie. I'm sick and tired of hearing about dear Mattie. It's like you sleep with her."

"Fifteen years she gave the firm. And now they've let her go."

"Your office has been closed for weeks," she says. "Everyone's been let go. That stinking nest where you rats worked is boarded up, and you rats are left to live in parking lots. Where do you go all day?"

"We should go see poor Mattie sometime," he says. "Cheer her up. See how she's getting on."

"All this mooning over Mattie. You should be getting work. You can't go through the motions every day. We have no money. Soon we will be living in the parking lot with all your friends. Soon enough we'll have no food."

"Ah, dinner," he says, and the paper drops to his lap. "What do I smell...."

"Nothing."

"Let me guess. Let me guess."

"You're wrong."

"Roast beef! Of course. Another cut of roasted loin from some rough beast."

"No! No!!" she says. She stabs the wool with her needles, and pulls the endless scarf, or some piece of scarf, or some piece of something red back to her lap and puts it in the basket. "No roast beef. Whatever I fix, you say, 'Roast beef.' 'Roast beef this, roast beef that!' We never have roast beef. I hate roast beef! It makes me want to puke. You and your roast beef fetish. It makes me sick."

"Corn, too, unless my senses deceive me. Creamed, as I like it, I hope. I love a good helping of creamed corn with my roast beef. Fresh from the can."

"And no corn. Corn is pigs' food. You might eat that slop, but it will never pass my lips."

"And do I detect garlic in the air. Tell me, my beloved, it's mashed potatoes and you have fixed them like Aunt Betty does. Roast beef, and corn, and mashed potatoes exactly like Aunt Betty." He closes his eyes. "Perhaps, my little buttercup, before our evening repast, another of your magnificent martinis. With an olive, please to tide me over until I have roast beef."

"Night after night. Dinner after dinner." She stands. She paces. She waves her arms. "You want something more than a wife who cooks, or waits on you, or roasts your beef, or washes your clothes, or picks up the hats you throw on the floor, you pig. You want a machine, that's what you want, a mechanical mother, as you suckle on martinis without end. No wonder you don't touch me anymore." With her back to him, she longs for something outside beyond the window.

"You chill them perfectly, dear," he says. "Always stirring, never shaking."

It is her reflection in the glass she sees, and it's as if it's outside, not in. "You come home, sit and drink until your brain is butter, and whatever you eat you call roast beef. Then you read that paper until you fall asleep. Every day, the same. I want to bite the head off a rat."

"Yes," he says. "The paper. The news. Shall I read to you?"

"The same paper night after night. We've cancelled our subscription. One paper which you read again and again. The same stories over and over about the same sorry people. We have no money for a newer newspaper so we can see how things change. We have no money for food. No money for roast beef. "

He stares into the corner of the room. He dips his brow. "Then, we're not having roast beef for supper?"

"We're not having supper."

"Well, one paper is about the same as another, I say," he says. "Nothing much changes, does it, really? But then again, it's good to know what's going on."

He straightens the paper and reads.

"See?" he continues. "It says people are still getting married. That's good."

"But different names on different days," she says.

"Yes. That's true."

She turns and looks about. "I seem to have finished my drink."

"And mine seems finished as well."

"Another then."

"Indeed," he says. "I'm hoping we have not come to the end of the olives."

"We have a barrel of olives. We always have olives. We measure out our lives in olive pits."

"Good, then," he says. "Then again, I'll have an olive in my drink."

"For me," she says, "I'm thinking onion."

"Onion? Indeed," he says. "Now there's a change."

"Yes, an onion," she says.

"But is it wise to change?" he wonders. "Change can be so dangerous."

"To hell with that."

"With change?"

"With dangers to our lives. To the hell of one day being like another."

"Well, then, yes, yes," he says. "To hell with that I say. Indulge yourself. Give onions there a chance. Live life with vigor. Be fearless facing the unknown."

"Olive for you," she says, preparing their martinis at the bar. "But I will do with onion." She pours the gin and vermouth into the shaker. Then with aplomb she drops an olive in his glass. An onion into hers. And shakes and pours. Then tastes her drink.

"And?" he asks. He has stopped reading, folds the newspaper in his lap and sits motionless.

"Nothing," she says. She shakes her head.

"Nothing?"

"Not at all."

"I supposed as much," he says. "After all, it's no martini."

"It's not?" she asks. "Then what is it?"

"There are those who call such things a Gibson," he says. "You see, the onion changes everything."

She sips her drink. "Yes." She smiles. "It's quite a different thing. I said 'nothing' only because I expected something else. And failing to be what I imagined, I came to think of it as nothing. It has a name. I feel like singing."

"Your scarf...," he says. He looks from her lap across the floor at the red thing she is knitting.

"Yes."

"It's growing longer."

"Than what?"

"Than what it was."

"And when was that?"

"When I came home."

She stops her work and looks herself. "Yes. I suppose that's true."

"It's not much longer, of course," he says. "But it's not the same as what it was."

"No. I suppose not."

"It's what it was only different," he says.

"Like the onion makes the Gibson. The onion changes everything. I don't feel so much like singing."

He reads. She knits. Time passes.

"Someone's worked my puzzle," he says, looking closely at page 13. His eyes are not what they used to be.

"You did that," she says. "Yesterday, I think, or some such day like that. Looking back they are all so much the same. You always work your puzzles. You talk on and on to me about your puzzles. But to me, they are all so much the same. Items that have answers and need answering. I don't care about your puzzles. I have never cared."

"It's a good thing it's not finished. There's still some work to do."

"Then do it, dear. You have time. Perhaps completed you will at last be satisfied."

"There are no pencils," he says, digging in the chair between the cushions and the arms.

The red scarf, or some part of a scarf, or some part of something, has fallen across the floor and wiggles against the wall. It then pushes against the wall and hits the edge of the page and then falls off the page. He has stood and gone to the window where he looks at his reflection in the glass. It's his reflection in the glass he sees, as if he's outside, not in here. With his tongue he laps the olive from his martini.

"We should drive up to the farm again and see Aunt Betty," he says. "Ah, to taste Aunt Betty's garlic potatoes once again. Those memories wash over me like a thousand frightened horses."

"You know nothing about horses, dear."

"Like ten thousand frightened horses wash over me."

"And Aunt Betty is dead. She died years ago. I am not driving up there again and sit while you throw yourself on her grave and cry while your tears wash over the earth that covers her."

"Not all day, of course," he says.

He wipes away a spot on his chin.

"A short visit," he says. "All day would be too long. There can be no such a thing as too much time with Aunt Betty. God love her. I can't wait to have another helping of her garlic mashed potatoes."

"We cannot go on," she says. Her red scarf, or some part of a scarf, or some part of something, has fallen on the reader's feet. The reader pauses, looks down to the feet and sees the whole event. "Go on like this," she says.

"Go on like what?"

"Like you go on to work every day to a job that doesn't exist. Like me not going anywhere, waiting here all day for you, knitting something that has no end, the next stitch like the last. Always hungry. Always angry. Always horny. Hoping a man–a real man–any man–will walk through that door and do something, anything, to me, that hasn't been done a hundred times before. Who will say something, anything, that hasn't been said to me a hundred, hundred times before."

"Of course I have a job, dear. Why else would I go to work every day and until I've bloodied my fingers to the bone?"

She waits. She knits. The red scarf, or some part of a scarf, or some part of something red, grows longer, behind and around the chair in which the reader sits. The reader pauses, looks around to see what surrounds him or her. "I don't know why you go to work when there is no work to go to," she says. "I know no one who does know."

"Well." He fluffs the paper as if he is reordering the news. "I see where the city council has taken up that senior center business again."

"I told you yesterday they are not building the senior center. They cancelled it months ago. Why do you keep harping on the senior center? I'm sick of it."

"I doubt it will pass anyway. Higher taxes, who wants that? Not I," he says. "No. I daresay, let the old and the poor go screw themselves."

"You don't make money anymore," she says. "You don't pay taxes. You have no job. We are the old. We are the poor."

"I am thinking, of course, of quitting that dreadful job, once we have the things we need. Then let the tax man see if he can get blood from a turnip. I should buy a gun and join the revolution."

"You have no blood," she says. "You are a turnip."

"Come sit by me, my pumpkin, and we will watch the sun together sinking into the sea."

"I am no pumpkin," she says. "I will not sit. I've sat all day."

"Relax, and let things flow."

She opens the door and stands in the frame and sees herself in the glass as it rains outside and she looks out. "I want to stand in the rain drenched forest until my clothes are wet and you can see my body underneath. I want to stalk the unknown beasts and bring them unto me."

"We have made it our point in life to live inside this space. To stay dry together in our love. To spend our hours, you and I, in the gentle breeze of passing time. To bare our souls and share our sufferings," he says. "Speaking of which, how was your day?"

"I hunger for wild meat."

"Your scarf is coming along nicely, dear. That's nice. And very sweet."

"To kill the beast is my desire. No cooking, waiting, cleaning up your mess. No scurrying about the dark like a cockroach for your love."

"I see you've finished your Gibson, dear. Did you find the satisfaction that you seek inside the onion?"

"I want to hunt wild cattle, slit their throats with cold steel knives, hang their carcasses by their haunches so they bleed clean, then cut away a bloody rump to feed on...."

"If not, I'll share my olives. I'm sure there's almost still a barrelful."

"I want to harvest mushrooms in the morning in the garden, kill snakes that slither up my legs, pluck apples from the limbs of trees, dig onions and potatoes from the earth. As the sun falls in the west, I want to ward off the evil one who embraces me in the shadows. Then in the gloam, suckle our dear children, rock them into stupor, then set them on the cliffs and give them up to ocean gods."

"But dear, dear, dear," he says. "We have no children."

"The fruit of my body return to the earth, fulfilling my duty to Goddess Death, and sing to Moon as dreams suck us into Sea."

"School lunches," he says, turning the page, and shakes his head. He licks his thumb and turns the page again. "They are serving the same lunches as they served last week. Nothing changes."

She sighs and returns to her basket and to the needles in her basket.

"You haven't fixed dinner, have you?" he asks.

"I feed only demons out of Hell."

"No roast beef awaits me, does it? Nothing from tongue to tail."

"No."

"And, I presume no corn, then, too, creamed or otherwise."

"Are you hungry, dear?"

"Oh, peckish, yes, a bit."

"Then call the children in. They are out back playing. Wash them up and sit them down beside their loving parents."

"I would, my sweet, but we have no children."

"Then, let them stay outside and play in the failing light of day while we linger in the quiet. We will listen while our unborn children scream as beasts from our unburied past scurry out from the dark and tear them asunder. Let the blood of the unborn flow across the land. Let the undead rise and devour their unborn flesh."

"If we had children, dear... Well.... We would have to share what little precious time we have."

"We should strip down to our sweaty meat and share the heat of our burning souls."

"No fire, no heat. We have no fire."

"In the fireplace."

"We have no fireplace."

"Our flesh would melt and fall away from bones." The red scarf, or part of a scarf, or part of something, has twined its way up the reader's legs and tightens. But the reader will stop reading. So close to the end.

"All day I've been thinking about apple crisp," he says. "I'm thinking it would be nice to cap our dinner with just one scoop of apple crisp. Remember how dear Mattie made it? Remember? Oh, poor Mattie. Gone now what? Afer she gave them fifteen years."

"Mattie."

"How I loved her apple crisp."

"It was Aunt Betty's apple crisp."

"Poor Mattie. They let her go, you know. We ought to visit poor Mattie."

"So you can ravish her."

"We might take her some apple crisp."

"There is no apple crisp."

"No." He looks somewhere where there is nothing. Nothing at all. "There never was any apple crisp, now, was there?" He stands and folds his paper carefully and tucks it in his chair.

She pulls the scarf from the reader's legs, from the floor around the reader's feet, back into the page and onto her lap. She folds it in the basket and pins it down with needles.

"It was the onion, wasn't it?" he says.

"We'll start a fire."

"Every night you say, 'We'll start a fire,'" he says. "But we never do. You need a better metaphor, my love. Something new."

"You come home every night, take off your hat and put it on a hook that isn't there, hang your coat on a hangar we do not have, and drink, and drink, and wait for my roast beef, and corn that's creamed or otherwise, and apple crisp. You dream of Aunt Betty's garlic potatoes. You long for children we have given to the beast. You lust for Mattie. Things must change, and so they have. Yes, I'll say the onion has changed everything. It's brought an end to your martini dreams."

"I thought it might be that." He stands. He puts on hat and coat. He picks up his briefcase on the floor. "Or something else that's just like that."

"Some day, my dear," she says before he leaves, knitting a long red scarf, or some part of a scarf, or some part of something red, "we must learn to love again."

"We should have stayed with olives. We have a barrel of olives."

"Some day," she says, looking closely at her knitting, the next stich exactly like the last one, "you will look at me, and see me."

But then he goes.

Then almost as soon as he is gone there comes a knocking at the door.

"I'm home," he says, and enters. Drops the briefcase on the floor. Hangs his hat and coat on hooks that don't exist in a closet that isn't there, and gravity pulls them down to earth.

Love Poem

$100 for 100 Words Contest Winner

Pamela Sumners

Darling, while I was gone for the summer
you heated gas on the stove and burned
down the house, and darling, while I was
gone, you invited a snake pit into the kudzu
and they strangled every last flower we had.
This is what I had heard but when I returned
the house stood true against the falling sky
but one dog was dead and another ripped
in his throat. I know my people always said
you were a little cold-natured for a Southern girl.
It must be those Yankee Calvinist parents you had.

THE NIKAH

PUSHCART PRIZE NOMINEE

KAYO CHANG BLACK

Tears rolled down my powdered face, dampening my makeshift lavender headscarf. I bit my lower lip and cried without making a sound. I could have said no to Gökhan and walked away from the *nikah,* the Islamic wedding ceremony—but my conditioning would not allow it. Growing up in a Taiwanese family, the concept of "losing face" was ingrained in me. I understood how unforgivable it was to humiliate someone in public. I felt compelled to submit to the conditioning that I have willfully fought against my whole life, to maintain my future husband's honor in front of his entire clan. But the obligation to compromise my integrity, whether it was real or imaginary, was crushing me. I hated having to pretend to believe in something to please my future mother-in-law.

Gökhan's mother was a gregarious Turkish woman. Short and squat in stature, she was the matriarch of the family. She had moved to Denmark with her husband in the '70s, and all her children had been born and raised there. However, she held onto the customs from the old country and behaved very much like a traditional Turkish wife and mother. I never saw her without her headscarf, even in the middle of summer. Gökhan's father, on the other hand, had adapted to Denmark. He was a quiet man with a handsome, honest face. He owned a grocery store in the neighborhood, and when he found out that I loved strawberries, he'd bring some back from his store every day during my visit. He was the type who would go with the flow and let his wife take care of all the traditions and rituals.

I had just arrived in Denmark a week earlier and had met Gökhan's family for the first time. We slept in separate beds because his mother thought it was improper for us sleep together until we perform the *nikah.*

That summer, Gökhan and I were in-between places—we had just left Dubai and in the autumn moved to Bahrain where I would start a new job. My new employers instructed me to move to Bahrain alone, or marry Gökhan so I could sponsor his dependent visa. Since we did not want to break up, we decided to elope in Canada. We made a pitstop in Copenhagen on our way to Vancouver to see his parents before we legalized our union.

Even though Gökhan's mother and I did not speak the same language, I wanted her to like me. I understood that the *nikah* was pivotal to his pious mother. I was not against it, but I also did not want to give her the impression that I was willing to convert to Islam. I am proudly secular, which caused major friction when Gökhan and I first started dating.

"If you want to be with me, and be accepted by my family, you will need to convert," he said—it was the only time I remember Gökhan being adamant about anything.

"No." I stared at him as if he had warped into a goat. Converting to Islam was *unthinkable.* Being secular is my mode in life, and I was not willing to change it.

He explained that all I had to do was to pretend, to do it for a show, which was what he had done his whole life. I still refused. He called me spoiled, stubborn and selfish. I cried but persisted. It was a battle of wills that lasted the whole day.

"If you love me, you will accept me for who I am," I argued, my eyes blazing. "You wouldn't ask me to compromise my integrity."

Eventually, I broke him down with a combination of persistence and tears. "You won't need to convert," he said, hugging me. "I will talk to my mother."

It was no surprise that Gökhan yielded—I was the girl who always had her way. "Don't smoke in the mall." Mama used to glare at me when I was on my way out of the house when I was in high school. "Someone might see you."

You don't want me smoking in the mall? I did just that with abandon. Don't want me dating white guys? I did, just to make you cringe. Oh, you would disown me if I got a tattoo? I did, just to test you.

Gökhan was right: I was spoiled. Mama relented, and Gökhan did too.

My initial experience with Islam was when I moved to Dubai for my first job as a librarian, about ten months before meeting Gökhan. My first impression was that it was strict and conservative. I had to abandon wearing skirts to work because it was indecent to show my knees. The religion forbade many things that I enjoyed, such as alcohol and pork. During Ramadan, even non-Muslims could not have a sip of water in public.

However, I kept an open mind. I wanted to be involved with my future husband's traditions.

When Gökhan told me about the *nikah,* I knew nothing about it. He described it as an engagement to tell Allah that he, Gökhan, had chosen me, Kayo, to be his wife. That did not sound awful—it seemed like a symbolic ceremony. I agreed that I was willing to take part in the *nikah,* as long as I did not have to convert to Islam. He talked to his mother who agreed that I would not have to. Overjoyed that her son would no longer live in sin, she invited the whole extended family, prepared an elaborate spread, and summoned the prestigious *imam,* a religious leader, who would officiate the ceremony.

I had no idea what I signed up for.

On the day of the *nikah,* I was in the center of the room wearing an ivory, ankle-length, cotton maxi dress with grey embroidered flowers at the hem. I'd bought the dress a few days before because it was long and covered my legs. However, the top portion was too revealing for Islamic taste, so I wore a grey cardigan, buttoned up all the way, which hid my tattooed arm and immodest cleavage.

Gökhan's three aunts were fussing around me, trying to pin a lavender pashmina over my head as a temporary headscarf. His little sisters, aged eleven and thirteen, whose room had turned into a bridal dressing room, stole curious glances at me. When I returned their stares with grins, they gasped, turned their heads and looked away. His boisterous aunts laughed and chatted in a combination of Turkish and Danish. They clamored and made animated gestures with their hands and clapped as they giggled over some anecdote I couldn't understand. I stood amid this commotion with a dumb smile on my face and nodded my head as Gökhan's only English-speaking aunt asked me if I was doing okay. Despite the chaos in the room, a part of me was having fun, soaking up his aunts' contagious excitement. I felt euphoric and found myself smiling more as time passed. I was putting the finishing touches on my makeup when Gökhan poked his head in the room. "Hey, can I talk to you for a minute in the next room?" he asked in a quiet voice, avoiding my eyes, his thick, dark brows furrowed.

"Is something wrong?" I asked.

How did I, my mother's rebellious and stubborn daughter, end up participating in a *nikah* with a Danish-Turkish guy she had only dated for less than a year? The truth was that the defiant teenager who continually stretched boundaries and pushed her mother's buttons found herself a lost and scared twenty-six-year-old woman in the Middle East.

I was born in Japan to Taiwanese parents and grew up just outside of Vancouver, British Columbia. I always prided myself on being an adaptable third-culture kid—I was fearless and foolish. Fresh out of graduate school, I moved to Dubai to start my first job as a librarian, even though I would not have been able to find the city on an atlas.

When I first got on the transport bus to the terminal of the Dubai International Airport, I burst into tears—the warm and humid air tinged with dust reminded me how far away I was from home. Homesickness was only one of the many challenges I faced in Dubai. For the first month, I tried to get an internet connection in my apartment to stay in touch with my faraway family and friends. I spent all my free time going to Etisalat, the national internet provider. Each time, I spoke to an indifferent woman at the counter who wore a black headscarf and emitted an intense frankincense perfume. Each time, she told me "two weeks, *inshallah.*" Each time, I left the building defeated and depressed. Before I knew any better, I was convinced that '*inshallah*' meant 'go away.' It took over two months for me to have an internet connection at home.

On the weekends, I would roam around the city wide-eyed, trying to absorb this strange, desert landscape filled with glitzy shopping malls and imposing skyscrapers surrounded by endless construction sites. As I walked by in my short-sleeve t-shirt and knee-length skirt, South Asian workers gawked at me with their unblinking, saucer eyes. I ran away to divert their gaze. I was confused, misunderstood, and isolated from everything and everyone I knew.

Within days of arriving in Dubai, I cried on the phone to Mama. After three days of crying, Mama broke down and came for a visit. She cooked for me, helped me settle into my new apartment, and we explored the city together. We shopped in the souk, went dune bashing in the desert, and had afternoon tea at the Burj Al Arab. However, after she left, I was even more homesick and lonely, which drove me to go out to meet new people. Eventually, I made friends with other expatriates, young women close to my age who had also moved to Dubai for their careers. But they did not ease my sense of alone-ness. What I wanted was someone to come home to and wake up next to every morning. Someone who would understand me, someone to go on adventures with, someone who would take me away from this loneliness and despair. After dating Gökhan for a few months, I thought he could be that person.

The truth is, my definition of a good relationship was simplistic and naive. I did not know a thing about a healthy relationship—as a teenager, I watched my parents struggle with their marriage. At the tender age of fifteen, I found out that Baba, my father, had been cheating on Mama.

Baba was a travel guide and was often away from home. At this time, Mama was in her mid-thirties, but she dressed and acted like a much older woman—a dedicated mother whose husband was away for long periods. Since Mama spent her days cleaning and cooking, she paid little attention to her appearance. Her clothing of choice consisted of dowdy, faded sweatsuits. Her world revolved around Baba, my younger brother Davis, and me.

Before school one morning, I was eating my eggs sitting on the high stool next to the kitchen counter when I heard Mama scream Baba's name. I am not sure what business Mama had poking around Baba's black nylon side bag—maybe she was putting something in there, or perhaps she was looking for something for him—either way, she pulled out a love letter in Baba's handwriting, addressed to another woman.

Mama lost her mind with this discovery. She wanted answers. She needed reassurance. She demanded Baba explain himself. He could not. He ran out of the door with his luggage to catch a flight and left behind Mama who had turned into a wailing mess. I do not remember how I got to school that day.

After school, I found Mama standing disheveled in the middle of the kitchen, wearing her frumpy, pale pink cotton nightgown even though it was three o'clock in the afternoon. With tears streaming down her face, she wailed and screamed that she wanted to die. She clutched a crumpled-up letter in one hand and with her other hand, made slashing gestures with a kitchen knife as if she was going to slit her wrist. I was terrified.

Several days later, I came home, and the house was silent. Before this whole fiasco, Mama always had a snack ready by the time I came back from school, like a brothy bowl of Taiwanese-style beef brisket noodle soup, savory braised pork with rice, or flavorful soy-sauce marinated chicken wings. But that day, when I wandered into the kitchen, she wasn't there. She was not at her usual station in front of the stove, engulfed in tantalizing steam coming out of a bubbling pot that she was stirring, telling me that my snack would be ready soon.

The eerie stillness was a stark contrast to what had happened in the kitchen only a few days before. I began to search the house to make sure Mama had not hurt herself. At the entrance to my parents' room, I held my breath, turned the doorknob, pushed open the door and tip-toed inside. I entered the room inundated with the stale, feminine odor of unwashed hair—the scent of desperate sadness. Mama was asleep and snoring loudly even though it was the middle of the afternoon. Her jet-black hair matted on the cream-colored pillowcase. Her usually smooth forehead crinkled with despair—even in her sleep, she was in agony. On the nightstand, I saw bottles of pills. Sleeping pills, seductive, secret sleeping pills that promised peace and a pain-free slumber. I picked up a bottle and rattled it—it was almost empty. I gathered every bottle in sight and took them. I rushed into my bedroom and threw them in the bottom drawer of my nightstand where I had stashed all the knives in the house a few days earlier.

At an impressionable age, I learned that my parents were not gods—they are flawed human beings. Watching my mother's meltdown caused by my father's infidelity, I discovered the dire consequences of being emotionally dependent on a spouse. I told myself back then that I would never want to be in her position. I would never allow my love for a man to turn into ammunition that he could use to maim me. I also learned the importance for a woman to be financially independent—with no economic means, Mama could not leave Baba even if she wanted to. She was an old-school, conventional Asian housewife who had never worked a day outside of her home.

During this dark time, I was overwhelmed and did not know how to process my conflicting emotions. On the one hand, I was angry. How could Baba betray Mama when she dedicated her whole life to us? At the same time, as a Daddy's Girl, I was confused. Baba was indulgent, showering me with his affection and bringing me trinkets from his trips. When I needed help with my chemistry homework, he was attentive and patient. He was also a fun-loving father who took me and Davis snowboarding on the weekends. I knew he loved Davis and me, but his affair broke Mama's heart and spirit. I did not understand how such an amazing father could be such a shitty husband.

I developed unhealthy relationship patterns around this time—I worried about men cheating on me or leaving me, but I also desperately dreaded being alone. My strategy was to become infatuated with a person and charm him with attention—the goal was to have him fall hopelessly in love with me, so he would not cheat or leave. At the same time, because I never wanted to be dependent on a man for my financial well-being, I moved around for my education and career. I never stuck around for anybody.

On the surface, I seemed accomplished and strong, but underneath, I was insecure and lonely. The tough girl who smoked and defied her mother was just a façade. Since having my first boyfriend at seventeen, I had not been single for more than a few months at a time. Like a rabbit chased by an unknown assailant, I dashed from one man to the next, looking for someone to validate me, to calm the nagging, neurotic voice inside my head: *I will never find someone who would love me because I am always "too" something. I am too fat. I am too emotional but also too ambitious. I am too crazy, too free-spirited. I talk too fast, think too much, and have too many feelings. I am too strong-willed, and at the same time, too needy.* Over and over again, this voice whispered to me throughout my relationships. With every failed relationship, it confirmed that I was unlovable.

When I met Gökhan, the nagging voice subsided. We connected on OkCupid and hit it off. He was living in Copenhagen and seemed like a reliable and attentive man. He was cute too, with wavy, dark brown hair, deep-set mahogany eyes, a straight nose, and a thoughtful demeanor. He quieted my anxiety with his patient, soothing voice. We fell asleep talking to each other on Skype many nights. I felt safe having him in my life.

The start of our relationship was a sweet and romantic internet fairy tale that spanned continents. After chatting online for three months, we met in person in Istanbul. On our second night together, Gökhan and I climbed several flights of creaky stairs to reach the rooftop of one of the budget hotels in the Old City. Opening the door to the terrace, the twilight before sunrise greeted us. Gökhan draped a blanket around me when he saw me shivering in the chilly, pre-dawn gust. Then, groping his way in the darkness, he led me to the shabby lounge on the far side of the terrace. We shuffled in our flip-flops, trying to suppress our giddiness. I looked up, enchanted by the constellation above me. As my gaze followed the horizon, I saw the flickering white lights from the boats and ferries dotting the Bosporus, the strait that functions as a border between Asia and Europe. The twilight was misty, making it hard to see where the sky ended and the Bosporus began. Over the railing of the terrace were the muted shadows of the shops, homes, and hotels of Old City, peacefully asleep. All around us, the shutters were drawn, the lights dimmed, and it was quiet. We sat bundled up on the lounge in the blanket. I was snuggling up next to a man whom, days before, I had only seen on a computer screen. He bent down and planted a kiss on my lips.

"Allahu akbar, Allahu akbar, Allahu akbar, Allahu akbar, Ash hadu an la ilaha illal lah..." The *muezzin* called out the first stanza of the haunting and melodic *adhan* at the crack of dawn to remind all Muslims it was time for the opening prayer of the day. My eyes flew open. To my surprise, my surroundings had transformed. Twilight had receded, and in its place, the sun emerged. The first pink and orange rays illuminated the sky, chasing away the stars. I rubbed my eyes as the sunshine warmed my face inviting me to crawl out of the warmth of Gökhan's arms. At dawn, the Bosporus was no longer

shrouded in a mysterious mist–it was bustling with ferries and ships moving back and forth between Asia and Europe. The city below was no longer sleeping; it was buzzing with horns and chatter as people arose from their beds to begin a new day. I was in awe of Istanbul's transformations between night and day. Looking at Gökhan's handsome face on this brand-new day, I kissed him before we headed back to our room. I was happy and in love.

Less than a year later, we faced a conundrum.

I followed Gökhan out of the room and closed the door as his aunts and sisters giggled behind us. We entered the next room, which was his parents' bedroom, and he sat me down on the edge of the bed. Averting my quizzical eyes, Gökhan said, "When the *imam* asked me what your religion was, I couldn't tell him that you didn't have one. So, I told him that you were a Buddhist. He said since you are of the Book—neither Christian nor Jewish, you would need to convert."

His words took a few moments to sink in. Once I understood the gravity of the situation, I started to panic. *Did he know this was going to happen before talking me into the nikah?*

"This is not part of the deal," I shouted, shaking my head. The pins keeping my lavender headscarf in place pricked my scalp. "You promised that I didn't have to convert if I go through the *nikah!*" I glared at him; my gaze was accusatory.

"I'm sorry I didn't know," he muttered, "You don't need to go through with it if you don't want to. It's completely up to you."

Is it up to me? No, it's not up to me! I started to cry. Gökhan looked at me with his thoughtful eyes. He handed me a tissue. I dabbed my eyes, blew my nose, and shed more tears. I looked up and saw myself in his mother's vanity mirror. The rebellious teenager inside me mocked my puffy face and smeared make-up—but I could not stop crying. Gökhan fidgeted next to me, occasionally patting me on the shoulder and repeating the phrase, "You don't have to do this if you don't want to."

Don't you fucking understand? I shouted inside my head. *From now on, we can never be truly happy together. If I don't convert, your mother is going to hate me forever, and I am going to feel lousy making you choose between her and me. If I do convert, I will resent you for as long as I live.* I kept my head bowed because I could not stand looking at the helpless expression on his face. I could not utter a word because if I tried to verbalize my feelings, I would start wailing. The teenaged me would have walked out of the door without looking back.

She was, however, overpowered by the decent Taiwanese daughter who did not want her future husband to lose face.

Looking back, I realized that I put myself in this messy situation on an impulse and through deeply rooted fear. I was in love with the idea of being in love. I also loved having an exotic boyfriend who had grown up in a set of cultures that were vastly unlike mine. I bragged to friends that between the two of us, we had four passports. At the same time, it was my fear of being alone that drove me to this irrational decision to go through with the *nikah*. Knowing what I know now, I should have walked away—coercion and compromised integrity are not a good foundation for marriage. However, as a third culture kid, I have been crossing borders and adapting to different cultures my whole life. I thought I was ready to cross a new one with Gökhan.

I was wrong.

I wept for an eternity, shed enough tears to fill the Bosporus. The girl with a cigarette dangling between her fingers, who dated white boys and covered herself in tattoos had turned into Gökhan's bewildered bride. On the other side of the door, the *imam* was waiting for me to change my wicked, wayward ways and Gökhan's entire clan was expecting us to profess our undying love and commitment to each other. I cried and cried like a lost child. I did not know how to get out of this mess.

Out of nowhere, Gökhan's father walked into the room. He was *smiling*. He closed the door behind him and started *laughing*. I gave him a look of bafflement as he spoke rapidly in Turkish. He paused and nodded his head. Gökhan looked at me and interpreted what his father had said. "My dad said you are taking this whole thing way too seriously."

His father grinned at me, said a few more words and nodded again. Gökhan translated, "He said it's totally fine if you don't want to go through with it. But you could also put on a show by pretending to convert, which would make everybody happy."

I stared at his father, shocked that he had just asked me to go out there and tell a lie in front of the whole family. He chuckled, nodded at Gökhan again and left without saying another word. What his father wanted me to do was what he had done, and what Gökhan had done his whole life: pretend and go through the motions to make peace. I felt defeated and exhausted. I forced my gaze back to Gökhan. *Oh, what I would do just to make this awful situation go away!*

After taking a couple of deep breaths, I asked Gökhan to fetch my makeup bag from the next room. I cleaned my face with a fresh tissue and wiped away the black smudges under my eyes. When Gökhan returned, I smeared on a thick layer of foundation and powdered my face. Then, I applied a sparkly lilac eyeshadow that matched my lavender headscarf. Staring at my reflection in the mirror, I grinned. My eyes were still puffy; my smile looked pathetic but convincing enough to those who did not know me. I smiled again and knew that my mask was secure. I reached for Gökhan's hand and led him out of the room.

Sadly, Mama's rebellious Canadian daughter did not have big enough guns to fight the rebellion in Denmark. After all, I was only one young woman trying to keep my integrity abreast in the face of a conservative, cultural tidal wave.

I followed the *imam*, who told me to repeat the *Shahada*, the Arabic script that would declare me a Muslim. "*La ilaha illa Allah wa-Muhammad rasul Allah*," which translates to "I testify that there is no other God but Allah, and Muhammad is God's messenger." The *imam* said it slowly, pausing after every few syllables to allow time for me to mimic the foreign sounds. Afterward, I signed a piece of paper that the *imam* had prepared. Shortly after, he declared us husband and wife.

From that day, I resented Gökhan. I never forgave him for putting me through a conversion.

Our union did not last long. Four months after we arrived in Bahrain, the Arab Spring broke out. A series of protests swept across the Arab world. In Bahrain, the government cracked down on the demonstrations, which created an environment of fear and uncertainty. The turmoil made it difficult for Gökhan to find work. A year and a half later, when he finally secured a job in Dubai, our marriage crumbled. Instead of following him, I got a job in Hong Kong to be closer to my parents in Taiwan. We broke up.

Many years later, I found the lavender headscarf in my wardrobe. I am still in Hong Kong, but now married to a wonderful man who loves and accepts me just the way I am. Though painful, I learned so much from wearing the headscarf that day, like communicating expectations, and accepting the people I love for who they are, instead of trying to change them. Even though going through the *nikah* and living in Bahrain was challenging, I would not trade that experience for anything else. Without it, I would not have learned how to be in a loving and equal partnership. Taking one last look at the headscarf, I put it in the trash bin. I have come a long way— the girl who smoked in the mall has grown up and learned how to love herself. I now know that I am strong enough to be the person that I have become.

Dear Dorothy

Janette Schafer

A man holds you precious until he has fucked you. You are an emerald or a diamond but his eyes glaze over and soon you are a sheet of glass.

You were a girl from the Midwest and he said you made him lose his brains, turned him into a scarecrow. Then he was a man of tin because you stole his heart: made it tick, made it break. Your ruby shoes left footprints on his psyche.

Then he became a lion, all rage and roar until he fell apart. He told you he was afraid of the dark and of the monkeys swooping in from his past. He could never be brave again if you forgot about him.

So you gave him the key to the City, removed the tinted glasses from his eyes so he could see there was no green, no emeralds; only white.

You let him under your dress, revealed that you were neither witch nor enchantress; only a woman. Then he hid behind a curtain and his hiding made him powerful.

PS: "Fucked" does not equal "precious." This lesson is hard.

Love,

Aunt Em

Suitable Match

$100 for 100 Words Contest Finalist

Melinda Winograd

You're the circus tent sewn
from red and white flags,
erected on a pillar of salt,
while I am the tiger in a box
behind concessions turning
tricks for scraps of praise.

THE CLEANEST ALIMENTACIÓN IN SPAIN

DAVID JOSEPH

The Alimentación was clean. It was clean and neat and had many things that people could buy. The shelves were filled with crisps, ramen noodles, dried cups of soup, and sauces including American ketchup. Inside the refrigerators, cans of soda were stacked neatly above chilled bottles of wine people in Spain prefer to drink on warm days.

Behind the counter, there was a freezer with bags of ice packed perfectly to maximize every inch of the space. In Spain, ice is like gold. It's rare and a real commodity in the Andalusian summers when the air gets thick and the temperatures rise. But the Alimentación was clean, impeccably clean. It was neat and clean, and it was easy to see that everything was in its place.

Each morning, around 9:30, Maria would arrive to open the Alimentación. She would slide the metal garage door upwards, revealing the large, glass window facing the narrow street. She would step through the doorway and enter the darkness that filled the store. She walked inside, placed her shoulder bag behind the counter and took quick visual inventory before even turning on the lights. She moved with purpose and precision. There wasn't a sense of urgency, but Maria possessed an attention to detail that wasn't always apparent with proprietors in Spain. She didn't look hurried, but she proceeded with a certain intent and focus that was undeniable.

Sometimes, when I entered to get a cold drink at the start of the day after an early morning walk, the lights were still off. The door had been opened, but the day's customers had yet to arrive. Maria would smile and say, "Buenas días" warmly. Over time, I had become something of a regular, and it almost seemed that Maria prioritized my arrival at the start of the day, often completing the transaction before even bothering to turn on the lights.

"Uno ochenta" she'd say, and I would have my coins ready. Each time, she accepted my money, she did so with genuine appreciation, and I liked going there. I liked Maria. I liked her store, and it was nice to go there in the morning. She was always friendly, and it was nice to get a drink and be friendly. This was one of the things I liked most about Spain. People were friendly and they made the smallest interactions pleasant.

Like most of the Alimentación owners in Spain, Maria was Chinese. Of course, Maria was just her Spanish name. Chinese business owners often adopted a Spanish name as a way to integrate with the locals, although it is unclear whether this approach was effective. They learned Spanish, and they opened their Alimentacións for business.

One day, I asked my friend Juan why no Spaniards owned or worked at Alimentacións. Although I admired the increased diversity in provincial Spain, I couldn't understand why no Spanish men or women operated these businesses. Juan replied that Alimentacións were open for more hours than other businesses. They began the day earlier, didn't close for siesta, and stayed open later into the evenings. Oh, and they worked Sundays too. "Spaniards" he said "simply aren't willing to work as hard as the Chinese families who immigrate to Spain" and, according to him, this was the reason no Spaniards had Alimentacións. Maria confirmed this work ethic one morning, sharing that her exercise was walking ninety minutes to and from work each day.

During the week, it seemed like Maria was always working in the Alimentación. Sometimes with her husband. Sometimes alone. But she was there from the time the store opened in the morning until long into the night when people stumbled out of tapas bars and through the door in search of a piece of candy, soda, or bottle of water. Regardless of the condition of the patrons, Maria employed the same poise and kindness. This was their business after all. They were in a foreign country, and they worked hard to accommodate the local culture as it was. From day one, they understood they were playing the long game. Trust would take time, but they were willing to do whatever they could to become part of the community.

The Alimentación was on a long street that ran from one area in the center of town to another. It wasn't a main thoroughfare, but it was an effective cut through for taxis and scooters. The street was mostly comprised of tapas bars and panaderias, which made it an attractive place for tourists, locals, and anyone traveling on foot. At the bottom of the street was a handsome plaza with great trees that rose into the sky and surrounded an impressive statue, which was the centerpiece. This allowed people to get something at the Alimentación and then wander down to the plaza with their snack or drink in search of a bench, with the sun streaming in from all corners of the Plaza, enveloping them in a warm embrace. I loved to bring my drink to the Plaza with a book and take up temporary residence on an iron bench. But the Alimentación was well located, surrounded by dozens of apartment buildings and easily available to residents and tourists alike.

In Spain, it isn't uncommon to enter an Alimentación and see the smoke rising to the ceiling or inhale the stale stench of cigarettes permanently suspended in a small space. But Maria never smoked inside her Alimentación. If she smoked at all, she made sure not to do it in her Alimentación, and the air in her store smelled fresh. The floor was also smooth and clean. There were never any signs of footprints that had been there earlier in the day, and Maria made sure of this. She swept and mopped throughout the day to ensure that people felt like they were entering their own home.

On the shelves, the canned food and glass jars were lined up, the labels centered meticulously, facing directly towards the customer. When a customer would come in and handle an item on the shelf, Maria would make note of this. However, in an effort not to embarrass the customer or make them aware of her obsessive nature, she would wait until they had left the store. Then she would peek out from behind the register and walk around the counter. She would calmly turn the label back, centered perfectly once again for the next customer who might enter the store. This did not bother her. It did not bother her that customers handled the items, and it did not bother her to return them to their original position. It was simply what she did, a measure in place to maintain the cleanest Alimentación in town.

On weekends, her son Jorge worked in the store in order to give Maria a break and allow her to spend time with her younger children. During the week, Jorge helped out with his brothers and sisters. He assisted them with their homework, made them dinner, and helped get them off to school. Jorge was 18 now, in his final year of Bachillerato at a colegio near their apartment. He was an excellent student. He was very responsible. And he liked to help his mother. On the weekends, he did this by working at the Alimentación. He was proud of his mother, and he liked the store. It was good to work at the store, and Jorge liked to help his mother out by working there over the weekend.

Jorge could move easily between, Spanish, English, and Chinese. Unlike Maria, who had command of two languages (Chinese/Spanish), Jorge had mastered three. He spoke each of them very well, and this was particularly helpful when interacting with tourists—many of whom came from the United States, United Kingdom, and China. Jorge was now learning German too and already knew a bit of Italian as well. This made him an asset in the store on Saturdays and Sundays when the volume of tourists increased. In fact, some English-speaking expats even waited until the weekend to purchase goods, since they knew Jorge spoke such good English.

Jorge was big for his age. Tall and big. A little overweight and not particularly athletic. He was the kind of kid that might be made fun of even if he wasn't Chinese. Being Chinese in Spain made things even harder, but Jorge was strong. His body was stronger than it might have appeared and his internal fortitude exceeded his physical strength—which was considerable. His family had come to Spain when he was young, and he was used to people rolling their eyes or muttering under their breath.

Moreover, this wasn't simply Spain. This was Granada, in Andalusia, where the tradition is rich, the culture embedded, and the region extraordinarily provincial. Granada was far less diverse than some of the larger cities in Spain. This made things harder for a new family, an immigrant family, particularly when they were taking business from Spaniards in such a difficult economic time. Jorge knew these things. He understood, and he carried this understanding with him when he went to work in the store each weekend. He thought of his place in the world as he walked to the Alimentación, and he wondered if things would always be this way. Times change, he thought. He hoped. Perhaps not as quickly in Spain as some other countries. But nothing stays the same. Not forever. Not the wars or the weather or the wind. Jorge wasn't holding his breath, but he had a degree of faith, and he would be ready when things were different.

One week after the conclusion of Semana Santa, the biggest festival in Granada, Jorge was working at the store on a Sunday when few places were open. A group of four boys his age walked into the Alimentación without giving Jorge so much as an acknowledgement. One boy said something with his hand covering his mouth while the others laughed. Jorge knew they were likely taking about him as he stood quietly by the register. He was a little agitated, but he tried not to show it. He stood up as straight as he possibly could, and he tried to remain composed. It wasn't difficult for Jorge to remain composed. He was mature for his age, and he took it in stride.

"Chino!" said one of the boys. "Mira" as he took his left hand and swept a row of cans off the shelf, sending them tumbling to the floor while the other boys laughed. Jorge moved out calmly from behind the counter and towards the boys. He knew they were trying to rile him up. He stood in front of them inside the store. It was Sunday afternoon. The air was warm and the light was streaming in. The streets were empty. There was nobody else around. It was just him and them, staring, basically eye to eye, although Jorge looked down on them slightly due to his height. The boys smiled, almost taunting Jorge, begging him to take at swing at one of them. Their eyes were laughing, waiting for Jorge to respond, to unleash his emotions, perhaps in the form of a clumsy, awkward punch in their direction.

As Jorge stood there in front of the boys, the long lens of history flashed before his eyes. This history of China. Of Spain. Of his ancestors. From the Great Wall to the Alhambra Palace, where the Moors once reigned supreme before Ferdinand and Isabella conquered southern Spain. He thought of his parents, the distances they had traveled to arrive here, the sacrifices they had made for their children, the dignity with which they carried themselves. He thought of the twelve lions at the Alhambra, carved in perfect stone, frozen for eternity, who could not roar even at the most infuriating moments. He thought of these great lions most of all.

Whenever he was forced to bite his tongue or hold back his fists, he would focus on the lions. These lions had been there for centuries. They were handsome and strong and chiseled in stone. They guarded the beautiful court, looked out from the inside at the surrounding walls, and were confined for eternity with a presence but no voice. Jorge understood what the lions felt. He understood, and he knew what it felt like to be rendered speechless and still need to stand tall.

"Perdone," he said as he moved past the boys only to reach down, pick up the cans, and return them to the shelf. He took his time with each one, reaching down carefully, grabbing them in his hand, and then lining the shelves with the labels facing out just as his mother would.

"Nada?" one of the boys said. "Nada? Claro. Ha-ha."

Jorge felt the anger rush through him from the inside. He wanted to wipe the smiles off their faces. He dreamed of shoving one of them against the wall and telling them not to come back. They had tried to humiliate him, and he felt the desire for some sort of retribution. But he knew that wasn't possible. His family had too much to lose, he thought. There would be other days. There would be other opportunities, different opportunities. But today was not that day. Jorge knew that and had to accept that his yearning for retribution would have to wait.

Jorge had been in Spain for the majority of his life, and in many ways he felt Spanish. He had been to Mirador San Nicolas when young couples would take photos after getting married in a nearby church. He liked to see the couples dressed up, the bride in a flowing white dress against the sprawling, stone backdrop of the Alhambra Palace and the groom dressed smartly in a dark coat alongside her. He had seen Spanish couples there, and he had been there when Chinese couples took photos as well. But he had never seen a couple from different backgrounds. This he had not seen, not once in all his trips to the Mirador with the Alhambra in the distance and the great Sierra Nevada Mountains peering over its ancient shoulder.

Her name was Lucia, and she was in Jorge's class. She was Spanish and she had long, dark hair and eyes that even seemed to shine on the darkest days. They lit up every room she entered, and Jorge waited each morning to see her walk through the door. Like Jorge, Lucia was a very good student, and he often found himself working alongside her at school. Jorge could tell by her eyes that she was kind. She was kind and understanding, and she never pitied him. Most of the Spanish kids at school either pitied him or resented him. Lucia did neither. Outside of class she always said a warm hello, even though her friends moved swiftly past Jorge as if he wasn't there.

By now, he was used to the cold treatment, but Lucia was different. She raised the temperature in the room, and she gave him hope. Hope for Spain. Hope for the future. Hope for himself. They shared a bit of an unspoken language, and Jorge wouldn't dare risk their quiet bond by revealing any deeper feelings he might have had. No, for now this was enough. This was more than enough. To dream was more than enough, and he looked forward to seeing her each day he went to school. He couldn't wait to be welcomed each morning by her smile. It was all that he needed in order to propel him through the rest of the day and into the weekend when he would work in the Alimentación that his mother worked so hard to run all week long.

The boys in the store laughed in his face, collected a few items they wouldn't be paying for, and walked haughtily out the door. I just happened to brush by the boys on the street before I walked in to the Alimentación.

When I walked inside, Jorge had returned to his place behind the counter. He said a respectful hello, and he tried to stand as tall as he was able, gazing cooly, as the boys disappeared down the street. Once they were out of sight and out of earshot, Jorge tallied the items they had stolen on the register. He reached into his pocket, took out his own money, and processed the payment to eliminate any profit loss that would have been evident to his mother.

On Monday morning, Maria entered the Alimentación in the dark as she did at the start of each week. The shelves were lined perfectly, with each label facing out, and there wasn't a speck of dirt on the floor. She checked the register and went over the books. The store had made a handsome profit over the weekend on the heels of the week following Semana Santa. Once again, Jorge had done a fine job. He was a good boy, she thought. He was a good boy and he had done a good job. She turned on the lights, propped open the door, and waited to greet the first customer of the day. Moments later, I walked in.

Life on Earth

Wynne Hungerford

Down a mile-long driveway,
travelled by mother and cub,
through woods singed gold—
a ramshackle farm in need
of seasonal help.

Burrata, sardines, granola.
Meadow, hoop house, gate.

Rusted screws like witch's fingernails
nick my shins and forearms.
Five missing piglets.

Either wandered into the woods
or the boar's belly, who knows.
Grunting fills the night,
and dead chicks fill an empty
feed sack by the door.

The world is full of gross recycling.
All gummy feet and shit-stained
feathers and blue eyelids.

One dies in my hand.
One grows naked.
One drags a flimsy leg.
One hosts mites.
One splits in half and spills wet grain.

What is life worth?
Six dollars per pound,
if you're a pasture-raised chicken.
They have orange eyes
and when I visit at dawn
they drink the dew covering my boots.

I cry and think about all
us animals trying to survive,
then watch the Presidential address on Syria.

There's black cherry yogurt
every morning and mist hugging
each hill like a horny old man.
A rooster humping a Rhode Island Red.
A boy whispering about his little nuts.
An older boy wondering
when he can get a blowjob.

A farmhand mends fence,
asking if I smoke cigars
or cook for the big man
or have sisters that look like me.

Enough.

I am not hay-flavored ice cream.
I am not cream cheese.
I am the bug beating your eardrum.
I am snakeskin in chicken wire.
I am impatient.

Remember Halloween in Missoula?
My friends and I saw a pair of men
dressed as breasts—
their peach-colored shirts
stuffed with pillows.
Plunger nipples.

It's different when you see
a sow's swollen teats gently
swing over seas of mud
and know that's what keeps
a baby from shuddering
and slipping to black.

Halloween night, my friends and I
played guitar and made up songs, singing
with whiskey and space heater,
I don't wanna die,
I don't wanna die.

That's what animals sing
in the long pasture,
hemmed by russet hills.

We catch two sheep in the corner,
carry them upside-down by the legs.
They look like angels, but unholy.

They go to slaughter in a trailer,
and come back as stinking hides.
Unrolled on a pallet and salted,
the sheaths of skin that once
held testicles are emptied out
and swinging like bells.

The cows chime, too,
when they see me.

Shuddering for a quick reprieve
from flies in merciless hoards.
The Angus tagged #5 likes head rubs
and cool evenings when I offer apples,
that thick black and pink tongue
curling around fruit,
slinging saliva missiles.

He avoided slaughter once,
but I don't know how.

The song plays louder
in some heads than others,
escaping through the wet
cave of a mouth
as a long, deep croon.

The song is forecasted into infinity,
with rolling fog
and clear skies
and thunder.

The idea seemed so beautiful then,
when I was twenty-one years old
and trying my hand
at life on Earth.

But now I know the truth—
half the stars above are airplanes
skirting outer space.

What Happened to Mr. Morrissey

Steven B. Rosenfeld

The spring of 1954 was the first time my father let me down. It was all about Mr. Morrissey.

When we arrived in school that May morning, we found a stern-looking grey-haired woman sitting at Mr. Morrissey's old wooden desk. She clasped her hands together on the desktop and looked at us over half-rim glasses.

"Good morning, class," she said without a smile. "I'm Mrs. Davis and I'll be your teacher for the rest of the year."

What happened to Mr. Morrissey?

"I'm not at liberty to say," Mrs. Davis told us, "but we'll do our best to pick up where Mr. Morrissey left off and carry on."

But, of course, we didn't. Yes, Mrs. Davis finished the prescribed sixth grade curriculum, but it wasn't the same. I missed many things about Mr. Morrissey, but what we surely didn't carry on were our derisive parodies of the Army-McCarthy hearings we'd all been watching on TV.

Before the live coverage of the McCarthy hearings, we didn't even have a television in our house. My parents read the *Herald Tribune* and Dorothy Schiff's liberal *New York Post*—my father often reading the *Post* editorials aloud at breakfast—and they listened to the radio, mostly classical music on WQXR and John Cameron Swayze's nightly newscast. We all tuned in to Edward R. Murrow's *Hear It Now* on Friday nights and, just for fun, Jack Benny on Sundays. But no television. My parents said it was a mindless distraction. "Intelligent people like us read books," my father told us, "we don't waste time watching television."

My father's study, just off the entry foyer of our house, was filled with books. Floor-to-ceiling shelves held complete sets of Charles Dickens, Mark Twain, George Eliot, Jane Austen, and much more. I wanted to believe Dad had read most of them. I too read books—the ones my grandmother bought for me, like Illustrated Classics versions of *Treasure Island* and *Tom Sawyer* and scores of Landmark History books—and the more ambitious novels like Jack London's and James Fenimore Cooper's urged on me by Mom, who'd earned her degree in American Literature at Brooklyn College while Dad was overseas in the Army. I also read comic books, although my parents frowned on them. They tolerated Archie and Bugs Bunny, but the ones I really loved, like Superman and Batman and Captain Marvel, were banned from our house. I had to buy them with my allowance, read them in school during recess, and then give them to my friends.

Even with no television at home, I had managed to see a few TV shows. My two best friends from school, chubby, jovial Andy and short, wiry Frank, both had 10" black-and-white TV sets with rabbit-ear antennas. Our three-bedroom colonial in the middle of a tree-lined side street, white with green trim and shutters, was only a few blocks from the old red brick elementary school, so I regularly walked to and from school with Andy, who lived on the next street over in a house very much like ours, except the trim and shutters were black.

When I went to Andy's or Frank's house after school, we'd sit in their living rooms, eat Mallomars and watch Superman or Roy Rogers or Captain Video. Once in a while, the three of us went to the Saturday afternoon movie matinees and then drank chocolate milkshakes at the ice cream parlor next door, although my parents carefully monitored what movies I could see. Westerns with John Wayne and Gene Autry and comedies with Martin & Lewis or Bob Hope and Bing Crosby were OK, but not the science fiction movies I yearned for.

"Those movies are too scary for kids, Davie," my mother proclaimed. "They'll give you nightmares and I don't want you staying awake all night." So I didn't go to movies Andy and Frank were allowed to see, like *The Day the Earth Stood Still* and *The Man from Planet X*.

Although our town was staunchly Republican, I knew my parents were Democrats who were going to vote for Adlai Stevenson in the 1952 election. In fact, Dad was on the local Democratic committee and wore an "All the Way with Adlai" button, although not to work. So, when it was announced in school—I was in fifth grade then—that we'd be let out early the following Wednesday to see General Eisenhower's motorcade come through town, I asked my father if I had to go.

"Yes, you do, Davie" he said. "Forget his politics. The man led our Army that won the war against the Nazis and the Japanese. You may not get another chance to see a true hero." My dad had been in the Army during the war and considered himself a patriot. Tall and imposing, with thick curly hair just beginning to grey at the temples, he was a successful trial lawyer in the city. He wore gold-rimmed glasses, three-piece suits to work and a tan cardigan and slippers at home, where he sometimes worked in his study at night or tinkered at his basement workbench on weekends. When he laughed, there were crow's feet next to his eyes.

Dad was very conscious of his standing in our community. He participated in the campaign to raise funds for a new hospital and bought prominent seats for High Holy Day services at Temple Sinai. And he taught us to "respect the Stars and Stripes," which he said symbolized "our sacred Constitution." So I went with my class to see Eisenhower, and we stood in the crowd on the curb waving the little American flags on wooden sticks they gave us, as Ike's open limousine went by and he waved back.

"Dad, what's an egghead?" I asked one evening during that election season. "A couple of kids at school said our family were 'eggheads' because we're for Stevenson. The way they said it, that didn't sound too good."

"Nonsense," my father said with a laugh that brought out the crow's feet. "An egghead is someone who uses his head. Someone who thinks. That's exactly what we are, and you should be proud of it." He tousled my hair.

I guess it was because we were all eggheads that Dad set very high standards for my sister and me, particularly how we were expected to do in school. If I came home with a 95 on a test, Dad would always ask, "so who got the other five points?" He enforced strict rules of behavior as well, but he rarely lost his temper. The closest he ever came was when I was ten. Andy and I got caught filching candy bars at the A&P, and they called our parents.

That evening, as soon as he got home from work, Dad summoned me to his study, closed the door and pointed to the chair opposite his desk. Then he sat at his desk with his grey-green eyes fixed on me. Before saying anything, he kept looking at me for several minutes, like Superman using his x-ray vision. When he did speak, his voice was calm but more intense than I'd ever heard it.

"Do you know what this is about, David?" he asked, not taking his eyes off me. He always called me "David," not "Davie," when he wanted me to listen carefully.

"Yes, sir," I said, looking at the floor. "What happened at the A&P, I guess."

"What *happened*?" my father said. "You mean what you and your friend Andy *did*, don't you?"

"Well, I mean it was Andy's—" I started to say.

Now he raised his voice and pointed a finger across the desk. "Oh, no. The one thing I won't tolerate is for you to try to blame this on Andy. Listen, son, we all are responsible for our own actions. Something like this most of all. Understand?"

I nodded, still looking down.

"Now I want you to look at me," Dad said, lowering his voice again. I looked up and he met my gaze.

"Your Mom and I didn't raise you to be a thief," he said. "I don't expect *ever* to have to say that again. If I did something like this when I was your age, your grandfather would have taken a belt to me." Dad didn't lift a hand to me. He knew he didn't have to. Instead, my allowance was cut off for a month—which meant no comic books and no movies—and I wasn't allowed to go to Andy's or Frank's house after school "until further notice." So, no TV, either.

But Dad was just as hard on himself. If he lost a client or a motion in court, he would berate himself for days, brooding alone in his study at night with his J&B on the rocks, hiding behind the evening's *New York Post*. I guess if he could have, he would have docked his own allowance, too.

When we started seeing the name Senator Joseph McCarthy in the headlines of *The New York Post* and hearing it on Edward R. Murrow's program, Dad sat us down and explained that McCarthy was spreading "a plague" that could strike anywhere.

"It's not just Communists and liberals he's after," Dad said, "it's also homosexuals."

Homosexuals? That was a word I hadn't ever heard before. "What are homosexuals, Dad?" I asked.

He stopped for a moment, glanced from me to my sister, who was only seven, then looked away. "You don't have to know everything, David," Dad said. "Let's just say that these days everyone has to be careful."

The next morning, on the way to school, I asked Andy if he knew what homosexuals were.

"They're fags, stupid," Andy replied. That wasn't at all helpful, but then Andy started talking about the Knicks game the night before, so that was the end of it.

Dad had said everyone had to be careful, but he was hardly careful when the school board tried to prevent Pete Seeger from giving a concert in the high school auditorium. He and a few others in town formed a committee and spoke out. "Pete Seeger may have leaned pretty far to the left twenty years ago," Dad told us, "but he and Lee Hays stepped up to support the war effort against the

Nazis. Not letting him sing violates the First Amendment right to free speech." In the end, Pete came and we all went to the concert. No one sang along more enthusiastically than my father.

As I turned eleven and started sixth grade in September of 1953, I had come to believe that my father was right about almost everything. But he was wrong when he said I might never see another true hero. When he said that, I hadn't met Mr. Morrissey.

Mr. Morrissey was the first male teacher I ever had, and nothing like the straight-laced middle-age women, some tall and skinny, others short and stout, who'd been my teachers since first grade. Mr. Morrissey was in his late twenties, medium height, with a high forehead and thinning brown hair. He wore horn-rimmed glasses that he was always pushing back up onto the bridge of his nose. Occasionally, a sheepish smile would cross his face when one of us asked a question he didn't know the answer to, or maybe didn't want to answer.

I quickly concluded that Mr. Morrissey was an egghead. He had a soft voice that made you lean in to hear him, which we always did because we didn't want to miss anything he said. When he wrote on the blackboard, it was never rote rules for us to copy into our notebooks because they would be on the test. Instead, he used colored chalk to draw bold diagrams and cartoons that made us laugh, but also helped us remember the lesson—funny little characters in the shape of Vs and Ns and As to depict verbs, nouns and adjectives, or three square-rigged sailing ships gliding across the Atlantic to discover America, or Tom Sawyer whitewashing the fence.

Nor did Mr. Morrissey ever stick entirely to what he was supposed to be teaching. One day, when we were reading *The Count of Monte Cristo*, he suddenly stopped and looked at his chalk drawing of sad-looking, bearded Edmond Dantes behind bars in the Chateau d'If prison, then stared out the window, as if he'd just seen something interesting in the schoolyard.

"You know," he said, "in a way, Edmond Dantes reminds me of one of my heroes, Eugene V. Debs." He turned back to face the class. "Has anyone ever heard of Debs?" None of us had. "He was sent to prison for leading a railway workers' strike in 1894. While he was in prison, he became a socialist and when he got out, he founded the Socialist Party of America and ran for President five times as the Socialist Party candidate." Before we knew it, Mr. Morrissey was explaining what socialism was.

When I told my parents about that class, I learned something about my father and grandfather that I'd never known. Dad's middle initial, E, stood for Eugene, after Debs himself. My grandfather had voted for Debs for President four times!

On the first day of class in September, Mr. Morrissey had told us he was a science fiction fan and urged us to read H.G. Wells, whom he called "the Shakespeare of science fiction," although no Wells novel was on the sixth-grade curriculum. Then, when we studied the great explorers, Mr. Morrissey pulled down a map of the world, but at the same time drew a diagram of the solar system on the blackboard. We knew from fifth grade science how far away the planets were from earth. Tracing the routes of Magellan and Vasco da Gama on the map, he then added a space ship to his drawing on the blackboard. "The distances those guys sailed back in the 16th century were so huge, it was like someone today taking a rocket trip to Jupiter or Mars," he told us. And suddenly we were discussing the feasibility of interplanetary space travel.

During the unit on the American Revolution, when we came to Benedict Arnold, Mr. Morrissey started a class discussion on the meaning of the word "traitor." That led him to Ethel and Julius Rosenberg, who had been executed the previous June for giving atomic secrets to the Russians. "Were the Rosenbergs traitors, like Benedict Arnold?" someone asked.

"Well, if they really did what they were found guilty of, then yes," Mr. Morrissey replied. "But a lot of people think they were framed and rushed to the electric chair as part of this red scare stuff that's sweeping the country."

When I came home and told my parents what Mr. Morrissey had said about the Rosenbergs, Mom suggested inviting him for dinner the following Saturday night. Having unmarried teachers over for dinner was encouraged by the PTA, and Mom thought that, "as a bachelor," Mr. Morrissey might "appreciate a home-cooked meal." Mom liked entertaining, although it wasn't often that Dad was willing to put up with dinner guests. This time, though, Dad agreed that we should invite Mr. Morrissey. He'd said more than once how he worried the Rosenbergs were victims of anti-Semitism, so he was eager to find out if Mr. Morrissey agreed.

As if we were expecting royalty, Mom polished the sterling silverware and took out the gold-edged china my father had shipped home from Japan. She made one of her best dishes, pot roast with mashed potatoes, and apple brown betty with vanilla ice cream for dessert. Once everything was ready to go in the oven, she went out to get her hair done.

That evening, there was lots of conversation, with Mr. Morrissey the center of attention. The grown-ups drank wine and talked about the Rosenbergs, Eisenhower, Pete Seeger and the "Red Scare." At one point, Mr.

Morrissey made me blush by saying what a good student I was. But what I remember most is when he told my mother it was OK for me to see those science fiction movies.

"Most of them have some grounding in scientific fact," Mr. Morrissey said, "they'd be educational for a smart kid like him. For example, my roommate, Matt, who's a real movie buff, says *The Day the Earth Stood Still* is a serious allegory about the threat of nuclear war. David's old enough to understand that, so don't hold back his intellectual curiosity."

When Mr. Morrissey mentioned his roommate, a strange look came over my father's face, and he shot an odd glance across the table at my mother. And Mr. Morrissey showed one of those awkward smiles I'd seen so many times in school. Soon after that, he thanked my parents for a lovely dinner and said it was time for him to go home.

"What a nice man," my mother proclaimed right after Mr. Morrissey left. "He'd make some lucky girl a fine husband." The way she said that, it sounded like she'd been rehearsing the line in her mind for delivery the minute he was out the door.

I'd never thought for a minute about Mr. Morrissey getting married, but for several days after that, I wondered if Mom had fallen in love with him and was going to leave us so she could be that lucky girl. Nothing like that happened, of course, but thanks to Mr. Morrissey, Mom did change her mind about sci-fi films. So that winter, I got to go with Andy and Frank to *Invaders from Mars, It Came from Outer Space,* and my all-time favorite, *War of the Worlds.*

When I told Mr. Morrissey one Monday morning in December that we'd seen *War of the Worlds* the previous Saturday, he reminded me that it was a novel by H.G. Wells. "Fine that you saw the movie," he said, "now get the book and read it." All I had to do was mention that to my mother, and for my birthday she gave me *Seven Novels of H.G. Wells*. By the end of the summer, I'd read them all—starting, of course, with *The War of the Worlds*. In the introduction to the *Seven Novels*, I learned that Wells was a socialist, just like Eugene Debs. But by that time, Mr. Morrissey was gone, so I couldn't tell him.

After the Christmas recess, it didn't take long for Mr. Morrissey to go from Debs and the Rosenbergs to Senator McCarthy. Hardly a day went by when he didn't find some reason to mention McCarthy, tell us how the man had made a career of forcing honest people out of the government and ruining lives based on unsupported accusations, and how "innocent folks all over the country are getting surprise visits from the FBI." He said he was disappointed that President Eisenhower refused to confront McCarthy. "He says he doesn't want to get down in the gutter with that guy," Mr. Morrissey said, "but that's just an excuse. The man who defeated Hitler's army in Normandy could get rid of McCarthy if he wanted to."

Then, in the spring, when McCarthy took on the United States Army in those televised hearings, my parents finally bought a television, which they put in the wood-paneled basement rec room so we all could watch. And Mr. Morrissey came up with the idea of staging our own version of the hearings on Friday afternoons.

Because most of us had been watching the hearings or the nightly news excerpts at home with our parents, we all knew the main cast of characters. Even if we weren't exactly sure who was who and what it was all about, we knew who the bad guys were—not only McCarthy, but also a rodent-like guy named Roy Cohn, and someone called G. David Schine—and that among the good guys were Army Secretary Stevens, the kindly old committee chairman Senator Mundt, and a Boston lawyer named Welch. When Mr. Morrissey handed out the parts, Freddy, the smartest and funniest boy in the class, was chosen to play Roy Cohn, and he cracked us up with his weaselly imitation. Jimmy, whom I'd always thought of as a good basketball player but dumb, nailed it as McCarthy. One of the girls, Vicky, who'd been the star of the school Christmas play, took the part of Schine. She dressed up as a shoeshine boy who kept forgetting what he was supposed to say, including his name—G. David Shoeshine. She was constantly rummaging through her shoeshine box, looking for her lines. My friend Frank was picked to play Welch, but he couldn't compete with Freddy, Jimmy and Vicky's antics. I got the part of Secretary Stevens, but I played him straight. At one point, Freddy, ad-libbing as usual in the role of Roy Cohn, pointed at me and said "I have reason to believe if you look in that guy's desk, you will find RED crayons!"

Mr. Morrissey insisted on being Sen. Mundt, probably so he could keep us from getting totally out of hand. He bought a plastic hammer at Woolworth's so he could gavel the weekly session to a close after half an hour. It was great fun, but Mr. Morrissey made certain that we were learning at the same time. The Friday before the Memorial Day weekend, as our mock hearing wrapped up, I raised my hand.

"Mr. Morrissey," I asked, "are you sure we're OK doing this? I mean, aren't you afraid the FBI might come after *us*?" He started to show one of those half-smiles, as if he didn't want to answer the question, but then he changed his mind.

"No, I'm not worried," he said firmly. "I think Senator McCarthy is finally on the rocks. That guy Welch,"—he pointed to Frank—"has his number." Everyone laughed. "Seriously, though, I hope some Friday soon we'll be able to play our version of The End."

At home, when I told my parents what Mr. Morrissey had said, Dad nodded. "Yes," he said, "Hopefully, McCarthy is nearly through."

Just as Dad and Mr. Morrissey predicted, the hearings soon ended—badly for Senator McCarthy. But the happy ending was never played in our classroom. Jimmy never got to point his finger at Frank and accuse one of his associates of being a Communist, and Frank never got to recite lawyer Welch's famous comeback—"Senator, you've done enough. Have you no sense of decency, sir? At long last, have you left no sense of decency?" By the time that dramatic exchange flashed on our TV screens, Mr. Morrissey had vanished, somber Mrs. Davis was sitting at his desk, and our Friday afternoon lampoons were no more.

The day he disappeared, the talk in the cafeteria, during recess and after school was all about Mr. Morrissey. Each of us had a theory about what had happened to him, although everyone agreed it must have something to do with what we'd been up to on Friday afternoons. The most common opinion was that somebody's parents—there were lots of guesses on whose—had sent an anonymous note to the Board of Ed, just like in *The Count of Monte Cristo*, and gotten him fired. Others thought Mr. Morrissey had received one of those visits from the FBI after all. Maybe the agents had been sent to his house by Roy Cohn, or by Senator McCarthy himself. There was even a view that Mr. Morrissey was in jail, like his hero Eugene Debs. We needed to know the truth and, if Mrs. Davis wasn't at liberty to tell us, we'd get our parents to find out—not only find out what happened to Mr. Morrissey, but bring him back to us.

So when my father came home that evening, I knocked on the door of his study. "Dad, I need to talk to you," I said. "It's about Mr. Morrissey. There was a substitute in class today, and she said she'd be our teacher for the rest of the year."

"Yes, I know," my father replied.

"You know? How?"

"I think all the parents know. We all got phone calls this morning, after you'd left for school."

"So then, you're going to get together, form a committee and get Mr. Morrissey back, right? Like you did last year when they tried to stop Pete Seeger from singing?"

"No, son, it's not the same."

"Why not? You told us then that it was all part of—you called it 'the plague' that Senator McCarthy was spreading." I could feel my blood rising, and my voice went up an octave. I repeated all the schoolyard theories about what might have happened to Mr. Morrissey. "We can't just sit here and let them turn Mr. Morrisey over to the FBI," I pleaded. "You said just last week that McCarthy was good as done for."

"Yes, let's hope that's true," my father said.

"So, what are you afraid of, Dad?"

"Look, Davie," my father said, not looking at me, "this thing with Mr. Morrissey isn't that simple. It's not like it was with Pete Seeger, not at all. Your mother and I just can't do anything this time."

By now, I was in tears. "I don't understand," I said.

He got up from his chair, put his arm around my shoulder and hugged me. "I know you don't. But you will when you're older." And with that, he poured himself a J&B and sat back down to read the *Post*.

Over the next few days, I found out I wasn't alone. Andy, Frank, Freddy, Jimmy, Vicky had all had more or less the same conversations with their parents. We still didn't know what had happened to Mr. Morrissey. All we knew was that we weren't going to get him back.

Gray-haired Mrs. Davis dutifully led us through the rest of *Oliver Twist*, Robert Frost's poems and whatever math and American history we still had to cover to be ready for Junior High School in the fall. And then the school year was over. Andy and Frank left for summer camp, but I wasn't going to camp that year, because Dad had just bought a new '54 Chevrolet Bel Air and we were going to spend six weeks seeing the USA in it, just as Dinah Shore sang on our new TV. The trip was planned for late July, so I had a few weeks to kill on my own. I rode my blue bike around the neighborhood, pretending I was Captain Video and the bike was my spaceship. I shot baskets in the driveway and read H.G. Wells' novels. And I went to the movies. It was the summer of *Creature from the Black Lagoon, Monster from the Ocean Floor, The Stranger from Venus,* and *Riders to the Stars,* and I wanted to see them all.

So there I was by myself one Wednesday afternoon in July, at the air-conditioned Orpheum Theater on Main Street, munching popcorn and riding to the stars. It was an amazing trip. But then, as the lights went on and I got up to leave, I saw something even more amazing. Sitting two rows in front of me was Mr. Morrissey. But he wasn't alone. With him was a young man about his age. I figured it was Matt, the roommate he'd mentioned at dinner that night, but, as the lights went up, I noticed that they had been holding hands during the movie.

"Mr. Morrissey!" I blurted out. He turned around, but as soon as he saw me, he turned back and slumped down in his seat. My first instinct was to come forward to speak with him, but I quickly realized that he was trying to pretend he hadn't seen me. Before I could decide what to do, the two of them got up, hurried down their row in the other direction and left the theater through a side door.

I skipped the milkshake and rushed home to tell my parents what had happened. Luckily, Dad was home early from work and sitting in his study reading the *Post*. I knew I was supposed to knock before disturbing him there, but I was too excited.

"Dad!" I blurted out as I barged in. "Guess who I saw at the movies? Mr. Morrissey! So, he's not in jail after all. He's still in town."

"I remember he told us you were one of his best students," Dad replied. "I'm sure he was pleased to see you."

"Well, that was the weird part," I said. "I know he saw me, but he pretended he didn't. And he and the guy he was with ran out of the theater without talking to me."

"The *guy* he was with?" Dad asked. A strange look crossed his face, like when Mr. Morrissey mentioned his roommate at dinner that night.

"Yes. I guess it was his roommate, but I think I saw them holding hands during the movie."

"Sit down, David," Dad said, folding his newspaper. "Your Mom wanted to tell you this when Mr. Morrissey was fired, but I thought it would be better to wait until you were a little older so you could understand. But you may as well know now."

"Know what?" I asked.

"Do you remember a few months ago when you asked me what homosexuals are?" Dad replied.

"Yes. You wouldn't tell me, so I asked Andy. He said a homosexual is a fag. Some kids in school were calling Adlai Stevenson a fag, so I figured it was like an egghead. Isn't it?"

"No, David, it isn't. First of all, that word, fag, is a horrible insult, and I don't ever want to hear you using it again, OK?"

"OK, but then what's a homosexual?"

"David, it's a man who is attracted to other men, not women. It turns out that's what Mr. Morrissey is, as you saw at the movies today, so the school board had to let him go. They had to do it to protect you and the other boys in the school."

"Protect us? From Mr. Morrissey?" I couldn't believe I was hearing him right.

"Yes, David. Homosexuality just isn't normal, it's unnatural."

"But Dad," I persisted, "you said Senator McCarthy was against homosexuals, and you hated him. You were so glad that he lost at the hearings. So why do you agree with him about this?"

"Look, David, I'm glad we're finally rid of McCarthy, but as I told you, this isn't the same thing. This country isn't ready to accept homosexuals, particularly not as schoolteachers. And, to tell you the truth, neither am I. In fact, if you must know, your mother and I ended up signing the parents' petition to get rid of Mr. Morrissey."

That ended the conversation. For weeks, I was devastated. I couldn't shake the feeling that my father had let me down. But I guess he was right about one thing. Back in 1954, I really was too young to understand. It would be many years before I could fully comprehend what had happened to Mr. Morrissey, and why, fifteen years before Stonewall, my own father had helped to make it happen.

IN THE DARK (A MICRO ESSAY ON *BLACK SAILS'* JAMES FLINT AND THE GAY VILLAIN TROPE)

$100 FOR 100 WORDS CONTEST FINALIST

LORY SAIZ

We're kids who grew with only villains to turn to for a hint of queerness, and then grew older to find ourselves between knowing better, knowing the dark heritage it rests on, and knowing we can't carry the shame of those who have done this to us in their place, knowing that our hearts are still in it and have the right to be. If so, then James Flint is catharsis, he's the gay-coded villain who is actually gay and not actually a villain, just as enraged as us at that unjust distortion, living in the process of undoing it.

BENEFIT OF THE DOUBT

MALLORY CHESSER

The police never admitted how Joel died, but we knew. The body facedown in the ditch was staged. The methamphetamine was injected by force. The bruises on his arms and grass stains on his pants were evidence he had been beaten, not the marks of a stumbling drunk, like the coroner said, and he had been clean for months anyway, had a wife and baby and showered with his wife's soap to show he was faithful. Joel was a good boy, if not a good man, Minnie said—Minnie, my grandmother, who I lived with summers—and I was never afraid of Joel the way I was of his brother, Shane, a born felon with shifty eyes who was not in prison only because he had never been caught. Shane was too smart to get caught, Minnie said, but Joel was not smart because he'd gotten an old egg from his mother. Minnie said Mrs. Turner had Joel after she was forty, and that was only to cover up a tryst with the Methodist preacher. On Mr. Turner's fortieth birthday she had brought him a beer and climbed on. Minnie waited until I was eighteen, on the occasion of Joel's funeral, to tell me his conception story, because it was not for young ears.

I met Joel at Minnie's when I was seven. Minnie was recently widowed and had renewed her zest for life by taking an interest in the lives of others. When she walked over to gossip with Mrs. Turner, I was sent out back with Joel, ten, and Shane, fifteen. I was too young to be of interest to either, but Joel, needing an ally against his brother, recruited me for his team.

While Shane dismantled old army men and crashed his brother's bicycle, Joel took me into the woods, where he had built a clubhouse in the ground using nothing but a shovel and a piece of plywood.

We ate Starburst from a tin and hid in the bunker all afternoon, smothering our giggles any time Shane got close, rolling on the dirt floor with silent laughter when Shane kicked a log and stubbed his toe. After our eyes adjusted to the light, Joel showed me the collection of treasures too precious to keep in his room: an intact-but-battered GI Joe, a collage of candy wrappers, a green glass bottle, and a very dirty rabbit's foot. We hatched plans for revenge that would involve a ransom note, Shane's secret magazines, and a deep pit covered in leaves. We pretended Shane was the sheriff and we were the outlaws.

Nearly four years after Joel died I opened an envelope from Minnie, no letter inside, just a news clipping with a Post-it attached. "This is the man," Minnie wrote, and all that time later, I knew who she meant—the man responsible for Joel's death. The headline read, "Gang Member Indicted in Stabbing Deaths of Three," none of them Joel, but his mother knew this man was the killer, and that had to be enough.

Joel died at twenty-two, barely older than I am now—I will soon surpass him—leaving me a wound in the shape of a question mark. Every time the scab forms some fresh doubt appears, preventing the wound from healing. I have learned to ignore it.

Mr. Turner's grief was enormous, bigger even than he was. And his love was boundless.

How else could he have hauled his weight to work every day, or sweated his life away in the sun, or raised two sons born to cause trouble? Mr. Turner was round and red with a stomach that hung over his pants and a heart so big it could burst. A year after Joel died, it did burst. Within two months Mrs. Turner had married the Methodist preacher, and although both parties were now widowed in the eyes of the law and the Lord, Minnie said that kind of behavior was why she didn't think much of preachers. But Minnie was a good neighbor, a good friend. She had the new couple over for dinner, but she never would call Mrs. Turner by her new last name.

The summer after it happened, Joel's widow started a new job in an office, and I volunteered to watch the baby. Before he even learned to talk, I told him stories about his father, just the good ones, to plant the seeds of memory.

One visit Joel and I watched *Robin Hood: Men in Tights* and decided to rob Shane of his valuables. Most of Shane's floor was covered in junk, a de facto security system against intruders—broken toys he'd stolen from neighborhood kids and board games ripped along the seams, minus their game pieces—but his books were his treasure. While Shane was at the movies—or so he said, before driving away in his mother's car—and Mrs. Turner was playing Bunco with the Ladies Who Lunch—or so she said—we perused Shane's bookshelf at our leisure.

"How about this one?" I asked, picking up a heavy collection of Jack London's greatest works. I was ten years old and imagined teaching the entire neighborhood to read. A thick book, I thought, would be most impressive.

"That's too big," Joel said, "too obvious. Put it back."

Joel pulled down two *Where's Waldo* books and put them in a sack. Whatever he touched, he carefully moved back into place. Being sloppy was how criminals got caught, he said. And it would be more fun if Shane suspected we'd done something but could never prove it. Bored with the books, Joel ducked under the bed. He was gone for a while before coming up for air, hair askew and covered in dust bunnies.

"Jackpot," he said. He was holding an old cigar box—the money, I hoped.

"Open sesame!" I said.

"Wrong movie," Joel answered. He sighed, sending his bangs ceiling high. Inside the box were several marbles, brightly colored. Pennies, nickels, a Sacagawea dollar—surely, Shane had something better. Beneath the pennies, opaque plastic squares, also brightly colored.

"What are these?" I asked, picking up one square and unraveling several, like a roll of stamps. Joel tore one off and snorted his superiority.

"Balloons," he said. "My brother's a clown." Joel ripped the package open and pulled one out, inflated it, and let it go. The balloon motored briefly around the room and sputtered to a stop on an empty pizza box.

My enthusiasm for the mission deflated too. "See you tomorrow at the bunker," I said, leaving Joel and the books behind.

Joel and I grew up close, as close as I could be to someone I only saw a few times a year. His hair got messier, and his brown eyes sparked with schemes. For five years, no matter how long it had been since my last visit, as soon as my parents' car left Minnie's, I could count on Joel's knock at the door. But after Joel hit his middle teens, his family's love for him became more complicated, and our friendship too. He started calling me "bud," and his presence around the homestead became less frequent.

"Jenny, Jenny, Jenny," came Joel's voice in the dark. Dad and I were visiting Minnie for the weekend. Dad wanted to mow her yard, he said, but I knew he was checking up on her. He thought she spent too much time with her gentleman callers. After Dad and Minnie went to sleep, I'd gone into the yard to stretch my legs and kick over crawdad mounds in Minnie's rubber boots. I turned toward the voice and saw Joel standing in the road between the two houses, in the gravel crotch before the driveways became two. He was smoking—a new habit—and I wondered why I hadn't seen him before.

"Nice cancer stick," I said, in my snottiest thirteen-year-old voice.

"Want one?" he asked, walking over. Joel exuded a sour smell that I later recognized as beer.

"No thanks," I said, taking a big step back and fanning my face with my hands. "Weren't you paying attention in health class?"

"Only to the good parts," he said, stepping closer again. "I guess I like to live dangerous."

He was a foot away now, too close, and a little wobbly on his feet. He was taller than before—he dipped his head so we would be eye to eye. The night was cloudy and his whole face was dark, except for his glinting teeth. His eyes lacked their usual sparkle. I shifted uncomfortably.

"You should take better care of yourself," I said. "You stink." His smile collapsed, and the moment ended.

"Sure, bud," he answered. "I'll think about it." He turned toward his house and took a huge drag from the cigarette. "See you tomorrow, maybe."

I gave him a wide berth the rest of the visit, and the next time I saw him, four months later, things were back to normal. I could tell by his scent he was still smoking, but never in front of me. It was a sign of respect, I thought, a sign he knew I was right—maybe he was even trying to quit. I gave him the benefit of the doubt.

One Thanksgiving when he was seventeen, Joel took the turkey, and his brother told us he had stolen it to court some girlfriend or another's mother. Shane loved to be the bearer of bad news, like when he first reported that Joel was hanging out with the roughneck cowboys at school. Now Shane had grown a goatee and was full of talk about moral relativism and other college babble. I carefully avoided him, confining myself to a quiet corner and insinuating I was on my period. Just as Minnie and Mrs. Turner had resolved to serve fried chicken, and as the family began to talk of disowning, there was an eruption of honking outside. We all went to see—me, Minnie, mom and dad, the Turners, the Baptist preacher and his wife—Shane couldn't be bothered—and there was Joel in his truck, with two of his friends in the back unloading a propane tank and a huge pot. Joel winked at me, and I felt a sense of relief. My friend was still my friend; he hadn't gone crooked after all. The boys fried up that turkey in less than an hour.

"I had to steal it," Joel said, "or it wouldn't be a surprise." His words trickled out thick and slow, an accent I was proud to avoid but liked, coming from his mouth.

"That was a good trick," Mrs. Turner answered, dabbing her eyes and looking grateful.

The boys had fireworks, too, and between the grease and explosives, it was the most dangerous Thanksgiving on record. I heard the whizz of the bottle rockets and saw phantom explosions for most of the dark, two-hour ride home.

Another year and Joel would beat up a man who had gotten Joel's ex-girlfriend pregnant but wouldn't do the right thing. Couldn't do the right thing, he said, because he had two pregnant girlfriends and the other was prettier. That fight would earn Joel three months in jail. The first Thanksgiving without Joel was a sad one, and a premonition, Minnie said later, of the years to come.

Joel's wife found the body on her way to work the day after. It was like he had been left for Tina to find, Minnie said—laid carefully in a ditch, on the very shortcut she used to get to her job at the beauty salon. The staging was an act of such cruelty that no twist of fate, no stranger, could be responsible.

His friends admitted they had been with him at the bar, but became evasive when telling what happened after. Somebody's house, razzing because he had to leave early—wife and baby at home—mysterious phone call, punches thrown. These weren't his real friends, Mrs. Turner said, but his prison friends—we knew the kind. He'd been trying to make a clean break, only met them for a drink to smooth things over. I couldn't imagine the person Joel had been, to get where he ended up. Minnie and I were indignant, stunned, crushed. Only later would I find my separate grief.

I had watched teen Joel's comings and goings whenever I was at Minnie's. I imagined the hometown Victory girls must be taken with him, felt proud when he gave me driving lessons, even in his brown and tan truck. We practiced at night sometimes, because Joel said I needed night driving skills. After I turned eighteen, he promised, he would give me drunk driving lessons: "Every girl needs to learn to drive drunk. You never want to be stuck at a party. That's how babies happen. And worse."

I nodded wisely, pretending to understand.

If only the girls at home could see us, sans the beaten-up truck. I wanted to meet some of Joel's hometown girls, and one Friday night in July, as we cruised Timberline Drive, I finally got my wish. They stood in a line outside TCBY, swirling their tongues in frozen yogurt and trying to get picked up. When I pulled up to the light and they saw Joel, each put her best feature on display: left, right, tush, tits.

"Jail bait," Joel said. "One of them got the vice principal fired last year. They found pictures in his desk."

I glanced to the right, curious whether these girls were like the girls that plagued me back home, tall and sculpted and skilled in the application of glitter shadow. We were paused at a light, and I was trying hard not to stall the truck—Joel said that if I learned on a stick I could drive anything—and though I'd be embarrassed by that old Ford back home, I realized those girls couldn't touch me.

"Hey, y'all," I called through Joel's window. "Careful eating ice cream at night. Anything you eat after seven goes straight to your hips."

One of the girls, who was wearing cutoff shorts and blue platform shoes, tottered over, pulling her top down low while she walked.

"Never seen you before," she said. "Are you a friend of Joel's?"

The light had changed and a couple of cars passed us, but it didn't seem to matter. Small town traffic, I wanted to say, take that girl down a few pegs. For Joel's sake, I didn't.

"You better believe it," Joel said. He slapped my knee, leaned away from the window, and pulled his hat down over one eye. He was putting on a show, and I wanted to see if the girl bought it. She rested an arm on the truck and inched forward to give Joel a glimpse down her shirt. There was not much to brag about, but she wasn't wearing a bra. Her tongue slid smoothly through the melting yogurt, and as she flicked at the cone seductively, a sticky pink glob of strawberry cream fell onto her chest.

"Shit!" she said, yanking at her shirt as the glob slithered its way down her front.

"What's wrong, Annie?" her friends called. They formed a hive around her, shooting evil looks at me and dabbing her with napkins. Joel was kicking the dashboard cover as he laughed.

A girl in a green bubble crop top glared at him.

"Hey, Joel, heard your ex-girlfriend's knocked up." She fixed her eyes on me, hoping she'd caught me off guard, waiting for me to blow. I didn't, and she locked in on Joel again.

"But it's not yours," she hissed, like a slow leak. Joel's face went hard.

"Shut up," said the first girl, the one with yogurt tits.

"Yeah," I said stupidly, sounding like I had a concussion. "What would he want with some high school girl anyway?" I hit the gas, wanting to drive off and leave them burning, but the engine sputtered and stalled. Stalled like this stupid town, like these girls with bump-it bangs and little minds. I turned the key again, hearing my humiliation in the turning of the engine. No matter his hurt, Joel came to my rescue.

"I hope you girls get a ride home," he said, just as the engine caught. "Make sure he knows your real age first." Then he leaned over to me, and before we sped off, planted a hot kiss on my cheek, barely catching the corner of my lips. It was my first, and I was stunned. We left in a roar of smoke that I hoped those girls would choke on. I was too embarrassed to look at Joel and watched the girls in the rear view instead. They went back to posing by the curb. Joel turned up AC/DC and sang along. But back in the carport at home, he shut off the music abruptly.

"That baby's not mine, Jennifer." When he called me by my whole name, I knew he was upset. Everyone calls me Jenny.

"I know," I said. "You'd do the right thing." He flinched.

"Whatever I do, I'm stuck." His hand approached my face then pulled back, as if controlled by a string. The kiss was fading now, and if he touched the spot even a little, it would wipe away.

"That's not true," I said. The words bubbled out of me—I registered Joel's anguish only in retrospect, remembering how the skin around his mouth had crumpled like paper.

"You're on to bigger and better things," he said. "I'm just here."

"You'll go to college," I insisted. "Everyone goes to college. Shane did."

"I'm not Shane," Joel said. He hopped down from the truck and bounded toward the trees, a line of pines that started thin but quickly thickened into woods. He disappeared in seconds, and I was the one burning with shame. Not the embarrassment of stalling out the truck, or getting into a catfight at the TCBY, or of receiving a confusing half-kiss from a boy who was like a brother. Apart from the smoking, I had never seen the difference between Joel's life and mine—I was here for the summer, went home every fall. Joel never got to leave and never imagined any different for himself. Visiting Minnie was an escape for me, this small town and these people I wouldn't admit I thought were small. They were living on the margins, working in chemical factories until the day the doctor said they couldn't anymore. They were ignored by FEMA after each storm, roads into town blocked by felled trees so that now the highway passed them by, some still living in temporary trailers, escaping into meth and God and bar fights and things that made headlines in Houston's "stupid criminals" page. I had never seen Joel's confinement, because it wasn't unusual in Victory, where almost everyone was poor, sick, or otherwise stunted. Even Minnie, who seemed invincible, lived on her social security. Joel had graduated that May, and I had been afraid to ask whether he would save up for a while first, or drive thirty minutes to the junior college. It never occurred to me that he wouldn't go to school at all. It was playing at living here, to think I knew about Joel's life. Some friend I was.

We weren't close after that. Joel went to Louisiana for a part-time job cleaning up the coast, and my only updates came from Minnie. Joel had a new girlfriend and a baby on the way.

I passed my driver's test, sent Joel a thank you note. Joel was caught with marijuana, intent to sell. Joel was on probation. My junior year was over, time to get serious about college—no more summers in Victory. Joel was married. Joel was in jail. At the next gathering at Minnie's, I was afraid to look him in the eye. He had let me down.

The last time I saw Joel was at my high school graduation party, a few months before he died. He filled his plate with soft foods—four different kinds of casserole, pinto beans, chopped brisket—and went for a walk, tipping his hat at me on the way out. I decided to follow, feeling guilty for averting my eye when he'd entered the room.

"Where is Tina?" I asked, after catching up to him by the old tree swing.

"At home with the baby. You probably noticed, he's not here either. If he were, you'd hear him."

He meant to be funny, I thought, but I wasn't sure, because he didn't smile. I remembered what Minnie had told me—Joel never smiled since coming back from prison, because he was self-conscious about the teeth he'd lost in a fight. I was glad he kept his mouth closed.

"Congratulations," I said. "I'm sorry I missed the baby shower. And the wedding. Studying hard, you know." I took a big swig of iced tea and splashed it all down my front. "I guess I have a drinking problem."

Joel reached into a pocket and pulled out his handkerchief, and I thought about Yogurt Tits and the night at TCBY. I was debating whether to try a "do you remember?" when Joel extended his arm to give me the handkerchief; the top button of his shirt came undone, revealing a nasty-looking tattoo I was afraid to ask about. In his hurry to cover himself, he dropped brisket on his boot.

"Sorry," I said, and "sorry," he said, and we both looked away.

The funeral was closed casket, family only, but Minnie said we were as good as family, and anyway, we weren't the ones who killed him. The Turners were in the first car with Tina and the baby, and Minnie and I followed right behind in her Buick. Shane brought up the rear— combing the funeral home for something he could sell, Minnie said. Minnie had practically lived with the Turners the past three days, running along behind Mrs. Turner with a box of tissue and providing Mr. Turner with a continuous supply of beer. I arrived three days after the call and pried Minnie away from them. I expressed my condolences but mourned only in private—I'd kept myself away these last few years and barely spoken to Joel when I had come, so what right did I have to grieve?

"The preacher did a good job," Minnie said, once we were driving to the cemetery. "He was respectful to the family but didn't sugarcoat things, didn't try to preach him into heaven."

I felt queasy from all the snot and phlegm I'd swallowed. If I replied to Minnie, I wouldn't be able to control the vomit. I knew Joel wasn't heaven-bound. Not even close.

"I can't believe they're taking us past the spot," Minnie said. "The very spot!"

She slowed the car, holding up the line, but there were only five cars, and I imagined their drivers were gawking too.

"Here? This?" The words choked out of me. Only in Victory could a funeral director be so thoughtless. The driver of the hearse had taken us right past the place Tina found the body, to the left of a bent tree and a telephone pole. As the procession crawled past, I lowered the window and stared into the ditch, like I would find an imprint of Joel's body. Of course I couldn't see anything—it had happened five days ago and rained since. That the evidence could disappear so quickly made the whole thing worse. The dam burst, and my grief broke through. We pulled up to the plot. The preacher's words were brief. I stayed in the car while they lowered the coffin into the ground, watching the scene through angry tears.

Back at Minnie's, I heard the rest of the story. The funeral had to be family only—present company excluded—because of the circumstances. His friends knew something they weren't telling, Minnie said, and maybe worse. They'd certainly been with him an hour before he died, filling him up with beer and whiskey, but they denied the meth, didn't know where he could have gotten that. Tina insisted that Joel hadn't been involved in drugs, using or selling, not since she'd caught him two years ago and cleaned him up. The stint in prison was a fluke. He was through with that mess, and he'd never have been friends with them in the first place, but for his own safety. He was getting out. To honor his memory, we should give him the benefit of the doubt. Family forgives, Minnie said, but people like that don't.

Friends could be murderers. A spouse could love you and cheat. Someone could be family and not family, your brother and your first love, a criminal and a gentleman. The police, the coroner, all were afraid to name Joel's death for what it was. The family kept their eyes on the news, looking for a sign. I was skeptical. I kept my eyes on Minnie, hoping to understand.

It was my first semester of college, and for the first time in memory, I hadn't gone to Minnie's for Thanksgiving—I was studying, I told my family; the airfare, I said. As it turned out, I would bomb those finals, cry my way into passing algebra and biology. I was back in my room after a cafeteria-style Thanksgiving. I missed Minnie's cooking. My roommate and most of the floor had gone home, turning the hall into a cold, fluorescent tomb. The ring was harsh and explosive.

"Hello?" I said into the phone. "Hello?" On the line was a heavy breather—probably some pervert who had called the same dorm room for years, lusting after the dulcet sound of coeds. I was surprised to hear my name.

"Jenny? Jenny?" Minnie had never sounded so old, or so little like herself. "Are you sitting down? Is there someone with you?"

I wasn't sitting down, and I refused to. Her tone warned me to prepare for flight.

"You need to come here," Minnie said. "It's Joel."

I felt cold in my arms; I couldn't hear Minnie's voice over the buzzing in my head.

"What do you mean?" I finally said.

"They found him by the road. They're not sure what happened. Not a car accident."

"You're not making any sense." The Joel she was talking about was not the Joel I knew, the boy in the bunker, my friend under the bed. Not the man who had given me his handkerchief.

"He was so young," Minnie said, in almost a whimper. "He was a good boy." There was a pleading note in her voice. If I agreed with her, it would be true.

Whiskey Mermaid

$100 for 100 Words Contest Finalist

AD Conner

When I lived with my parents in the shotgun house, I'd hide in their bathroom and pretend to be a mermaid stranded in a stranger's tub. In the living room, they'd drown out life with glass bottles and loud music. I'd bargain: God, make them normal, and I'll never ask to be a mermaid again. I have my own family now, but in the bathroom, I crawl into the bottle hidden under the sink, searching for normal. I drink my way out and find the toilet. I'm a flushed goldfish spinning down, praying: let me live with the mermaids.

Saint Magpie of Loserville

Pushcart Prize Nominee

Tiffany Promise

I like sleeping in Wal-Mart parking lots because they have spaceship-sized fluorescents that deter rapists, junkies, and hobos. I don't consider myself a hobo since I have a car, though I'm not too uppity to tangle with a hunky one if he has black enough hair or lungs.

My car's name is Ian, after a sexy, goth boy who was a couple years ahead of me back at Summit High (A.K.A. Slum-it High). Ian always had CD's, cigarettes, and mice in his trench coat pocket. I almost failed Biology because I spent the whole class daydreaming about climbing deep into that pocket: nuzzling up close to Ian's favorite stuff, turning myself into something sacred, something necessary, something that he'd never be able to live without.

The less attention he paid me, the more I pined; and unfortunately, I can count on my hands just how many times he let his baby browns pause on mine. I attributed it to his depression or his always being stoned. But really, I just hoped he was shy, and someday we could be shy together—far, far away from my whiskey-pickled Daddy and his punch-drunk knuckles and whatever Ian's slovenly excuse for a home-life was that forced him into smoking a pack of Marlboros every day and drawing pentagrams all over his backpack.

Five years after leaving Slum-It High, I'm still hoping with all my might that our paths will cross again someday; that I'll get to kiss him this time, maybe even fuck him. I especially want to do it in the back of my car. Ian inside of me while we're both inside of Ian—that kinda shit usually only happens on TV. *Serendipitous,* I think to myself, whenever I imagine us banging away in my backseat. I'm not quite sure if that's the right word, but it sounds sexy and slithery and filled with magic.

It's unlikely that I'll run into Ian any time soon though; I'm much too busy Losing. As my tires criss-cross state lines—from one side of the country to the other—I'm laboriously laying to waste all the bits and pieces of my body that were busted-up by Daddy. I already tossed a coffee-can filled with scabs behind a washboard factory outside of Columbus; dropped some molars into a wishing well in Gainesville; and buried a couple of petal-shaped fingernails in a donut-shop dumpster near Gary. I've still got a ways to go, but by the time I'm through, there won't be a speck of Daddy left in my blood.

This morning, while I was rummaging in my trunk for clean-ish socks, a bearded guy nodded at me as he walked by. Since a girl can't live on hope and good manners alone, I took his nod as encouragement to hit him up for the usual: a little change, a smoke, half of his BBQ sammie, a roll of toilet paper, whatevs.

Beardy surprised me by pulling a box of donuts out of his Walmart bag. I figured I was really pushing my luck, but I asked for some milk or OJ to wash them down with anyway; either would do, I'm not picky. As he abracadabraed a carton of Vitamin D, I spread a quilt on the concrete behind Ian. I figured a breakfast-picnic would repay any debt I might owe.

As the donuts dandruffed their powdered-sugar sweetness down the front of my shirt, I consciously chose to ignore Beardy's patchy facial hair and the flannel lumberjack get-up he was sporting. Instead, I focused on how much his Adam's apple bobbed just like Ian's when he swallowed. It reminded me of a Red Delicious plunked into a tub of water to be pecked at by blindfolded kiddies at Halloween-time.

After breakfast, Beardy tried to talk me into going home with him; I resisted. Men are always doing that to me: thinking they've found some lost child or broken-winged bird and their weird fatherly instincts kick in and all they wanna do is put my face on a milk carton or set my wing with a popsicle stick. Of course, sometimes they just wanna fuck me.

If I'm low on gas funds, could use a new pair of boots, or if I've been hankering for an unrequited banana split for too many weeks, I'll sometimes take them up on it.

You're much too busy to get caught up with this fella, Maggie Mags, I told myself, *even if he does have the good kind of donuts, the good kind of milk, nice manners, pretty brown eyes, and when he smiles just the right way his incisor protrudes like Ian's...*

Just a week ago, I'd ditched my buddy, Hatred, near the tracks in El Paso (A.K.A. El Trasho). He wanted to spend one last night swilling moonshine and smoking rollies with those homespun Texas homebums before heading off to Los Angeles. He tried to talk me into going with—his devil mouth extra slick—but I stuck my boots firmly in the dirt.

"C'mon Mags, Hatred'd purred, petting one of his thick-as-a-corncob dreads. "I'll take you to see X play at The Roxy and eat Oki-Dogs whenever you want. We can bang on that table where Darby Crash planned his suicide; it'll be killer."

Sure, punk rock and hot dogs are cool as shit, but I'd taken a break from Losing for a couple of days to hang with Hate, and I was itching to get back at it. It's not easy to Lose body-parts when there's someone else's eyes following you around, no matter how mashed up with junk they might be. And even though I secretly pine to Lose a toe in those famous California tar pits, I figure it's highly unlikely that Hatred'll even make it there in the first place. He'll get off-track somewhere along the line, tempted by some blue-eyed baby punk with bad skin and a homemade anarchy tattoo whose boyfriend's lip is in desperate need of a splitting.

"Looks like you've been living in this car," Beardy observes, fingering my empty toilet paper cardboards. We've been done with breakfast for forty-five, and he still hasn't skedaddled.

"Only for about sixteen months. Before that, I was squatting near Chi-town with this one-legged fucker named Chuckles. Since then, I've been doing my own thing, picking up a hitcher here and there," I say, feeling extra gritty.

"Really, kitten, you should take a load off. Spend a couple of days with me; it'd be nice," he offers. Some girls wait their whole lives to hear words like that. I'm, obviously, not one of those girls. Though when he says "kitten," I'm reminded of the time when dissecting cats in Biology class, Ian speared a cat eyeball on his scalpel and handed it to me like a rose.

"I'm right in the middle of something.... Something that works better when I'm alone," I try to explain.

"What are you, some kind of werewolf? I ain't skeered," he says, winking. The way the skin crinkles at the edge of his eye socket looks exactly like Ian's did when he'd listen to Nine Inch Nails on his Discman during Lunch, air-drumming to the beat.

"Maybe," I growl, liking the idea of somebody thinking I could be part-beast.

"Listen, baby girl, I'll just drop you off before I head to work. I work eight-hour shifts, five days a week. Maybe more since we're right in the middle of this big highway project. How's that for alone time?"

He promises to throw in a couple bottles of Boone's Farm, some strawberry air fresheners, a car wash, and a whole Costco pack of toilet paper if I'll chill with him for a bit.

"Fresh razorblades, too?" I ask, only semi-hoping it'll push him over the line.

"Razorblades, cocaine, popsicles, pie, whatever you want, pretty girl," he acquiesces with a grin.

When we shake on it, I notice that his thumbnail looks like Ian's: a little jagged half-moon filled to the brim with dirt. I have a hankering to take my tooth to it—to scoop out the tobacco flakes, grit, oil, whatever it is that's got his hand looking so goddamned manly.

Instead of actually taking me to his house (he lives with his mom; "taking care of her" is what he calls it), Sorta-Ian springs for a hotel room. I'm not sure if the woman behind the counter thinks I'm a prostitute or drug-dealer or what, but she stink-eyes me so hard that I reckon I might sprout an extra head under her cursed gaze. I let Sorta-Ian finish checking-in on his own while I investigate the lobby.

I don't say it out loud, but I'm pretty stoked by this whole hotel situation. I've spent enough long nights picking ants off my underpants and trying to keep mice from shitting in my knapsack to know that I'm not into dirty dude rooms. Putting me up in a hotel is the kind of thing Ian would do if he had the cash.

It's been at least fifteen years since I've been to a place like this: That one time Daddy decided to act like a real daddy and took me and Bubba on a weekend trip to Galveston. Everything was fine until he left us alone with a handful of quarters to get dinner out of the vending machine while he spent the rest of the night getting wasted at the titty bar. But this hotel doesn't smell like sunscreen and bleach, it smells like rich folks instead: lilacs, warm leather, and verbena—whatever the fuck *verbena* is.

As I walk through the lobby and into the breakfast room, my eyes get swimmy in my head. It feels like I drank too much boxed wine too quickly: just unplugged that nozzle right in my mouth and let the sweet, red nectar flow. There's a little fake pond/waterfall near the omelette station, catty-corner to the glass elevator. Everything's so fancy-schmancy and rimmed in gold that I figure it's only minutes before security guards come over and escort me back out to the parking lot where I belong.

I sit on the edge of the pond, digging through my pockets for a coin to toss in. I take all wishing-opportunities equally seriously: coins in fountains, falling stars, wayward eyelashes, four-leafed clovers; I'm not one to squander. I find a penny at the bottom of my bag; it's tarnished and mottled and looks like it came from inside a homebum's butt, but a wish is a wish is a wish.

I turn around, close my eyes and whisper: "I wish to run smack-dab into Ian. Not Sorta-Ian, or car-Ian, but Ian-Ian. I don't care when or where, though the sooner the better, obvi. He doesn't even have to fall instantly in love with me. I just want to see his handsome face, kiss his salty skin, etcetera etcetera."

When I turn back around to try and spot my penny as it sinks into the water, I notice for the first time that the pond is filled with loads of delightfully glittery goldfish.

"Hey, Mags," Sorta-Ian says, coming up from behind and startling me. "I've been looking for you everywhere." He kisses my neck right at the hairline. I didn't realize we'd made it to the kissing stage already, but I'm so stoked on the fish (and the omelette station! and the glass elevator!) that I let it slide.

"See these sweet fishy babies? I love them sooooo much!" I squeal, pointing into the pond. I tell Sorta-Ian about my pet goldfish, Flushy, that I'd had for years as a kid—like for way more years than you're supposed to have a goldfish—because Flushy had magic powers that made him impervious to everything from starvation to Mr. Bubble to cat claws and beyond.

"Good ol' Flushy," Sorta-Ian says, like he's actually listening to me talk.

"He was made up of sun particles," I say, remembering his effervescent shine. "Magical, death-proof sun particles.... But, then, when I was twelve, our stupid fucking neighbor, Mister Maggot—I really have no idea what his real name was that's just what I've always called him—came over with his dumb poodle-doodle dog and that stupid-ass stuck its snout right into Flushy's bowl and sluuurp!"

"Damned mutt! I'm sorry baby," Sorta-Ian says, pulling me into a hug.

"But don't worry! I'm like one hundred percent sure that Flushy is still alive in that fucker's belly. He like turned it into his perfect habitat or whatever: swimming around, pooping everywhere, and living the good life."

"Phew!" Sorta-Ian exhales dramatically, "I'm glad there was a happy ending, you had me worried there for a minute, girl."

"And what's even better is that *these* fish are orange and glowy *just like* Flushy." I point into the pond. "Which means he sent us his offspring! Or his clones! Shit, I don't know what they are exactly—*doppelgangers*?" I realize my voice is about four times louder than it should be, so I make it just a smidge louder, hoping it can reach all the way up to the top of the cupola or whatever that domed ceiling way-up-yonder is called. *Cupola?* Sounds fancy enough.

"Looks like you made the right decision coming with me then, huh?" Sorta-Ian says, winking at me—that wink that reminds me so much of Ian's NIN-listening face. "C'mon, giddy-up, your suite awaits, princess.

"But my Flushies...!"

"You can come back down and visit your Flushies later; they ain't goin' nowhere." He wraps his big arm around my waist and pulls me with him to the elevator. He smells like pennies and summertime highways—somehow familiar—and he carries all my bags, even though they are pink leopard print and only held together with safety pins.

I spend a couple of hours in the hotel room just walking around and touching things while Sorta-Ian is at work. There's a kitchenette with an electric stove with no macaronis glued to the burners, a big bathtub without cigarette welts, and central heat/air that switches back and forth with a click.

I take the longest, hottest bath of my life, not worrying about cranky water heaters or water bills. It's been a long time since I've had access to a tub—trucks stop showers and McDonald's sinks just don't compare. Whenever the water starts to chill, I refill with abandon. I use a whole bar of soap on my oniony feet, and empty the entire teeny shampoo bottle onto my head. It's too hard to wash each individual dreadlock—they puff up like sponges when they're full of suds—so I focus my attention on scraping the oily crust from my scalp.

I try to boil-boil-toil-and-trouble myself into a shiny, more-respectable version that Ian might want to take to prom, or that Sorta-Ian might wanna screw. I pretend to throw in a couple of newt eyes, some frog's breath, a pinch of mugwort, and I say a fake magic spell with mostly made-up words. Before getting out of the tub, I feed one of my dreadlocks down the drain. *R.I.P. hair; Memphis, Tennessee,* I think, recording the Loss and location in my brain.

In an effort to look my sexiest, I dig my least-holy tights out of my knapsack, put on a little leopard nightie, and slosh apple cider vinegar under my pits. I rub glitter into my Chapstick, and then spend a couple of minutes at the window tapping Morse code messages to Ian—the studliest Hyundai in existence—down in the parking lot.

I love you the most. I promise I'm not cheating on you by sleeping somewhere else. Nothing will ever come close to cradling my ass the way you do, my tapping says.

I smash my glittery lips into the glass extra hard, leaving greasy kiss-marks speckled with tiny roses of blood. Losing a bit of hair and blood will just have to be enough for now.

A *Wife Swap* marathon is on TV, the mattress is memory foam, and the pillows aren't just made of wadded-up toilet paper, so I let myself daydream about a future with Sorta-Ian. There could be major benefits to marrying a nice union man who has money and health insurance and all that other blue-collar crap. Him: coming home from work tired and grease-stained; me: making Velveeta-stuffed-meatloaf in a cute, wifely apron. He would mow the lawn on weekends while I learn to knit. I've always fantasized about making my own socks and car-blankets and tiny booties for Ian-Ian's mice.

By the time Sorta-Ian gets back from work, I'm conked out on sleepers, and mostly-dreaming, but his body next to mine feels like a giant praying mantis, so I push myself into his prickles hard—hoping for at least a little bruising—and let his antennae graze my cheek. I will myself to learn insect-speak, thinking that maybe this thing could work—even if only for a little while.

I've always thought of Losing as a solitary act, like religion is for some folks. I wear it like a crucifix, I fuck it like a lover, I use it to light candles, and alter my body over and over again in accommodation. But maybe, just maybe, me and Losing and Sorta-Ian could have some kind of threesome. A menage-a-trois if you will; whatever the fuck *menage* means.

When I finally wake up in the morning, Sorta-Ian is gone. But, in his stead, he's left an ice-bucket-full of Flushy-twins pilfered from the downstairs-pond. I spend the first part of my morning whispering secrets to my new friends, and picking dry skin from the heels of my feet, cuticles, elbows, and lips to feed to them. When I sprinkle the skin-flakes into their bucket, all the Flushies dart to the surface at once, fighting over me. Gifting me with a bucket of Flushies is the exact kind of thing that Ian would do for me.

Later that night, as we're sitting down to dinner at a real-restaurant-not-Taco-Bell, Almost-Ian tells me to order whatever I want.

"Whatever I want? Are you sure?" I ask, batting my lashes at him over the menu. There are roughly fifteen kinds of margaritas listed here, all with different kinds of tequila, different kinds of fresh fruits. I can't remember the last time I drank liquor that didn't come in a plastic bottle and/or bag.

"Anything," he says winking. "I've got myself a credit card." He pulls it out of his wallet and slaps it down on the table with authority.

"Holy shit, no way!" I squeal, grabbing it and instinctively sticking it in my bra.

"Don't make me come over there...." Almost-Ian is practically drooling like the Big Bad Wolf.

"Or else what...?" I lick my lips; I know how to play the part of the yummy Little Pig pretty darn well.

When Almost-Ian orders guacamole, I decide to give it a shot. Something about him makes me want to try new things, to be a new kind of person. As a kid I was really freaked out by avocados; I was sure they were some kind of evil alligator-demon food that would turn my skin green or make me sprout extra teeth. Then sometime around junior high I heard they were fattening and figured I wasn't missing out on much. Practicing Losing for so long has made me quite the pro at avoiding anything that could possibly lead to gain.

But, here, with Almost-Ian, swimming in tequila, I decide to indulge. Even if that means more meat, fat, fingers, eyelashes, a tail, what-have-you. I grin at him through filled teeth, and his mouth puckers just like Ian's would whenever he'd listen to Marilyn Manson in his Malibu.

"I wonder what the poor folks are eatin' tonight?" I say, suddenly remembering how my Paw-Paw (who I haven't thought about in years) would say that whenever we'd sit down to a fine meal.

"Looks like they're eatin' Mexican," Ian ribs back.

I try not to ruin the moment with my weirdness, but I secretly hope that depositing my next, hefty cheese enchilada crap into the Memphis sewer system will be enough of a Loss for now. I could always try to bury it in the flowerbed by the parking lot—something a bit more ritualistic than a flush—but I'm not sure how to transport poo without a plastic baggie.

After dinner, we have sex. It's more vanilla than I'm used to, maybe because neither of us is starving to death and having to break each other open like bread. He's on top, I'm on bottom. There's some humping and some groaning, his dick is a little smaller than I expected, but it does the trick. He definitely knows what he's doing with his hips and fingers. He flicks my clit until I come, he licks my neck in long, languorous strokes. I worry a little bit about my skin still tasting like street-grime, about the fact that one bath can't do much to combat years of no-baths.

After it's all over, I feel cozy and complete. Like I'm a woman who has just made love to her man. Not like I was hacked open—from bellybutton to asshole—with a rusty chainsaw, how I usually feel after sex. I congratulate myself for engaging in something so grown-up.

Almost-Ian falls asleep quickly, cum drying on the tip of his wilting dick, his breathing heavy and ragged. I stay up late writing in my journal, carefully memorializing the Lost hair, blood, and skin of these last two days. But I'm having trouble figuring out what to call this new womanly-sex thing. Sure, I popped my cherry years ago; in fact, my virginity is stuffed deep in an underwear drawer at a closed-down Victoria's Secret in Houston (A.K.A. Bruise-town). But, suddenly, I've got this second hymen to commemorate. Maybe I'll call it *chastity*—that rings of sexual maturity.

As I record, I fantasize about a future in which I'm the kind of woman that can love every inch of herself—even the broken parts. Retracing Ian's tire-tracks—hopefully with Ian in tow—I'll keep the trunk filled with forget-me-nots to sprinkle on the graves of all of my Losses.

Our life together morphs into a sitcom; everyday a mimicry of the one before. Almost-Ian gets up early and goes to work, leaving me drooling on the goose-down pillow. I spend all day popping zits in the Hollywood starlet mirror and wiping the pus on the inside of the medicine cabinet. I waste electricity and water, watch *Buffy the Vampire Slayer* on the gay channel, nap, and feed my Flushies pieces of dead skin and scab. I make cup after cup of coffee on the weird little one-cup coffee maker until I run out of grounds.

"Hi honey, I'm home," Almost-Ian shouts as he walks through the door.

"Hey babe, how was work?" I ask, jumping off the couch and wrapping my arms around his neck. I've started painting my toenails with Sharpie and brushing my teeth twice a day.

"Same old same," he says, "Lookie what I got my girl!"

Digging my fists into his Santa-sack today, I find tea lights, roses, and a *Rolling Stone* magazine. Everyday it's something new. I've already been gifted a Hello Kitty doll, whiskey, cookie dough ice cream, nag champa, fish food, cans of Coke, a book of Emily Dickinson's poetry, a carton of Newport 100's, some quartz crystals, lavender/kelp bath salts, *The Satanic Bible*, and hella weed. It's almost like he's got mind-reading abilities. Or X-ray eyes that see straight into my heart. Or maybe he's just been following me around for years and taking careful stock of all the things my fingers have paused on in stores while contemplating that ol' free-ninety-nine fleece.

I'm officially the imp who got lured into a candy house. My witch just has a beard and drives an Oldsmobile.

After he's passed out from whiskey and dicking, I use the thorns on the roses to carve delicate lines into my skin, drawing just enough blood that my Loss feels sufficient for now. The tea lights make burning myself feel ritualistic. I'd always just used Bic lighters and books of matches before; I didn't realize I was forsaking so much romance for convenience. Even blisters look prettier when coerced by candlelight.

It's hard to keep track of time without mile markers accumulating in the rear-view, a gas tank that's always threatening emptiness, and when someone else is washing your sheets for you. So, I don't even realize that Christmas has come and gone—the lackluster old tramp that she is—until Almost-Ian shows up with champagne, strawberries, Twinkies, Cool Whip, and a sly smile peeking out from under his beard. He's ready to party hard.

"Happy New Year, baby girl!" He shouts, brandishing a champagne bottle like a holy grail. The droplets of condensation on its necks look like diamonds, but I don't even care.

"Oh no," I groan, "Hasn't been a New Year yet that I haven't ended up weeping." I pull my knees to my chest, stretch my t-shirt over them and hook it to my toes. I pull my arms inside, plunk my face deep into the neck-hole: snail-mode.

"It'll be different this year; you'll be kissing me!"

"Doubtful," I say, popping my head and arms out of the cocoon and yanking the champagne bottle from his hand.

"That's for midnight, silly," he reprimands, taking it back.

"You can do whatever you want with that other bottle over there, but this one's mine. Gimme!" The pitch of my voice makes him loosen his grip.

I wrestle with the cork until it zings across the room, sending a bolt of lightning down my spine. I'm not good with loud noises, even the ones I have control over.

I suck at the foam that's pouring from the mouth of the bottle, not wanting to let any of those precious dizzy-bubbles go to waste. I grab the tub of Cool Whip, the box of snack cakes, and the plastic crate of berries, and sit my ass down on the couch for a gorge-fest.

"Can I join you?" Almost-Ian asks, scooting in next to me before I have time to say *no.*

"You can do whatever the fuck you want," I say turning away from him and using the Twinkies like giant fingers to scoop out dollops of whipped frosting. I top each bite with a whole berry, and I have to stretch my mouth as wide as it will go—almost dislocating my jaw like a snake—to make it fit. I wash each bite down with a swig of champagne, straight from the bottle.

NYE was never any different than all the other days of the year; but something about the promise of a new beginning made Mom hanker for something better. Those nights she'd talk back to Daddy, or pack up the car, or do some other *strong woman* shit that she'd heard about on Oprah. Daddy would just keep getting madder and drunker and madder, and by the time midnight finally struck, Mom would be crumpled up on the kitchen floor and wailing. I'd be running around looking for somewhere safe to hide.

In an effort to protect myself from my memories, I set the A/C as cold as it will get and build an igloo-fort out of all the sheets, blankets, and towels that I can find.

"Can I get in there with you?" Almost-Ian asks, peeking his head into my fort.

"Hell no!" I say, sinking further into myself. I know it's not fair to be mad at him—he didn't make it New Year's Eve—but to have the audacity to want to celebrate this shit, there *must* be something wrong with him.

"But it's cold out here and you took all the blankets," he whines, his tongue thick with alcohol.

"You're a man; deal with it," I say, wishing he would just go away or fall asleep or something—anything—as long as it is far away from me.

Even though I'm hunkering deep inside my igloo—cotton balls stuffed in my ears, wearing both bathrobes at once—when the fireworks start blasting outside, I feel them reverberate through my bones. They sound like gunshots and behind my closed eyes I see a rain of blood.

My breath gets trapped in my chest, like when a bird accidentally flies into an open window and gets stuck in a room when all it's ever known is outside. The bird flies around in screwy circles, not understanding that the window it just flew into is right there and if it could just fly back out, everything would be okay.

"Must be midnight!" Almost-Ian hollers from the couch. "Come out here and give me some sugar!"

I make myself count to ten, I look around my fort and remind myself that I'm safe. I visualize clouds and balloons and kites flying in the sky. I attach Mom and Bubba to the end of the kite strings; hoping that they can help pull me out of this panic. I do my best to imagine my lungs as envelopes coming unsealed, but nothing happens. My ribcage is bursting with the ferocity of one thousand bewildered pigeon wings.

Suddenly, when another firework blasts, this time even closer to the hotel, Ian—my trusty black stallion with door dings for days—begins honking in the parking lot: *Beep! Beep! Beep!* The lilt of his familiar chirp allows the breath to flow in and out of my pipes again. I gulp the air, tasting its crispness on my tongue, letting the coolness of it wash through my chest. It's the best thing I've ever tasted—even better than booze.

Once my body is properly re-oxygenated and I can use my limbs again, I run to the window and tap Morse-code messages to Ian: *I love you. I'm sorry I've been away for so long. I lost track of time. I forgot what was important. I'll be down soon.*

He beeps back: *I love you too. I forgive you. It's time for us to hit the road. We've got a lot of Losing to do. I'll always wait for you.*

I run back to my fort, avoiding Not-Ian's grasping hands. *I'll just spend one last night in my igloo,* I tell myself. *I'll be out by morning. I'll make like a library and book!*

"Why you runnin' around here like a headless chicken, baby girl? Come gimme a kiss. It's a new year. You and me together."

Suddenly, the idea of kissing Not-Ian makes me wanna hurl. I can't remember if I've been with him for a week or a month—everything's blurred into a memory-foam-infused fog of television/sex/weed/booze/ bubble baths/ Pizza Hut delivery.

I've gotten lazy, I haven't Lost anything more substantial than hair, blood, skin, shit, pus, cum, or spit—just the mundane stuff that regular people slough off every day. Not to mention that everything I've laid to waste for weeks (?!) has been in this one shitty hotel room in this one shitty city. When I mark it on my map, it will be at least the size of a quarter: the Memphis Mausoleum (A.K.A. Suckerville)—a big black smudge of ink. A testament to Losing my Losing. Losing myself when I'd meant to Lose something else entirely.

As I go to crawl back into my fort, I bump my head on the coffee table, hard.

"You dumb sonofabitch!!" I wail, pushing the table over with both of my hands. I notice that one of its legs wobbles more than the others, so I yank on it. *The squeaky wheel gets the motherfucking oil,* I think.

My fear transformed to anger, I feel as powerful as a superhero, like one those mothers who can lift a car when her baby is trapped underneath. I hate this stupid, fucking table, I can destroy this ugly piece of shit, I can make this crap my bitch.

"Babygirl, please chill the fuck out," Not-Ian urges, "It's a holiday, remember! We still have time to celebrate. Just you and me and a bubble bath?"

"Shhhh, I'm busy," I say, pulling and twisting the leg, not noticing that my palms are getting red and agitated with blister.

I twist and pull with all my might, until suddenly the leg pops free. It feels like popping that stubborn knuckle in my left thumb: a sigh of relief.

In my hand this table leg feels like a weapon. It's dense and erect with a sharp nail protruding right out of the end. It's archaic, a torture device; I could pluck Not-Ian's eyeball right out of his skull. But he isn't the one who needs to Lose something; I do.

I've been trying to Lose all the pieces of myself that were ruined by Daddy; to wipe him clean off the map of my body. *But that doesn't really make sense, does it?* Because he broke my rib in second grade when he hugged me too hard, and that sucker is still weaved into the basket of my ribcage, thicker now with callouses of calcium bound around the snap. Daddy gave me more black eyes than I can count—especially during summer when teachers weren't around to get suspicious—turning my whole socket a deep eggplant purple, the same color the bad girls in high school wore as lipstick.

Daddy, being Daddy, burrowed his way straight into my brain, my heart, my very soul; he's everywhere, like God. The only thing that could really snuff him out completely would be a gallon of bleach or some anthrax. A noose, a gas oven, a head-on collision. But I don't go there because I can't go there because I won't go there because...

"I want to live!" I scream to myself, to my memories, to Daddy's ghost that's always right here inside of me no matter what I do to try and get rid of him.

"I'm serious, Magpie, why don't you just calm down? We can order some chocolate mousse from room service! We can watch whatever you want on TV!" Not-Ian's freaking-the-fuck-out squeal breaks my reverie. I wish he would just leave already. I have this one last thing to do, and then I'm outta here.

"Get away from me; I'm busy," I growl, turning the table leg over and over in my hand, marveling at its size and shape, how shiny with lacquer it is. "I told you I was busy when we met. You should have listened."

"Seriously, girl, they have my credit card on file," he says, attempting to take the table leg out of my hands. I imagine his brain formulating Mr. Fix-It ideas: wood glue, hammer and nails, duct tape maybe. But I know that none of those things will work. It's impossible to really ever fix something that has been this broken.

"Miiiiiine!" I scream, grabbing it back from him. I need to Lose something right now or else I will never forgive myself.

I look at my hands. No. They are good hands. They feed me, they hold Ian's steering wheel, they record my Losses. They take better care of me than anyone else ever could.

I look at my legs. No. I need them to walk, to run, to carry me far away from places like the Pear Tree Trailer Palace. Places like this.

I look at my feet—that's it! I remember hearing once about how ladies in the olden days had their baby toes removed so they could fit into pointy shoes. I remember how Cinderella's sisters cut off their own toes so they could easily slip into that glass slipper and fleece the Prince. I remember how Daddy used to always put his feet in a bucket of baby powder before he put his boots on; he was a hard man, but he had such soft feet. I remember someone telling me once that you break your little toe hundreds of times in your life, those times when you're just walking around your house and you stub it on the bedpost or the coffee table and it hurts like the dickens for a quick minute, it's actually broken.

"This little piggy cried wee, wee, wee, wee all the way to the grave," I say, turning away from Not-Ian and sitting down on the carpet to face the window. Fireworks are still blasting in the sky, flooding the room with weird red and blue glows, but I feel calm now that I have a plan. Memories can't hurt me when I'm living in the moment.

I curl my right leg up and under me like a lotus flower. My left leg points straight out: an open highway, a freeway to freedom.

"Goodbye, little friend. We've been through a lot together, but this is where our journey ends. Losing you will set me free. Thank you," I say to my littlest toe, that cute cranberry-shaped thing with not much of a nail.

I take a deep inhale and as I exhale, I make one swift hack with the table leg. I feel a sharp, shearing pain run through my whole body. *Out of the frying pan and into the fire,* I think. The nail on the end of my weapon goes deep, hits bone. Blood spurts up like a fountain. *That's a good name for a metal band:*

Fountain of Blood, I think, as I hear Not-Ian start retching somewhere behind me. I hope he makes it to the bathroom quick; I hate the smell of vomit.

I whack rhythmically, like a clock ticking, and pretty quickly, the nail has gouged a deep crater. In order to sever, I need to change my position—I need to stop poking this one hole over and over again, but poke more holes around the circumference of the toe. Eventually, the holes will just meld into one another, and tear like a perforation.

I have to bend my knee and bring my toe in a little bit closer to my body. It smells like the meat department of the grocery store.

I hack and hack until finally I can no longer feel pain. The nerves have been severed and all that's left is an intense throbbing. It feels like my heart has moved down to my foot and is beating harder than it's ever beat before. "We've got the beat, we've got the beat," I sing.

There's more blood than I expected. The beige carpet fibers suck it up thirstily, turning a deep maroon. I remember when I was four and spilled grape juice on my comforter. I hated that ugly, blah-colored thing and reckoned if it got ruined, maybe I could get a Care Bears one. That was when Daddy introduced me to his belt.

"Silent night, holy night, all is Lost, all is quiet," I sing, lopping away.

All that's still connected is a bit of bone. I'm going to have to crack it in half with my fingers; my instrument has done all it can do. *Blood on my hands,* I think, as I drop the table leg.

I pull my left leg up to me, now I'm sitting criss-cross-applesauce, which reminds me of kindergarten, which reminds me of learning the alphabet and finger-painting, and how many times I had to switch schools because teachers kept asking too many questions about my bruises.

I hold my foot steady with my left hand. It feels like a dying bird, heaving its last jot of life, still warm, but barely. I wrap my right fist around the wet, mangled pinky, and with all the force I have left in me, I snap downwards. My elbow hits the spongey carpet with a thud.

I look down and my toe is sitting quietly in my cupped hand.

Disconnected from my body, it looks like a gnawed-on chicken nugget, a piece of earthworm, a wad of chewed-up bubblegum. Definitely not human.

I start to sing "Hush Little Baby" as I cradle the toe in my palm, rocking it back and forth, putting it to sleep.

I reach over and grab my bag, I dig around until I find my favorite pair of underpants. They are red and silky with a black lace edge: the perfect funeral shroud. I carefully wrap the toe up tight—like a present. It will rest in the bottom of my knapsack for now, it will be safe there.

Standing up, I realize that I'm still too drunk to drive, the loss of blood has got me pretty lightheaded, and the way my foot is throbbing reminds me of that time I did a lot of Ecstasy at a rave and the deep thrum of the bass bumped up through the floor and made my body feel like it had to dance to stay alive. But I don't think I should try to dance right now. A bath sounds like a better option. Water has all kinds of magical healing properties that are good for sucking out boozy toxins and cleaning wounds. I haven't had gangrene yet, but Chuckles down in Chilly-cago warned me of its wickedness and taught me a bunch of hobo-medicine tricks like how to stop bleeding with spiderwebs and vinegar and how to dress a wound with toilet paper and a handkerchief. He even showed me how to fill a deep wound with honey, to kill bacteria and stanch the stank.

As I limp to the bathroom, I look over at Not-Ian. He's strewn across the bed with little chunks of barf all imbedded in his beard. I'd kept hoping he'd shave off that scratchy, ugly thing, but now I don't care if it grows so long that it touches the floor like some weird old Rip Van Winkle freak. Thinking about him touching my boobs makes me gag.

"What the fucking fuck, dude?" he slurs at my backside.

As I'm pouring my bottle of apple cider vinegar into the bathtub, getting the water all hot and fragrant, I remember how Bubba and I used to pour table salt in the tub with us to simulate swimming in the ocean. That time we'd gone to Galveston with Daddy, we were mesmerized by the way the sea seemed to patch up our wounds right quick, better than Mom's kisses even. I had a split lip and some belt-burn at the time; he only had a skinned knee, but when we got out of the water, we were halfway to healed. Bubba never had nearly as many ouchies as me.

"Boys don't need the same kind of manhandling, it's you womenfolk that's all full of sin," Daddy'd always say, trying to make sense of why he beat me and Mom so bad but left Bubba alone. I always figured Daddy himself was the most sinful of us all though.

I pour in the whole canister of lavender/kelp bath salts that Not-Ian had brought in his Santa-sack. This is bound to be my last bath for a while, so I might as well make it good. Since my water's as saturated with salt as the Gulf of Mexico, I decide to dump the Flushies right on in; *Surfin' USA!*

I hobble out of the bathroom and over to the bed where my fish-bucket lives. I have to be careful not to put too much weight on my left leg.

"What're you doin' now?" Not-Ian asks without even lifting his head to look up at me. Damn man can't hold his liquor, that's for sure. What kind of wimp have I been shacked up with for weeks?

"If you honey-buns are anything like the real Flushy, then you're only partially fish, but mostly magic," I tell them, as I carry the bucket into the bathroom. "Do a girl a solid and patch up this wound, kay?"

The Flushies are happy to break free of their confinement. When I climb in the tub with them, they nip lightly at my skin before jetting away. I probably taste familiar since they've been surviving on skin flakes and fish flakes for God-knows-how-long. I sing songs to the Flushies about sunshine-colored sea monsters biting the heads off of blood-clotted creatures while I soap and sponge. They tickle.

"Send your magical sun particles to my toe to hamper the bleeding, please?" I beg them, feeling awkward about my use of the word *hamper* but liking the way it sounds and knowing the fish will get it—they do have me inside of them after all.

The blood from my toe creeps into the water, changing the Flushies scales from traffic-cone orange to a more sunsety shade. I scrub myself with Not-Ian's loofa, hoping that I'll be able to slough off a smorgasbord for the Flushies to indulge in; they deserve it, they've been such faithful pets.

I splash around happily, less guilty now that I've Lost a toe; only slightly bummed by the fact that I'm gonna have to leave my Flushies with Not-Ian. They don't seem like they'd be very good road-dogs.

I'm not sure where to bury the toe. I reckon I could stick it between the mattress and box spring, though I don't know how often the maids flip the mattresses. Leaving it anywhere in this hotel room means that it would end up in a landfill, and that's a dismal place for such an important part of myself to rest eternally. I'll have to ponder it when my head's a little clearer.

I wake up from what feels like a minute of sleep—one of those weird, falling-off-a-cliff, heart-in-your-throat moments where your eyelids blink open and you can't remember ever having drifted off to begin with. Not-Ian is sitting next to the tub looking like he got bit by a rabid skunk. For some strange reason, he's naked. Maybe he barfed on his clothes? Or wanted to climb in the tub with me, but saw my Flushies and realized there wasn't room?

"Mornin' sugar-lumps. I's gonna git in there, but I fell," Not-Ian mumbles from the floor, his words sloshing around in his mouth.

"Um, okay," I mutter.

When I look over at him, some kind of veil lifts from in front of my eyes and I actually *see* him for the first time. His body is a weird mix of old man and baby: there's a blanket of thick, coarse hair lining his chest and privates, but underneath the fuzz he's pale and soft. No tattoos bleed from his forearms, no scars from knife fights or razor wire lace his chest, there's not even a fucking ingrown hair or a cat scratch to be found. He's pristine and unadulterated—life has barely grazed his shoulders. I want to carve an upside-down cross between his eyebrows. And lop off his pointer finger.

When I turn my eyes to revel at my own lived-in and martyred body, I realize that while I was sleeping, all of the bathwater drained away and I'm lying here dry as a bone, covered in dead fish. A few of them are cluttered down near my feet, but most of their tiny, shiny bodies are resting on my belly and chest. They tremble with my every breath.

"My Flushies are dead!" I wail.

"S'okay, baby girl, there are plenty more downstairs. I'll get ya another bucket-full later on."

"Don't you get it? There is no later on! You fish-killing bastard!" I don't know why I blame Not-Ian—I know that it's not his fault—but I can't bear the weight of thirteen deaths on my own shoulders.

I want to close the Flushies eyes for them, like I've seen priests do in movies, but since goldfish don't have eyelids, I have to think of something else. "We're all in this together now," I whisper longingly, looking down at my legions of dead friends. I guess these fake Flushies weren't nearly as tough as the original Flushy after all.

Since these poor, innocent souls consumed my skin and blood, the only right thing for me to do would be to eat them back. That should give them a chance at eternal life. It's the least I can do.

"Rest in peace, sweet, golden Not-Flushies," I blubber, carefully plucking their limp bodies from the graveyard of my chest. One by one, I place them in my mouth, making sure not to bite or chew. They slip down my throat, quietly, like secrets left unsaid. Washing them down with water from the faucet, I swallow and swallow and swallow—until they're all gone.

"Whut the fuck ya doin'? Anti-Ian slurs. "I must be fuckin' dreamin'." He goes to stand up, but his knee slips in a puddle of vomit. When his flesh slaps the floor, it makes a sucking sound.

"Listen, dude, thanks for everything. But as you can see, this just isn't gonna work," I say, trying to climb out of the tub without stepping in his mess.

"Where' ya goin'?" he mumbles from his spot on the bathmat, rolling over just enough to keep from getting stepped on. "I was gonna git in with ya...."

"This has nothing to do with you. I mean, yes it does. You just aren't the kind of person a girl like me can be with. I need someone who knows what it feels like to have razor wire rip their skin. Someone who's played one too many games of five-finger-filet." When I look down at the empty place where my toe used to be, pride swells my chest—which inevitably makes my boobs look bigger. I try to wiggle my four remaining toes, but it hurts too much.

"I've no fuckin' idea what yer goin' on about," Anti-Ian groans from the floor; he's holding his head in his hands. "Just come over here and sit with me. Daddy has a lap for ya. I'll make it all better."

"Daddy? Daddy? You've got to be fucking kidding me. Go *Daddy* yourself. I don't need you! I don't need anyone at all. I'm totally good on my own." I pull the towels down off the rack, letting one of them fall right on his head. "Actually, I'm better than good. But if I were to hook up with someone *for real* for real, they'd have to know how to make a shiv out of melting the elastic waistband of their underwear. They'd need to know what it smells like in the underbelly of the underworld. And they'd never ever—in a million years never—refer to themselves as 'Daddy'!"

"Huh? Under what?"

"Underworld, dummy. It smells like bellybutton and earwax and period panties and junkie swabs and puke. Like that time I threw up on Chuckles' white suspenders and turned them pink 'cuz all I had in my stomach was boxed wine and Saltines. And he just kept on wearing them like that for weeks."

I wrap a towel around my midsection tightly, and another one around my head. I want to feel like an Egyptian queen as I step out of this bathroom and into the next phase of my life.

"Uggghh, everything hurts. 'Mind me never to mix champagne with tequila again." Anti-Ian's shoulders heave as he retches yellowy spit into the rug.

"I need someone who isn't afraid to slice me open, debone me if that's what it takes. *You'll* never be the Sid to my Nancy. Someone might be, but it's not you." I pull the bathroom door shut behind me. I try to slam it for emphasis, but it just thumps lamely in the frame.

My belongings are strewn all over the room, mixed up with the bait-&-fuck goodies from Anti-Ian's Santa sack. I don't want any of his gifts though; excess stuff is not an asset when the primary goal is Losing. I hobble around—trying to keep the majority of my weight on the un-wounded foot—plucking my junk from amongst the rubble. It feels like an Easter egg hunt. Except this time Daddy didn't fill the plastic eggs with dead bugs and bullet casings for a laugh. This time, I'm hunting for what's mine.

Everything I own fits perfectly into my two backpacks and one duffel—just like it always has. I check three times to make sure I've still got the toe; I apply extra eyeliner and dress my wound with coconut oil, tissue, and as much self-love as I can muster.

"Later, alligator," I say to the bathroom door as I'm leaving.

Anti-Ian doesn't respond. Or if he does, his voice is too hushed for me to hear.

It's early in the morning, so the continental breakfast bar is still steaming. I'm not hungry now—I'm too full of fish—but the Hobo Code of Conduct states that passing up free food is a sin worse than murder. I fill my pockets with toast, sausage, dry pancakes, and honey packets—which I'll be able to use on my wound when my coconut oil supply has run dry.

As I walk through the parking lot towards Ian, I feel my spine straighten; the sun tangles itself into my dreadlocks like a crown. Crawling behind the wheel, I thank myself for having had the foresight to Lose the toe on my left foot instead of on my accelerator foot.

"I'm not psychic, but my Losing is," I whisper, giving Ian's dashboard a celebratory kiss.

Everything feels just right, like when Goldilocks found the porridge that wasn't too hot or too cold. The way Ian's seat cradles my butt, the way my hands feel on his wheel, even the way he smells like a mix of strawberries and the stuff you pick out from under your fingernails with a toothpick. Perfection.

Ian doesn't care that I have fish burps, that no matter how much I Lose, I'll always have Daddy's eyes staring right back at me—out of my very own face—in the mirror. Hell, I might even still have some of Anti-Ian's sperm swimming around in my lady-parts; Ian always accepts me exactly as I am.

"First thing's first, lover," I say, pulling the map out of the glovebox. "We've gotta find the proper resting place for this toe. Just anywhere won't do. This sucker's a testament to my Losing, my survival, my whole damn life. This thing woke me the fuck up! We have to bury it somewhere super special."

I lay the atlas across my lap and the whole United States opens up before me like a fully-bloomed rose. I close my eyes and swirl my finger over the map, drawing invisible snakes and ribbons and hearts in the air. I count to thirteen—Ian's favorite number—and then plunk my finger down.

When I open my eyes and look, I'm pointing right at Texas. The motherfucking Lone Star State: full of big-ass stars and perfume-blooming sage, my dang birthplace, Daddy's homestate, and all that other hokey-pokey shit I've tried to forget. Of course Texas is the destination; it's always been the reason.

As I drive from one broken-down town to another, I'm scared of running out of gas— filling stations are few and far between in these sparse Mississippi-to-Louisiana parts—I play Nirvana's *Nevermind* on repeat for luck. I once saw Ian writing the lyrics to "Drain You" on the back of his binder; it's my favorite song on the album.

A few hours in, the Flushies start rumbling in my guts. Before I have time to find a regular bathroom, I pull off the highway and pop a squat in a stranger's backyard garden—which, of course, is a much more respectable resting place than the sewer system of Bumfuck, Nowhere. I reckon the fishiness of the shit will add more nutrition than regular fertilizer. Hopefully the gardener will win World's Biggest Tomato at the state fair and Flushy's magic will live on. Daddy always loved tomatoes; especially with sprinkles of salt, pepper, and vinegar. I fantasize about him sitting down to eat a big-as-a-house motherfucker, and the thing rolling right over him and squashing him flat.

It takes a good nine hours, but once I hit Houston, skyscrapers, spaghetti-bowl interstates, and Chili's restaurants sprout up at every angle. I decide to head to Galveston to look for that sunscreen-stinking hotel where me and Bubba'd stayed with Daddy. I want to connect the dots between the two hotels of my life, to see if there's meaning in the mapping.

When Daddy'd left me and Bubba alone in the hotel that night, we'd had actually had a blast. He left enough quarters for us to get Cool Ranch Doritos, Twix, salted peanuts, gummy worms, and a Coke from the machine. Bubba didn't want stupid nuts with so many other more-delicious options, but I made him eat them for the protein. I had tiny bites and sips of everything—I was already deep into my Losing—and let Bubba take the bulk. We jumped from bed to bed, watched TV all night, and wrapped the whole room in toilet paper as if we were decorating for a birthday party.

The next morning, when Daddy got home from the titty bar—still-drunk and broker than before—I got less of a beating than I'd anticipated: his knuckles were just sloppy enough to barely break the skin. My lip swelled up some, but I just pretended it was a gummy worm that got stuck to my face when we were partying, a relic from our bygone night. Then, Bubba and I got to swim in the ocean while Daddy nursed his hangover; so overall, it was a win-win.

"Galveston, here we come. I'm gonna lay this toe deep in your tar-riddled sands, right on the edge of that stinky, old Gulf. She'll sit everlasting, just waiting to be swallowed up the next time the earth quakes on its axis and forces the sea to open her mouth too wide."

Out of nowhere—a sign pointing towards Sugar Land pops up in the ditch. Something old and reptilian, from the backwater part of my brain takes control; I veer onto the exit ramp. Holding the steering wheel with my left hand, I run the right one through my dreads, over my cheeks and lips and chin; I let my thumb linger in that concave of my collar bone, the place where the tendons of the neck meets the width of the chest. "The thumbprint of our family's sin lives on our skin," I tell Ian. "Sometimes we have to shed our entire selves in order to find freedom."

I'd forgotten all about Sugar Land (no nickname needed), how as a kid I imagined all the houses were made out of graham crackers and gumdrops, but had been disguised to look like regular houses so the grown-ups didn't get mad. I'd spent the best summers of my life there, in my grandparent's rambling, trinket-filled farmhouse. They'd always catch me licking the walls, looking for frosting. But instead of a spanking, I would get a kiss.

"Whatcha know good, Miss Magpie?" Paw-Paw would say whenever he saw me, wrapping me up in his big, cigarette-reeking arms, a piece of hay stuck between his teeth.

"I know nothin'!" I'd holler, hoping that if I could be empty enough, he'd be forced to fill me up.

Driving down Treasure Trail, it all comes back to me: Paw-Paw plucking his old guitar, while I played fake-hopscotch on the checkered floor. Me-Maw baking and baking so the whole house smelled just like the inside of a gingerbread house should smell. How both of them would tuck us in bed at night under hand-loomed quilts and take turns reading stories.

There was always a jar of candied apricots sitting on the kitchen counter, and when no one was looking, I'd sneak a bunch of pieces into my pockets. Since the apricot chunks were goldfish-colored I thought that if Bubba and I ate enough of them, they'd make us more like Flushy: strong, brave, safe from Daddy's belt.

"Screw Galveston, Sugar Land is where thou shall be bequeathed," I tell the toe. I don't really know what *bequeathed* means, but it feels like the right word for the moment.

As I drive through the old neighborhood, I notice that the houses all looks smaller than I remember them, their lawns are all deader too. But there's something in the air that surges with life, like when it's really hot outside and the space above the asphalt vibrates in rainbowy waves. It's January, so it can't be heat. Maybe it's memory. Or ghosts. Though, really what's the difference?

As I pull in front of Me-Maw and Paw-Paw's house, I'm disappointed to see the windows boarded up and the garden waist-high with weeds. I wonder who moved in after my grandparents died. I wonder if they had kids that played in the yard, if they ate hand-churned, strawberry ice-cream in the summertime. If they swam in a cleaned-out horse trough when it got up to over 110 degrees, if they hunted crawdads, if they made crowns out of clover. I hope that these kids got to do some of the things that Bubba and I did before Daddy decided to end to our visits.

"The old folks are spoiling these little leaches. The stink that comes off this one especially..." Daddy would say, grabbing my arm, "...worse than shit on a stick."

One night when Daddy had socked Mom harder than ever before—so hard that a chunk of her septum was hanging out of her nostril—Mom told me to go and pack up mine and Bubba's clothes; that we'd be staying with Me-Maw and Paw-Paw for a while.

But when Daddy caught us piling into the car near midnight, he grabbed his shotgun from the rack in his pick-up and used the butt of it to smash out the headlights and windows of Mom's El Camino. We couldn't drive anywhere like that.

It was the middle of the night, so me and Bubba were in our pajamas and barefooted. As we were shuffled out of the car and back into bed, little bits of glass got all stuck up in the soles of our feet; we knew better than to complain.

When I woke up the next morning, there were bloody footprints tracking our steps from the driveway through the house; it reminded me of how Hansel and Gretel left breadcrumbs in their wake. I wished that someone would stop by, see the blood trails and set out on a mission to rescue us. But, since no one ever did, it was up to me to pick the glass shards out of our feet with Mom's eyebrow tweezers.

I put Ian in park, shut off his ignition, and crawl out of my seat. I stretch my arms and legs. The air smells clean here, even though it probably isn't. I remember Me-Maw always worrying about the chemical plants nearby and then Paw-Paw went and died of brain cancer and proved all her worrying right. I take a deep breath anyways.

Right smack-dab in the middle of the front yard, the same old pecan tree is still standing; a ladder to damn-near heaven. This very tree produced the nuts for Me-Maw's award-winning buttermilk/pecan pies, the recipe of which she took to the grave.

I wrap my arms around its trunk, pretending for a minute that it's my grandparents.

I'd had so much fun as a kid, sitting here and kicking these nuts around, arranging them in fake-hieroglyphics across the yard. Because I liked to collect things, Paw-Paw gave me an emptied-out coffee tin to keep my treasures in. I put a ton of pecans in there, along with other special things like heart-shaped leaves, locust skins, and wishboney twigs.

Before bed, I'd ceremoniously pluck a couple of pecans out of the jar and use the Christmas nutcracker to bust them open. I was always extra careful not to drop any of the nut pieces into Me-Maw's mustard shag. After arranging the nuts meticulously on big leaves (what I called "fairy plates")—in a happy face formation—I'd set them on the windowsill, shell-less and glittering with easy consumption. This was my offering to the outdoors kingdom of critters. I wanted to give as much as I could. I wanted to make lives outside of mine feel taken-care-of and special.

When I'd check in the morning, the nut chunks would always be gone.

I'm thankful for the trees' presence, for its strength, its hope, its ability to withstand destruction, pollution, hurricane, drought. Here it stands, crown almost touching the sun, a symbol for all the pain and suffering and Loss that I've survived. That *we've* survived.

At the base of the tree, I start digging a hole with my hands. The grass comes up easy. Under the grass, the dirt is moist just like it always is in this part of the country: ripe for growing rice. The perfect resting place.

As I dig, the soil and sludge creep up underneath my nails, it reminds me of digging my fingers into Me-Maw's homemade playdough. She put almond extract in it, so it always smelled like cookies.

I'm careful to avoid disrupting the roots. I wouldn't want to do anything to disturb this tree's stalwart growth. But I dig deep, finding bugs and stones and worms. I remember when Paw-Paw taught me that if you cut an earthworm in half, it would regrow its tail. I've always wondered if the same thing might happen to me, if my Losses would come back. If someday I'd just wake up and all the spots that I thought were bound for eternal emptiness would be full again.

My fingers move through loam, humus, and bottom-soil—all kinds of dark substances that have never known sunlight. I dig and dig as the moon moves across the sky: a big glowing belly guiding my hands.

I'm almost shoulder-deep, when finally, a silence arises from the opening and I know I've gone deep enough. I put the toe at the bottom of the hole, still shrouded in my red-&-black panties.

"Ashes to ashes, dust to dust. Give us this day our daily bread. Like a snake eating its own tail, I hope to return someday. Like I have today. Again and again and again to honor this baptismal Loss. Blood sugar sex magic. Peace be with you." I throw a handful of dirt on the toe, look to the heavens, and smile.

Filling the hole back up is much easier than digging it. In only a few minutes, the ground is back in place. I stamp down hard with my boots, making the earth look as if it were never disturbed. I mark the grave with pecans, clover, and some honeysuckle filched from the neighbor's vine.

I sit down on the burial plot and take a deep breath. "What's next?" I ask the tree, Me-Maw and Paw-Paw's empty house, the moon. Things suddenly feel different. But I'm not sure what to do with this difference. I dig around in my pocket for a cigarette; I need something ritualistic to mark this moment. But my fingers come in contact with a tiny box of razorblades instead. Aha, a blood-letting! Even better.

I slit the pointer finger on my right hand, it' a quick, sharp burn; nothing I can't handle.

I think about writing *Magpie + Ian 4-Ever* inside of a heart: the same thing I've written time and time again: on notebooks, on the bottoms of my shoes, in the dirt of Ian's windshield, on bathroom stalls in truck-stops across America.

But instead, I write *Magpie Forever* right on the bark of the old pecan tree.

"If I keep on Losing with the patience of a saint, then maybe, someday, it won't even hurt," I shout, my voice echoing off the emptiness of the cul-de-sac.

A bird caws somewhere in the distance, but I doubt he's talking to me.

Maybe someday it won't even hurt.

Snow Drift

Jose Trejo Maya

Inscribe:
    stones covered in snows/storms.
        The view from the *Observatory of Tulum:*
        skies refract in jade iris glare.

        It began as a flashpoint from
        the sun on the sand.
        It's your viewing the *Equinox of Spring:*

        walk towards new heights colonnaded rites.
        the passage of centuries past:

The Truth About Swans

Christina Robertson

The flock of Sandhills are so high up in the cold that their peculiar rippling call sounds as though echoing off God herself, falling to the earth as perhaps evidence of her existence. They are migrating in long hatch marks, south over the city of Chicago today. I'm down here, flying solo, tramping through slush puddles to my coffee place, yet the falling sound easily seduces me into feeling something more important is going on, something I need to be part of. That faint undulation makes me want to let loose something wild inside myself. I make good on a difficult promise to fight this all too familiar urge—I need to tighten up for goodness sake. It is not actually my coffee place, just the neighborhood hub where I'll make another effort to join the legion of beings I have been, for better or worse, conscripted to. I decide to wait to cross with the light. There was a terrible accident here last summer.

The café is busy, warm, its windows steamy. It isn't packed with cyclists as it is on mild days, filled then with impossibly lithe bodies in skins of black and yellow, orange and blue, red, green and white, narrowed shoulders emblazoned with bold endorsements for Schwinn, Bianchi, Ridley, Condor. There is laughter and gear talk on those days, routes and speeds and hammerfests and breakaways, and rough tales of epic fails and crashes, brutal "endos." Tucked in, here and there amongst them is usually a young mother or two, their gooey toddlers disassembling a blueberry muffin or some such. I like to nurse my coffee, letting the yarns and convivial one-upmanship become background music for me while I absently watch crumbs fall to the floor and work on my Reality Journal. I confess, I find perverse satisfaction in witnessing the ruination of a perfectly good muffin. Besides, to be precise, the journal is a droll therapy assignment. I am trying to change my life for the better. Or so I'm told.

Today's crowd is different. A few annoyed commuters are being edged out by a hulking mob of texting, heedless teenagers. The fancy prep school down the block must be going on some kind of field trip. This privileged youth no doubt lobbied for a little up and coming soccer mom and dad extravagance before boarding the yellow bus. I study the girls. They are mascaraed and tautly sullen. The boys, still baby-faced, seem awed by them, mulling the tantalizing possibilities they hope will present themselves at the back of the bus. One boy with an especially angelic face stares full on at the barely contained breasts of the girl beside him, mesmerized, as if they are Death's last light.

Towering over the fray, darkly handsome Derek pulls frothy works of genius off the La Marzocco. Occasionally his dawn blue eyes rise to read the room. A masterpiece of roses climbs his arm and a cascade of pines tumble down the other. No skulls or thorns or Chinese characters. No excerpts from Thoreau or Whitman. No bike tattoos. Warm red blooms and brisk, majestic evergreens, as if he's got a secret hero's life in the enchanted forest of A Midsummer Night's Dream. He's mine.

The café owner offers greetings to each customer, entertaining observations designed to stroke ego: *It's cold! But just the sight of you warms us up, right guys?* Derek might offer a nod, but otherwise remains silent. It seems like the tall, beautiful ones always do, right? OK, let's call a spade a spade. Derek isn't really mine, but at times he peers at me over his handiwork, abstractions of ferns and hearts and wheat shafts to top drink orders, and the edges of his eyes lift in what I read as a nuanced message. He always makes a swan for me. It's why I come to this place and not another café where I might better fit in—or in which I might disappear. His swans call me out.

It's not a crush I have. I'm too old for that, too far from anything that could connect us in real life. I'm long divorced, and the mother of a son in college. In fact, I could, just about, be Derek's mother. In my higher mind I certainly don't flatter myself in thinking he sees anything other than the silver thatches in my hair and the flaccid tone of my arms. But he must perceive something else, something that inspires swans. I imagine it as a courtship ritual in one of my many parallel universes. God, I love those places.

This is the thing—I lie. Paula, my therapist, uses that word freely in our sessions. Telling her I lie was probably the only truth she got out of me in the beginning. But eventually she wore me down. Not that I couldn't bite back at any time to protect my mental creations, nor that she succeeded in prying out some violent trauma that had left me with a compulsion to rewrite the past. I'm just getting tired of this marathon. Paula seems as good a place to stop as any.

The fire in my gut when she first explained her extravagant diagnosis, pseudologia fantastica (compulsive lying, to you), has subsided. I might get a little defensive when she questions me, but I no longer feign rage, no longer panic and leap into fight or flight the way I did at first, soon after being mandated to treatment. Then Paula's dimly lit office with its painstakingly predictable décor made me sick. I hated its unrelenting calm and multiple framed degrees from smart, but not the best, universities. I hated her nauseating patience. How, whenever I thought I had her indoctrinated, when I thought I'd won and she was going to join me in my preferred version of the truth, my alternate story, she'd yawn. Or ask me what really happened and why I felt that account wasn't good enough; what pushed me to lie. I would try to up the ante then; I'd get friendly with her, appeal to the girlfriend in the therapist. *I know, I know, it's a lot money, but I needed it...and they wanted to pay! Yeah, I thought I'd give it the old college try, but, you know how it goes, Paula...once he was interested, I wasn't.* After a while I got tired of trying to convince her of things I wasn't so sure of myself anymore. She started to win. She succeeded in making me feel like crap. And that crap was fascinating.

Listen, here's a little-known fact about Sandhill cranes: once they begin to mature their plumage fades from cinnamon to a dishwater gray. They begin an odd Springtime ritual then, industrious preening with Midwestern mud, rich in iron oxide. Streaks of it seem to restore some of that youthful glow to their feathers.

Sometimes I find the truth outside is really distant, like watching a movie. And the truth inside is small and ugly, alien and insatiable as a damp little hatchling. What is wrong with reaching? Expanding my concept of self? Is it wrong to share things with people the way I want them to be? The way they should be—inspiring praise, providing excitement, diversion, refuge? Paula calls it "manipulation". I call it *outwitting.* She calls them "fabrications". I call them *reasonable assumptions* and *suspensions of disbelief.* After all, isn't the world filled with BS? Rife with things that seem insupportable, untenable, illogical? Impossible? That five hundred tons of metal can take a running start and lift off the ground; that a deaf man can write emotionally kickass symphonies, that two people can find trust in one another though they are strangers? That children can grow, even when deprived of everything that is dependable and right. That for millennia, those dirt gray cranes have flown thousand-mile journeys simply by waving muscle and rust tinted feather.

I believe they are working on increasing their odds when they adopt that mud-rusty patina. I get it! Out there in the great muck and flow, stifled by the pitiless drudgery of it all, the ongoing attempts on the life of your soul, you have to make yourself desirable, distinctive, viable. It's part of an elaborate plan for survival. If one doesn't wake with a surge of anticipation for the day ahead, one fabricates it with "attitude adjustment;" *fake it 'til you make it.* One coaxes it with a swipe of lipstick and eyeliner, borrows it by tuning into a favorite station, stokes it with a cup of coffee. Are those lies? Putting your "best foot forward", "wearing many hats", "pitching" your idea, "wooing" a mate, "winning someone over". C'mon, isn't that all a little suspect?

You know, it used to be that I enjoyed stirring in a bit of sugar and disrupting my swan with the spoon. But lately I've begun to feel a knot of guilt over destroying the beautifully crafted creature. Guilt is something I can only recall experiencing way back in childhood, when my shining exaggerations (if I must) took their first steps onto the wire. I wasn't sure why I was fibbing. It just seemed a better answer in the moment. I wasn't interesting enough to be a nerd, brave enough to be a jock, sexy enough to be a slut, caring enough to be a best friend. I had a secret intelligence, animal cunning. There was a thrill in embellishing my stories, relief in upping my test grade, in elevating my inconsequential social status. Lying got easier. It became a game, something I excelled at. The sense of accomplishment made it ok. The guilt went away. I could do without the friendships I lost. Those people weren't smart enough anyhow; dummies dulled by a compunction to be polite and moderate, i.e. boring.

I steal a glance at Derek as, with each pass of my spoon, my swan becomes a cleaved heart, then a formless striation. He is working on the next order. Silly for me to feel bad. He doesn't know what I've done to his swan and, really, why would he care? Everything is made to disappear here. That's what's great about food and drink establishments: everything is presented with as much appeal as possible, it is consumed, and disappears.

Sorry. I attribute these bloated insights to Paula and her dogged round up of my "falsehoods". Without Paula I wouldn't be feeling bad about Derek and his foam. I'd have sold him a bill of goods about myself by now, tried to get to him, briefly, until he would undoubtedly distance himself. Still, it would work just enough for a quick stroke to the old ego. For a short, dreamlike moment my silvering hair would rewarm to chestnut, the slight dragging of my cheek would rebound and age spots would unbind back into freckles.

This brief time—the time I might have had him convinced I had something he wanted—would be a badge of achievement in human desirability. That was something I never thought I'd have back on the day I was dying of shame, having my eight-year-old head shaved, the treatment for lice at the Night Ministry family shelter. It was something I gave little consideration long ago, in those days of chaos when mom was out of her head on methamphetamines, before I was taken away. It was something I finally gained, then lost again years later, when I found Steve's wedding ring on the kitchen counter, Steve gone to live with the pretty young Apple Genius who'd fixed his phone. Rising above, fooling people, has been my balm in Gilead.

I haven't mentioned Derek to Paula. I'm afraid I will offer up a variation of the truth that will be too creative for her to stomach...where he actually asks me to meet him after work and confesses he is attracted to me—a May/October—OK, November—thing ensues. We stroll off, kicking stones, touching, brushing against each other, swapping humorous anecdotes. We end up on a park bench gazing at the swans that glide in the lagoon...or we climb out onto the rocks at the lakefront and count the scrappy gulls on the break wall. Either way we are most assuredly leaning against each other for warmth, marveling at our spiritual connection, the one we read clearly in each other's eyes. Our dissatisfaction with the paltry cards life has dealt, dissatisfaction so deep it is blooming on his skin and rushing off the cliff edge of my brain.

What? It could happen.

One of the bevy of mocha sipping teen vixens is holding court near the condiment table. She draws from her to go cup, blue eyes twinkling, perfect cleavage on display beneath an unzipped parka, then fingers a fan of ski tags dangling from her pocket. Her nail polish is dark blue and badly chipped. Nevertheless, she is a particularly pretty girl with a face that had probably launched a thousand likes. There is sotto laughter from her associates, three attractive, if less luminous wannabes. She—Breck I think her name is—is telling them something with her eyes and a couple of strategic grimaces. Just behind her, trying to stand so close it would look like an accident should they touch, is the reason. It is the cherub, a boy Norman Rockwell would have painted in the simple hues of a past era. Boys often look benign at this age, plain as donuts, until that mysterious moment when Nature takes them by the hand and leads them to a full costume change. Somewhere in the midst of high school they become men. They still don't know what to do with what they've gained, but the girls quickly help them figure it out.

Breck seems to me to be one who may have already helped a few. She glows, as a sun, the others huddled around her. As far as I can see, the calculation of her movements, her attitude, one of sublimely casual disinterest, the perfect weight of her lashes and contrived sexiness of her hair convinces me that she'd snacked on boys from an early age.

The rougher cut girls around her are feeding off abundant innuendo in her cute-mean sign language. It is quick and easy for me for me to decipher. They are planning to toy with the naive, baby-face behind her. She has sensed his hopefulness and, like a spoiled child given a balloon, has a primitive, irresistible urge to pop it.

His name is Scotty and gullible is written all over him. Like most boys in the grips of infatuation, he is dumb as a rock. This I'm thinking as I see Breck strategically back into him—accidentally on purpose. With contact, a deep flush blooms in his cheeks and the creamy foam from his hot cocoa splashes across his knuckles. He quickly pulls his hand away in an effort to avoid spilling on her, unfortunately flipping the cup onto himself. The drink slops down his pants. Breck stifles a giggle with her squad. She knows she has innocence cornered.

He winces looking down at the very suggestive stain on his tan jeans—the stain that would be there all day. The guys all lose it. But it is when Breck, grabbing a handful of coffee napkins, kneels down before him and makes a coy attempt at rubbing off the stain that the uproar really begins. He pushes her away and the whole coffee shop sways its attention. It is too late. The soldier has risen. She glances slyly at her gal pals from her suggestive position on the floor. Scotty's expression strains between utter torture and rapture, his cheeks now purple. The guys have commenced to howling and yipping like a pack of hyenas. The boy doesn't know how to play this as it becomes apparent he...doesn't know how to play this. Misery wells in his eyes. The girls erupt gleefully.

Here is the truth about swans: they are not the proverbial brainless beauties they appear to be. They are highly intelligent creatures that can actually distinguish between people; remember who has been kind to them and who has not. They seem ethereal, but are muscular, hollow boned, yet strong enough to inflict serious injury, even to larger animals, even to humans. And, for all this high drama, they are, as a species, nothing more than close cousins to the obnoxious Goose.

I don't need Paula's voice in my head asking what's really happening. I know both sides of this scenario, just as a swan can float and fight, or plain gray cranes sense the benefit in rouging themselves. I know humiliation. I know nakedness. And I know the intoxicating effect of crafting a win. Over the years I've learned how to control the characters in all my plays.

I sidle over to the pack and ask Breck if I can help her up. The boys freeze. The girls freeze. Before I know what is coming out of my mouth, I am introducing myself as a documentary filmmaker working on a very interesting project about human conscience. I tell her she has all the qualities we have been looking for in a subject: being highly photogenic (she smiles and glances at her entourage), having leadership quality, and a streak of cruelty. She stares at me in disbelief. I've got to give her credit for that. I take out one of my ambiguous business cards, the one that reads itsastory.com and has an MFA after my name. I hand it to her and review what I'd seen her do to her friend that caught my eye. I frame it, objectify it, glorify it, sounding quite professional, if I do say so. I restate its callousness and perfect lack of conscience. Call me, I say. I even hand a few cards to the other girls, telling them we might be interested in them as well.

A harried teacher appears at the door of the coffee shop, annoyed at having had to wait so long. She points to her watch and signals them all to hustle. Derek's eyes watch from their clean heaven as the kids start shuffling out, some leaving cups and stirs behind. To my satisfaction, Breck still looks confused and embarrassed, chewing on a ruined fingernail. From the doorway, her gaggle of hopefuls all glance back, excited. I smile and wave one of my cards overhead as they depart.

I look down at my deflated latte. No time for another. I shift my gaze over to Derek. He is, of course, staring at me, as is most everyone else in the place. Bending forward over the counter, propped on his trellis of roses, he asks with genuine interest if I am really a filmmaker. I fix him with a direct eye—BS lesson 101 is never glance away—and reply with all but a nod, *I'm always working on a good story.* I figure that's true enough.

I realize I haven't the time to make an entry in my Reality Journal now. Paula will chalk this up to "resistance". But Hell, it's just that participating in life's theater has a more interesting pay off. Feeling the pressure of the hour, I zip up my jacket and try to catch Derek's eye once more on my way out. He is gone. It's for the best; I only have a minute or two's walk to decide which version of what made me late to share with Paula. I mean, frankly, I don't really mind her so much. She's like one's loyal dog. I don't actually want to mess up our thing, whatever it is. This is what I am thinking about as I step out onto the street. And there he is, Derek, leaning against a sunny wall, shivering, hunched, hands in the pockets of his jeans. *Can we talk?* he asks, gazing at me with those sky-eyes. My youth comes rushing back, lifting curves, pinking me up, adding heartbeats, erasing the mileage of years, husbands, children, careers, mistakes. The air out here feels clear and compelling.

It could happen.

The Bar at the Bottom of the Hill

$100 for 100 Words Contest Finalist

Thomas Boos

Where our fathers met our mothers in the lampless gravel parking lot. Where there was nothing at all. Where we ended up spending the best part of our twenties. Where the sky at night was a black upturned bowl that we never gazed into—never wondered what was beyond because we knew there was nothing. Where the neon flag hummed above the door, and the taxidermy deer stared from every wall. Where they sang *West Virginia, mountain mama.* Where our lives came to an end. Where there was nothing at all.

THE DOLL

PIERO SCHIAVO-CAMPO

TRANSLATED FROM ITALIAN BY SARAH JANE WEBB

On March 9, 1902 Alma Schindler married the musician Gustav Mahler. From then on, she was known as Alma Mahler. What do we know about her? Everything and nothing. History informs us of the countless lovers and affairs that made her the most intriguing and talked-about woman of the twentieth century, eclipsing her artistic production. The daughter of a painter, from a tender age she mixed in the intellectual circles of Vienna and became acquainted with their foremost representatives. She was still very young when she met and had a love affair with the artist Gustav Klimt, and possibly others (Max Burckhard? Alexander von Zemlinsky?), but at twenty-three she decided to settle down and marry the famous conductor, twenty years her senior. Alma loved music. She wrote some Lieder and sang one to her husband, accompanying herself on the piano. Mahler listened attentively, then, without saying a word, he got up from the sofa and retreated to his studio. What estranged the couple, though, wasn't Mahler's indifference towards his wife's artistic efforts, but the death of their first daughter, Maria Anna, who contracted diphtheria at the age of five. It was then that Alma, devastated, realized what her fate would be: to love madly, and to lose her beloved–along with the fruit of their intimacy.

First, she fell in love with Walter Gropius, the future founder of Bauhaus, the school that would boast Paul Klee and Wassily Kandinsky among its teachers. Alma couldn't help putting her whole heart into everything she did: she would have died, rather than lead a mediocre existence, and secret encounters she would have viewed as cheap. That's how Mahler learned what was happening to his wife: she told him forthrightly, except for the most intimate details.

The Maestro tried to restore their relationship–he even consulted Sigmund Freud, in the hope that the eminent psychologist would give him some advice–but refused to divorce his wife. He hadn't long to live: he was in New York when he fell ill, in 1911; he returned to Vienna, but died that same year. In 1915, Alma married Gropius; the two separated in 1920, when Alma discovered that she was pregnant by the poet Franz Werfel, whom she married a few years later.

Between Mahler's death and her wedding to Gropius, Alma Mahler had a tormented affair with an intemperate genius, the expressionist artist Oskar Kokoschka. It was Klimt, one of his teachers, who introduced Kokoschka to the general public in 1908, but the young painter's art didn't appeal to everyone. It was hard, strong, clumsy, full of contrast–almost as if Kokoschka were determined to depict his troubled soul, rather than reality; or as if reality itself were nothing other than the sheer projection of Kokoschka's mind: in short, of his folly. Alma Mahler fell in love with him, but realized that they would never form a stable relationship. Insufferably possessive, he demanded to see her at all hours, to spend all his time with her. He surrounded her with care and attention, lavished praise on her paintings; yet Alma was well aware that, in their rapport, she was nothing but a piece of Kokoschka's soul. After two years of passion and strife, Alma Mahler decided to leave her lover.

Kokoschka was devastated. He'd let Alma inside. Kokoschka hadn't given her his heart, as the average bourgeois would have done. No: Alma was a part of his own soul that had suddenly become independent and had decided to walk out on him. It was as if carmine and ultramarine blue refused to be brushed onto the white canvas that he stretched across wooden frames with wide-jaw pliers. He had never intended to restrict the freedom of his beloved: Alma had every right to do what she wanted with her life. Yet he needed her presence, just as his paintings needed carmine and ultramarine blue to come alive. He went to the most famous milliner in Vienna, Hermine Moos, who also crafted rag dolls, and ordered a life-size doll whose features he designed himself. She had Alma's expression and round face; her sensuous lips, curled into a perennial smile; her high, generous bosom; her large thighs (which she had no reason to be ashamed of). Her long black hair fell softly to the shoulders, and her skin was warm and soft: Moos had used the best plush fabric on the market, and its flesh color had been obtained with a dye created by Kokoschka in person. When the doll-maker finally delivered her, the artist was enthusiastic. He placed her on the large red armchair in his studio, and gazed at her at length with loving eyes.

"You're beautiful! But we can't have you sitting there all naked like that. Wait, I'll go and get you some clothes and underwear. Don't move, my love, I'll be right back!"

Kokoschka had no idea about sizes. The haberdasher on the corner of Banhofstrasse made some suggestions, and he returned with a pillow-case in which he'd crammed two pairs of underpants (a change would be useful, he thought); a corset; a pleated skirt, very similar to one Alma had worn; a lace blouse; and even a large hat with an ostrich feather. He dressed her, scrutinized her. Everything was fine, except for the hat.

"We often talked about it, remember? I always said that you'd look even prettier in a fashionable hat, but I didn't want to force you to do anything against your will."

He removed the hat and threw it into the fireplace.

"And now, sweet lover of mine, we can resume our strolls on the Ring." He picked her up by the waist, dragged her down the stairs and into the street.

"Look, darling, a motorcar! That's the third I've seen, this month. They're manufactured by Herr Ferdinand Porsche, the greatest engineer ever born in Austria. He's one of my fans, you know? I've sold him two paintings, and he seems to want a third one. When I get paid, we'll buy a bottle of champagne from Felix Strauss and drink it together."

During their long stroll on the Ring, they came across a couple of Kokoschka's acquaintances and nodded politely. As usual, people stared, mesmerized by Alma's beauty. Not until their elongated shadows projected themselves onto the trunks of the plane trees did the two go home. There they ate, then lay on the perennially-unmade bed until they fell asleep, exhausted.

In the following days, Kokoschka resumed the life he'd always led, or perhaps the one he'd always dreamed of, together with his darling Alma Mahler. He took her with him wherever he went: to the park, to coffee shops, to the store where he bought paints and brushes. Alma's presence gave his strength, inspiration. He went back to painting every day, which he hadn't done since she'd entered his life. One month later, however, he started to feel that something was amiss. Sitting on a stool, in his studio redolent of oil paint, he gazed at his beloved reclining in the red armchair.

"Why do you sit like that in the shade? You look like a ragbag... Why won't you talk to me? Are you feeling depressed? I know how it feels, I get like that, too: every time I finish a painting, my soul feels drained. But believe me, you need to use your willpower and overcome this torpor. When steeped in darkness, the worst thing you can do is curse the light."

He observed her silently. Where were her laughter, her smart comments, her sense of humor? Where was her eagerness? He realized that what he loved in Alma Mahler was, in fact, her passion, her hunger for a fast-paced existence. He would have loved it if she'd squeezed his hand, or suggested they danced together, in the middle of his studio, without accompanying music, surrounded by easels and with all his paintings propped up against the walls. He drew nearer, started to undress her. When she was completely naked, he carried her to his bed and lay down beside her.

"Why don't you embrace me? Why don't you hold me tight? You don't seem to like me any more..."

The next day he showed up with Alma at the front door of the imposing house of Herr Porsche, in Mozartgasse. The famous engineer and captain of industry had sent him a note the day before, and Kokoschka was keen for such a wealthy man to become a collector of his art. Under his right arm, wrapped in brown paper and tied with string, he carried the painting that he intended to sell to him. As usual, his left arm was wrapped around Alma's waist. He rang the doorbell. Shortly after, Porsche's butler appeared.

"I'm Oskar Kokoschka, and this is Alma Mahler. Would you announce us, please? Herr Porsche is waiting for us."

The servant nodded and opened the door wide to let them through. He showed them into a sitting room furnished in the fashion of the previous century: satin-covered armchairs; gilded stucco work; exquisite china on burl-wood furniture. The walls were covered in paintings, among which Kokoschka recognized the two that Porsche had bought from him. They hung alongside a couple of works by Klimt, and a self-portrait by Egon Schiele, a young man he didn't see much: Kokoschka considered him extremely talented, but as mad as a hatter. On a table in the center of the room, the master of the house had placed a glass case containing a model car.

"Were you admiring my model, Herr Kokoschka? It hasn't been manufactured yet, but I hope it will be. An inexpensive car that everyone can afford. When I manage to produce it, I'll call it 'Volkswagen.' What do you think of that? But do sit down, please. A glass of liqueur?"

Porsche wore an elegant double-breasted gray suit. He was well-groomed, clean-shaven, his moustache seemingly trimmed to size with precision instruments. As he entered, the air was stirred by a subtle drift of Cologne. He gazed at the artist with his slanted eyes. For some reason, to Kokoschka they looked like the eyes of an engineer: Herr Porsche could have had no other occupation, and those eyes–he thought–showed a sort of predestination to excel in mechanics.

"Thank you. I've brought the painting. Just like you wanted it: two lovers in the countryside, with a white cat nearby..."

Porsche continued to observe Kokoschka's eyes: restless, and seemingly incapable of focusing steadily on anything.

"But I asked you to bring me the *Bride of the Wind*, remember? When I came to your studio, I was deeply impressed with that painting. The two lovers, recumbent between crumpled sheets, unexpectedly morphing into desolate valleys and mountains bathed in nightlight..."

"I do remember, Herr Porsche," interjected Kokoschka, "but I can't part with that work. You see, Sir, in that painting I portrayed my darling Alma as she appeared to my intricate soul at the happiest time of my life. She wasn't merely beautiful: there was a fire in her, and a perfect candor that turned into voluptuousness, into endless desire; until, sated and spent, she would drift off in a dream that she alone could understand. This is what I retain, in the depth of my yearnings. But now... Look at the state she's in. You see? She's so detached, nothing concerns her anymore. It's as if she were permanently at the window, pining for another man. I shower her with attention, but she ignores me. She doesn't even move!"

Porsche turned his engineer eyes towards the doll. Having slipped halfway off the seat of the smooth satin sofa, she was almost kneeling on the floor. Her long skirt had climbed up to reveal hefty thighs, but this didn't seem to bother her. Slowly, Porsche returned his gaze to the painter.

"If I succeeded in making her move, would you give me the *Bride of the Wind*?"

Kokoschka stared at him goggle-eyed. His lips parted. If anyone in the world could accomplish such a feat, it was Porsche.

The whole of the following month, the painter stationed himself in one of the automobile manufacturer's workshops, remaining in close proximity with the mechanical engineers in charge of the *operation*. He was anxious, of course. Such complex surgery had never been attempted before. Porsche himself had designed the skeleton of light but sturdy aluminum to be installed in Alma's body. The bones were held together by universal joints and moved by string tendons. Though the muscles couldn't be recreated, Porsche had invented an ingenious system of reinforced balloons: once inflated with compressed air, they would move her limbs, head, torso, hips.

Naturally, an energy source was needed. The eminent engineer devised, for Alma Mahler, several small two-stroke engines, gasoline-powered and extremely quiet. There was the problem of how to supply these systems with fuel. In the end, they decided that the liquid should pass through Alma's mouth. This would enable the couple to enjoy a drink together: champagne for him and, for her, the fuel blend she needed for her movements. She was fitted with an artificial esophagus, and the engines were attached to the corresponding joints. When the skeleton was ready, Alma was sawed in half length-wise. Overcome with fear of losing her forever, Kokoschka refused to attend in person. He left the workshop, retreating to the small entrance hall. There, on the wooden table, someone had left the previous day's newspaper. The painter started to leaf through it, hoping for distraction. Tides of war. Once again, European powers are arming themselves, ready to send off hundreds of thousands of peasants disguised as soldiers to battlefields that no-one cares about. History is here and gone and we're its witnesses, dragged along by a river of which we don't know the origin–or the destination. We should be content with bar chatter; with evenings out at theaters full of bright lights and bejeweled women; with the love of our sweethearts, their black hair fanning out on the pillow. There is absolutely no sense in this world, and looking for it at all costs is the only real sin that human beings can commit.

Over two hours went by before the radiant technicians came to fetch him and showed him into the workshop. Before Kokoschka's eyes appeared Alma Mahler, seated on the counter. There were still wood chips and sawdust all around, testifying that the surgery she had undergone had been radical. As he entered the room, he saw her get off the counter and walk towards him on her own, with no-one to support her. He burst into tears.

Kokoschka decided to wait a few days before resuming their strolls on the Ring. He thought his loved one should have a little time to recover from her dreadful operation, though she didn't appear to be suffering. Herr Porsche had devised a special mechanism–a wooden tablet with brass buttons–to control her movements. Depending on the combination of buttons, Alma got up, sat down, walked forward, moved her arms, and so on. At first, Kokoschka was a little disappointed with her movements. They were slow, mechanical. In order to walk, his darling Alma had to lift a thigh, then bend her leg forward, push her limb and straighten it until the heel touched the ground, and only then advance with her torso. By pressing on the right keys, she turned her head: the joint enabled her to rotate it at any angle, and even to complete several turns. The painter had to use the system carefully, to make sure the result didn't look unnatural. Eventually he would get used to the situation, he told himself. Alma Mahler was like someone who had been in a serious accident: because he loved her, he would take care of her; he would arrange for her to have everything she needed, and make sure that her awkward movements wouldn't be derided by the gossips of Vienna. Every ten days, he got her to drink the mineral oil recommended by the mechanics. He never left her alone. Every evening he helped her undress, and every morning to put her clothes back on. Having realized that the necessary movements were beyond his lover's capabilities, he didn't want this inability to make her feel embarrassed–*different*, so to speak. One evening he observed her at length, in the semi-darkness of his large studio lit by a single incandescent light bulb. She sat straight, immobile. Of course, until he used the tablet, she couldn't move.

Suddenly he felt sad: for her, first and foremost, but also for himself. Was this the result he'd planned to obtain? As a painter, Kokoschka was a perfectionist. Despite their apparent instinctiveness, his pictures always aimed at an objective, at an innermost principle that mustn't be betrayed: when he felt that he hadn't managed to express satisfactorily what he'd had in mind, Kokoschka would destroy his painting without mercy. As he observed Alma that night, he realized that she looked like a botched painting. Her face smiled at him. It smiled all the time: there was no way to make it not smile. True, she moved, but only when he made her do so; and even if she did move, there was no trace of the dazzling light and deep shadows that he once perceived in her gaze. He got to his feet and started to walk up and down his studio, his arms behind his back and his head bowed. He followed a row of blue tiles, making sure his steps never touched the white ones. With all his mechanical skill–he reflected–Porsche would not be able to give his adored Alma a soul. The engineer had done all he could, but in order to move forward he needed someone else, an expert in that inner element that distinguishes us from metal skeletons, plush covers, and two-stroke engines.

Doctor Landauer.

No one else could help him. The artist knew him well: he was another collector. He had sold him a self-portrait in which the face was all patches of green and blue. Landauer had graduated in mechanical engineering in '99, only to discover that his true calling was medicine. As a doctor, he was a pupil of the famous Maximow, who in 1908 announced the discovery of stem cells. Landauer then pursued his own research on stem cells in a direction that Maximow, and German medical circles at large, considered less than ethical; he was even obliged to flee from Berlin, taking refuge in Vienna, where his name was only ever mentioned in whispers. One evening, while they sat in a bar having a beer, Landauer had told him something of the results of his work: self-replicating organs, tissue that regenerated itself... The doctor maintained that life could be manipulated, just like anything else, though his opinion had come up against the moral prejudices of the majority of his colleagues.

Landauer lived in Dunkel Strasse, a side street of Hütteldorfer Strasse not far from the Schmelz. The painter rented a town carriage, but on hearing their destination the coachman told Kokoschka that he had no intention of taking him and his companion that far: he would leave them at Hütteldorfer, one block away. When the two got off, the street was deserted. A thin fog enveloped the buildings, creating mysterious pools of shadow all around. The wistful sound of a Barbary barrel organ reached Kokoschka from a distance. The painter and his beloved slowly covered the short stretch that separated them from a noble but run-down building that towered massively in a narrow lane, stifling it. Kokoschka rang the doorbell and stood waiting. It was a while before an old man with strong features and dark rings under his eyes decided to unlatch the front door.

"I'm Kokoschka, the painter, and this is Frau Alma Mahler. Please announce us. I know I wasn't invited, but it's a matter of great importance, and I hope that an enlightened man like Doctor Landauer will forgive the inconvenience of our unexpected arrival.

Without saying a word, the servant closed the door on them. Kokoschka and Alma were obliged to wait several more minutes before the heavy door opened again, and the old man let them in. They found themselves in a hallway. The ceiling had stucco decorations in high relief and walls painted with zigzag motifs in strongly contrasting colors. In the middle of the room stood a man of medium height, whose round spectacles flashed in a sinister manner at the flickering light of the candelabra held up by the servant. Landauer was smiling.

"Herr Kokoschka! This is such an honor: your visit pleases me immensely! Do come in and make yourselves comfortable.

He showed them into a large studio that opened directly onto the hallway, and invited them to sit on a sofa with a diagonal-stripe cover. Kokoschka, who was tense, sat bolt upright. Alma smiled.

"Tell me, Herr Kokoschka: to what do I owe the pleasure of your visit?

While the artist explained the situation, his haunted, watery eyes couldn't help but reveal his misery. He described the operation carried out by the Porsche technicians, and told him all about the engines and pumping mechanism that enabled Frau Mahler to move. Landauer listened attentively, interrupting occasionally to ask for further details, and didn't express an opinion until Kokoschka had finished.

"This is a difficult case. You did well to come to me: I believe that your unexpected visit will pave the way to an interesting experiment. Ordinary people believe that we are animated by a vital spirit, something that goes beyond matter: a mysterious *res cogitans* over which man has no power. But we scientists know that this is not the case. The secret of our soul lies in our nerves, which intertwine along the limbs and inside the inner cavities of our body to form the brain–the real seat of thinking. And this is the point: your loved one doesn't have a brain.

"Wouldn't it be possible to get hold of one for her? I beg you, Doctor, I'd do anything to have her back for real..."

"If you're thinking of implanting a brain–purloined, so to speak, from another man (or perhaps I should say from another woman)–I must tell you immediately that this wouldn't work. First of all, the resulting individual wouldn't have Alma Mahler's personality, but that of the person who originally owned the implanted organ. In any case, based on current medical knowledge, this sort of operation would never succeed.

"The brain requires a constant supply of oxygen, which is delivered by the blood flowing in the arteries. If deprived of oxygen, the brain dies within minutes. The cardiovascular system and lungs would have to be recreated... For the moment, science is unable to transfer all these things from one living body to another. However, there may be a solution... Let me think this over."

While the doctor was engrossed in cogitation, Kokoschka, on edge, did nothing but stare fixedly at him.

"Yes, I have it! Come with me to my lab," exclaimed Landauer.

Kokoschka rose abruptly from the sofa, his features drawn, his eyes haunted. He operated the tablet so that Alma, too, got to her feet, and together they followed the doctor up a flight of marble steps. Even the staircase had been painted with a zig-zag motif. For a moment, Kokoschka feared that the strange decoration might have a confusing effect on his beloved and cause her to trip; then he realized that it was he who risked falling over: Alma was climbing the stairs with slow, steady steps. While he ascended ahead of them, Landauer glanced briefly over his shoulder.

"You must be asking yourselves the reason for these geometrical motifs... This house used to be inhabited by Doctor Caligari... the director of the mental hospital, you know? He decided to decorate his home in a style in keeping with his occupation. At first, the effect is disconcerting, but one grows used to it. Just think: one day, the famous film director, Fritz Lang, came to visit me. He would have liked to use my home as a film setting, but I refused, of course. Anyway, I can't afford to redecorate the place.

They reached the landing of the first floor, and the doctor showed them into a room entirely painted black. The central light barely illuminated the long shelves, with their array of large glass jars containing biological specimens: lizards, mice, but also human hands and feet, preserved in formalin to prevent decomposition. There was an enormous wooden table in the middle of the room, clear except for a tray of surgical instruments immersed in a bluish solution.

"This is my lab, Herr Kokoschka. As you can see, it doesn't look like a hospital; since I expounded my ideas to the hematologists congress in Berlin, I've been obliged to operate with great economy of means. I've been attacked all round: they said I wanted to subvert the work of God; that life and the nature of organisms depend exclusively on the will of the Lord; and that science shouldn't meddle with such things. But I've told you before, I think... Getting back to us, my idea is to put stem cells to work in order to generate the living tissues that Frau Mahler needs, particularly the nervous system, whose main part is the brain. Obviously, this is far from easy: as I was saying, the brain needs a constant supply of oxygen. Ideally, the stem cells should be guided in such a way that they equip her with lungs, but perhaps these can be replaced with the bellows that drive air into her muscles. In any case, it won't be possible to deliver oxygen to her brain cells without using blood, so we'll need a heart and a network of blood vessels."

"Are you saying that, with your stem cells, you can reconstruct an entire human body?"

"I believe I can. I discovered there are different types of stem cells: some develop in a manner that can only result in the production of certain types of organs, such as the liver or lungs; but others are like child-cells: they have no schooling in life as yet, so they can evolve in any direction. In all these years, I've done nothing but study how to make them grow, 'programming' them, if I may call it that, for the purpose of producing certain tissues, exactly where they are needed."

"That's fantastic, Sir. But I still don't understand: if you grow a brain inside Alma's head, how can you be sure to reproduce Alma's mind, and not someone else's?"

"That's the whole point. You see, Herr Kokoschka, I'm convinced that our cells contain a sort of code: something capable of lending each one of us our specific individuality. Unfortunately I can't prove it yet, but I've conducted a number of experiments, and they all seem to support this assertion. Besides, this is the only explanation for Mendel's observations and for the Laws of Heredity that he set out. In order to reproduce your loved one correctly, I will need tissues that were part of her body. Any fragment that is sure to have come from her person will do: a flake of skin, a fingernail clipping, even a hair.

An image flashed through the painter's mind: the bed in his studio that was always unmade. He had slept in it with Alma Mahler. It was possible that a hair or two of his beloved had remained on her pillow. He must run home and check.

"I think I can get you what you need."

Retrieving a sample of Alma's hair from her pillow on their bed in his studio was not a problem for Kokoschka. Her hair was long and black: so different from his own, which was short and blond! Kokoschka easily recognized one and rushed back to the house in Dunkel Strasse, where the experiment was started.

In the following days, the doctor and the artist silently observed the evolution of the new Alma Mahler, a miracle of life created by the science of Man. She lay on the bed prepared by Landauer in the black-painted lab. The scientist's scalpel had dissected her along precise lines, uncovering the metal skeleton created by the Porsche engineers, and the two-stroke engines that enabled her to move. Landauer illustrated his project to Kokoschka in a whisper, to avoid disrupting the almost mystical silence of the place.

"You see? These mechanisms transfer the motor-generated movements to Frau Mahler's limbs and to the other parts of her body. As you can see, they're hydraulically-operated systems; but what we need is nervous signals, which are of an electrical nature. Fortunately, Nikola Tesla recently patented a device that's just right for our purposes. We'll arrange for nervous signals to replace those transmitted by the tablet."

"With a patent, doesn't one have to pay to make use of it?"

"We'll deal with that later. I'm well-acquainted with Tesla, and I know that he puts science before mercenary interests."

The liquid with the stem cells was placed inside rubber sacs attached in various points to the metal bones. As the days went by, biological tissues started to develop and to grow, forming throbbing rosy-colored structures. Landauer was in ecstasy.

"Veins are forming here." The doctor indicated a point in Alma's open torso. "If you look carefully, you can see that blood is already circulating in them. And the glottis is forming here."

The doctor pointed to Alma's throat. Kokoschka was filled with both admiration and concern. On the one hand, he admired the power of science, the fantastic quest for knowledge that mankind had embarked on the previous century, and that was already yielding such incredible results. God died and was reborn in us, in his creatures. On the other hand, he was concerned that mankind didn't really know where their quest might lead. Would Alma really recover her thinking processes; and along with those, the ability to love him?

"What can you tell me about her brain?"

"We can't admire that. It's forming inside her skull, of course."

"At the end of all this, will she really be Alma Mahler? I mean: how will she remember things, the time we spent together, our walks on the Ring, our nights full of passion?"

"Naturally, she won't remember anything. Thanks to the life codes contained in the hair that you brought me, she will be Alma Mahler to all effects, but as if she were reborn, and ready to start a new life."

"Will she still be in love with me?"

Landauer smiled.

"That doesn't depend on what we're doing here, but if you managed to make her fall in love once, I reckon you should be able to do so again."

Over the next few weeks, the tissues created by Landauer's stem cells continued to grow. One day, the two men noticed that one of Alma's arms had started to tremble, as if she were trying–unsuccessfully–to move it. Hours later, the trembling had reached the other arm, then her legs, and finally her torso, until her whole body was moving convulsively. She was arching her back, shaking her head, fisting her plush hands in mid-air, as if trying to grab something, then distending them in violent spasms. Suddenly she started to emit a prolonged whimper, like the subdued cry of a wounded animal.

"It's time to stitch up her body. No point in trying to monitor the cells' growth any further: we'll soon find out if the experiment has worked. I'll have to tie her to the bed..."

With knitted brows, Landauer started to prepare the surgical needles and dozens of yards of suture needed for the operation. To Kokoschka, those needles didn't look so different from those used by the dollmaker, Hermine Moos, but of course he didn't know much about surgery.

"Will she survive?"

The doctor glanced at him through his round spectacles and frowned.

"Let's hope so."

Ten days later, Kokoschka and Alma Mahler left the house in Dunkel Strasse. Alma was able to walk now, with the aid of a stick. According to Landauer, exercise would improve her mobility; she should be encouraged to talk, to move. She shouldn't be kept at home–he had recommended–but taken out and about, to enable her young mind to make the sort of progress that both men expected. The doctor's instructions had been extremely detailed. The biological tissues with which Alma was endowed had to be nourished, and gasoline was no longer enough: Landauer explained to Kokoschka how to prepare the sugar-and-salts solution that she needed. In order to enable Frau Mahler to assimilate it, she had been fitted with a modestly-sized stomach and bowel. Kokoschka was to give her the solution once a day, using the tablet's commands to prevent the liquid from ending up in the tanks of the Porsche engines. Fortunately, this was the only operation still requiring the use of that rudimentary control device. Kokoschka was delighted that he had thought of Landauer. It was only because the doctor mastered both engineering and medical skills that he was able to accomplish such a miracle.

"Let's take a carriage, my love. True, you need exercise, but I wouldn't like you to get worn out."

"Ahhhaaghaaaa," replied Alma.

"You must learn to control your tone of voice, my darling. There's no need to talk so loudly: it's not done, you know."

"Gheeegaaaahooo."

"Of course, my love, I agree. Let's go home now, so you can lie down a little. You won't have to do anything, I'll get dinner ready. Would you like some boiled potatoes? We could dress them with the horseradish sauce prepared by Frau Shoenberg, our neighbor..."

"Ghu."

Those were days of ecstasy and forgiveness. Kokoschka had to admit that he had hated Alma when she left him, but as they lay side by side on the bed in his dimly-lit studio, their old conflicts melted away like ghosts in the light of a new morning. As Doctor Landauer had predicted, Alma had reawakened to life. She was still the old Alma, and yet she was like a child, eager to learn about the world, and always full of wonder. On the second day, taking advantage of a moment in which the artist had gone out to buy milk and eggs, she got hold of a paint brush and filled a canvas with irregular marks. The picture was still unfinished and Kokoschka, to begin with, was annoyed. But then he looked at her, and his heart filled with tenderness.

"Pure abstract art. Is this what you aim for now? The value of gesture? That irregular trail of carmine across the canvas ... I see you squeezed the whole tube out... Never mind: you obviously wanted to lend substance to your stroke; you needed a tactile structure to strengthen your concept. Well done."

"Gheeee," replied Alma, with the eternal smile that not even Landauer had managed to wipe from her face.

The weeks went by. Kokoschka was happy to have his lover back, yet aware of a budding anxiety which at first he couldn't explain. He took her with him to the usual places for their strolls; he had her sit next to him, holding her large plush hand in his, feeling more and more clearly that she was restless, as if she were looking for something that she couldn't find in her everyday life. That was Alma Mahler: nothing could be done about it; yet he was afraid of losing her. One day, on the Ring, they met the painter Egon Schiele, with his wild hair and usual crazy look in his eyes. Kokoschka greeted him with a nod. After all, their relationship was entirely formal: though both were considered expressionists, Schiele and Kokoschka interpreted the artistic spirit of their times in opposite manner. Kokoschka detested the obsession with nudity that emerged from his colleague's work: he found it lacked those inner whirlwinds of emotion that inspired him, particularly when making love at night. He bowed his head respectfully, and in that moment registered that Alma had fixed her smiling eyes on Schiele's lunatic features. Schiele smiled back, and Kokoschka couldn't help but notice something sly in his expression. Were they acquainted? Of course, they must be! Alma Mahler knew all the intellectuals in Vienna–many of them intimately. Had she slept with him? She never mentioned her love affairs, not even the notorious ones that the whole city gossiped about in outraged whispers. Klimt, Mahler, Gropius... why not Egon Schiele? He felt a wild rage well up inside. Suddenly, the reasons for his anxiety were clear to him. Of course: as time went by, she learned more and more; as her awareness of the world deepened, she became increasingly independent from him. She was more and more herself, Alma Mahler, the one he loved because no man would ever be able to claim her as his own. This drove him mad. Perhaps, he told himself, it was the inevitable price to pay for giving her arms and legs, engines to make her move, nerves and muscles, so he could make love to her on the bed in his studio. He gave Schiele a curt parting nod, grasped his beloved by the waist, and literally pushed her away and along the crowded street.

Reclining on the bed, he observed the light that the lamp post in the street projected, forming patterns on the ceiling. She slept alongside him, immobile. What is it, inside us, that makes us constantly unhappy? What are we looking for, in this moment of awareness that we call life? Why can't we give ourselves over to simple everyday pleasures? He thought about the light dinner he'd had; about her face, as she delicately sipped gasoline from a ceramic mug. He thought about Egon Schiele, and the mere idea that she might be attracted to him rekindled the fury that he'd felt that afternoon. His eyes roamed restlessly, pausing occasionally on the shadow of an object. An ashtray. The vase in which he kept his paintbrushes: in the half-light, it evoked the silhouette of Egon Schiele's head, his coarse hair standing up on end. The easel in the middle of his studio looked like a giant warrior with a triangular head. In the grip of anxiety, he couldn't sleep. The thought that his beloved could fancy another man while being at his side nagged him relentlessly: he stared obsessively at his vase of paintbrushes, that grotesque head of Schiele which had somehow made its way into his existence and now lurked in the shadows. In the end he fell asleep; when he awoke, his studio was awash with the grayish light of dawn. Alma was up. Seated on one of the rush chairs, she was staring fixedly at the street, as if that house were too cramped to contain her spirit, and he a stranger who had chanced to end up in her bed. Or was she thinking of a way to meet his rival? He got out of bed quietly. She didn't even nod a greeting. He dressed quickly, trying not to look at her. Enabling her to have thoughts had been a mistake. Before, at least, she had depended on him entirely and couldn't have tried to get away.

That evening, he took her out to dinner at Lambert's, an inn run by a Frenchman in Pfullstrasse. The food was good, the patrons few, and they wouldn't be disturbed. A light rain veiled the night along the gray streets of Vienna. He held his umbrella over her so she wouldn't get wet. Lambert showed them into a small, private dining room.

"What shall I bring you? I have oysters, fresh from Trieste..."

"Oysters will be fine, Monsieur Lambert."

"And the same for Madam?"

"No, thanks. Only some gasoline for her, thank you."

There was a long silence, while he concentrated on what he should say to her. Alma stared straight ahead.

"Are you happy?" he asked her. For a moment, he thought he perceived something strange in her gaze, like a soundless cry that her permanent smile rendered even more harrowing.

"So you're not happy? Why not? Talk to me, my love. Please explain. I'd do anything to keep you satisfied."

"Ghaauuuu."

"So that's how it is! I knew it. Can't you be content with what we have: the moments when we hold each other tight, when we dream together?"

"Ahguuooohhhh."

"But why? What is it you miss? I bet you don't even know. Go on, admit it. That's the way you are. That's why I love you madly, and that's why you run away from me. You drive me out of my mind! You're looking for something without knowing what it is–something that doesn't exist. And now you're thinking of Egon Schiele, aren't you?"

"Guahhhooo."

"That's not true. It's *my* business too. I won't let you go anywhere near that man. Did you know that he raped a young girl, when he was in Neulengbach? He was sent to jail, then somehow managed to get acquitted. He's an evil creature..."

"Ahggahaaa."

"Don't interrupt. I know him. He'd make you unhappy."

"Ghu."

Kokoschka bowed his head. For a long moment he observed the dead oyster shells. Again, a wild rage was welling up inside him, uncontainable, like the flurries that stirred the sheets in the *Bride of the Wind*.

"So you want to leave me again? I won't let you..."

From the adjacent room came the indistinct drone of patrons intent in conversation. Someone, somewhere, was playing the piano: the notes arrived muffled, as if absent-mindedly caressing their ears. Kokoschka lifted the sharp knife that Monsieur Lambert had left on the table, and with frenzied thrusts started to stab her. When he saw her immobile, he grasped her by the waist and dragged her outside, into the garden. He lay her on the damp grass, then stood over her, looking down.

"You don't deserve me. You never did. We had something special and you threw it away. Adieu."

Head down, heedless of the heavy rain, he set forth along the gravel path towards the exit.

From what I've heard, it was Monsieur Lambert himself who called the police. He reported what he had seen, as well as what he had imagined, and pointed out that Kokoschka hadn't paid the bill. One of the policemen bent over what remained of Alma Mahler. There were large splashes of red on her chest.

"What are these stains, Fritz?"

"I don't know. Red wine, I imagine."

The End of the World?

$100 for 100 Words Contest Finalist

Claudia Reed

The smoke pumps darkness. I focus on Frankie's profile as he passes through and we emerge. It was industrial, that time.

Now it's happening again. The forest combusting to the north yellow-grays the sun. The local trees are stunned with empathy. The little dog lies down beside the road, panting and blinking. Frankie is just to my left. I remind him that he died seven years ago but he doesn't say anything. Never did say much, except to answer a question. So I ask for the second time: "Is this the end of the world?"

The Black Iris

Single Word Contest Finalist

Katherine Todd

"Is it supposed to be a cave...
Or is it a stylized flower?"
I giggle a bit at her
wide eyes when I tell her that
no, this painting is not of a
cave or an iris, but, "It is
a cunt," I turn and stage whisper.
Her little cheeks flush crimson
and a liaison saunters
over to us, about ready
to kick us out, but I screech, "Run!"
We push our way out onto
the street, laughing at the fear of
one simple word, because it had
not been said to one of us yet.
But it will, and it will sting more
than where he slapped you, more than when
a stranger snapped photos under
your skirt and you saw them online,
more than everything said to
you that night you broke his nose.
But neither of us knew that was
our future, so we stole some
fresh fruit and laughed at its core.

TEAR STACKS

WARREN DECKER

北京站到了
We are arriving at Beijing Railway Station
HELLO SIR WHATS YOUR NAME WHERE ARE YOU FROM

Passport
Wallet
iPhone
2000 RMB
Beijing subway map
Contact numbers
Antibiotics
Textbook

apocalyptic
boisterous
clandestine

The teacher of the Level 1 class is beautiful like a friend's tough big sister. The teacher of the Level 2 class is intimidatingly beautiful with stark cheek bones, a tight black skirt, and high tan leather boots. But it is the teacher of the Level 3 class who is the beautiful woman you knew you would meet in Beijing and fall in love with so intensely that you would have to leave your job and home and wife and children behind and start everything over. You see her through the glass classroom door where she is smiling as she listens to a student, and nodding with wide sympathetic eyes. She brushes her long black hair behind her ear and turns to face the whiteboard, pausing with a red marker in her right hand, her left hand resting on her side with her slender fingers extending over the soft white fabric of her skirt.

Once upon a time a man and a woman lived in a small apocalyptic village. One boisterous spring, they fell in clandestine love. The woman wanted to get

> **married. The man said, "Let's go to Beijing. In Beijing I can make money. I can buy you a house. Then we can get married."**

"Sir, we understand that this visa was valid for three years when it was valid. However, it is no longer valid."

"It doesn't expire for another two years."

Walking alone through Beijing, there are people. There are people wearing pink high heels, zebra-stripe tights, green skirts, black fur coats, opaque-lens tortoiseshell-framed sunglasses; people eating roasted pork on sticks, Kentucky-fried chickens, fermented cabbages, salted peanuts, duck intestines boiled with chilies; people licking green-tea ice cream; there are people...

崇文门站到了
We are arriving at Chongwenmen Station
HELLO SIR WHATS YOUR NAME WHERE ARE YOU FROM

Passport
Wallet
iPhone
1756.2 RMB
Beijing subway map
Contact numbers
Antibiotics *disillusioned*
Textbook *ephemeral*

Misty makes you nervous by always leaning too close and smiling and putting her breasts on the counter and speaking to you in fast Mandarin. Your lips are chapped when she talks to you. You swallow. You forget words you once knew. You tell her you want to be in the Level 3 afternoon class with Lǎoshī even though it is too difficult for you. That afternoon you meet the only other student, a woman from France with pink-pastel framed glasses who takes up three desks with her bags and coats, and two iPhones that are both plugged into the classroom's only electrical socket. All afternoon, you listen as she speaks in Mandarin and makes Lǎoshī laugh. She says something in Mandarin and they laugh. Lǎoshī says something in Mandarin and they laugh. You can't understand anything. You can't speak. You need to tell Lǎoshī.

So the man and the woman travelled to Beijing. It was a long bus ride from their village. When they arrived they were <u>disillusioned</u>. They had to live in a very small room. It was a hot <u>ephemeral</u> Beijing summer. They had no money for meat.

"We understand that your visa has not yet expired. Unfortunately, this particular visa is not valid in conjunction with your passport."

"But I just renewed this passport."

...drinking civet-shit coffee; people listening to transistor radios and spinning in the Summer Palace courtyard; people screaming into phones; people riding rented bicycles, scooters, motorcycles, three-wheeled carts piled high with enormous loads of Styrofoam-stuffed plastic bags which bounce under tightly cinched rubber cords; people driving black BMWs, blue emission-free cars; people beeping horns; there are people...

前门站到了

We are arriving at Qianmen Station

HELLO SIR WHATS YOUR NAME WHERE ARE YOU FROM

Passport
Wallet
iPhone 1632.5 RMB
Beijing subway map
Contact numbers
Antibiotics
Textbook

fermented
graceful

The girl at the Qianmen Station luggage inspection gate is girlishly beautiful, a young woman in the big city for the first time. She waves the metal-detector wand around your crotch. She pats your phone in the chest pocket of your blue North Face down jacket. She smiles.

Every day they ate <u>fermented</u> vegetables stir-fried in oil. Then one day, in the fall, the woman

> **found work. She did very well at her work. Soon she gracefully made a lot of money. The man did not do well at his work. He felt very sad. Soon the man and the woman felt embarrassed to be together.**

"Sir, I'm afraid you are not allowed to remain here without valid identity documentation. Unfortunately, you are also not allowed to leave."

"Wait-wait-wait-wait-wait. I don't understand."

...smoking Zhonghua cigarettes, hand-rolled cigarettes; people hawking, coughing, spitting; people selling eggs, sesame biscuits, chicken feet, raw noodles; people playing cards, chess, mahjong; people praying at Yonghe Temple in clouds of smoke; people with skateboards and bulky headphones walking through dusty hutongs, looking for the real Beijing; there are people...

和平门站到了

We are arriving at Hepingmen Station

HELLO SIR WHATS YOUR NAME WHERE ARE YOU FROM

Passport
Wallet
iPhone
1402.5 RMB
Antibiotics
Dictionary
Textbook

hierarchical
impartial

The French woman and Lǎoshī are laughing and looking at you expectantly. You understood a single word in their conversation, *winter*. You don't say anything. You have to tell Lǎoshī through the homework stories. You could write about travelling to Beijing and falling in love with your teacher. After a month of romantic courtship, walking hand in hand in the Temple of Heaven, you travel with her to a village in the outskirts of Xian where you meet her parents and stay with them for the Spring Holiday. At dinner, you get the coin in your jiǎozi and the whole family thinks it is auspicious. Later that night, Lǎoshī collapses with her head on your chest, sobbing and laughing after a convulsive orgasm. You stroke her long black hair behind her ear, pulling it away from her tear-filled eyes and her bewildered close-lipped smile. Her delicate nostrils flare as she tries to catch her breath.

> **The woman moved out and bought a <u>hierarchical</u> house. She was very busy. Soon the cold, <u>impartial</u> Beijing winter came. The man could not pay for his room anymore and he moved into a park.**

"You do have the option of revoking your current passport."
"Can I get a new one?"

...shouting "Hello sir what's your name where are you from" at Tiananmen Square tourists; people being young and beautiful beautiful beautiful beautiful beautiful; there are people digging plastic bottles out of trashcans; people begging for money with buckets and misshapen swollen heads; there are people...

宣武门站到了
We are arriving at Xuanwumen Station
HELLO SIR WHERES YOUR NAME WHAT ARE YOU FROM

Passport
Wallet
Phone
943.8 RMB
Antibiotics
Textbook

jubilant

A woman with densely freckled skin, a warm smile and black teeth, gestures for you to sit at a rough, sticky table across from a frowning man who leans deeply into his plate and smacks his lips as he eats. You point to something on the menu that has the Chinese character for vegetables. Five minutes later, the woman serves you sour fermented cabbage stir-fried with salty fatty meat steaming on a red plastic plate. It tastes like greasy kimchee.

> **Every day the woman would <u>jubilantly</u> stack her money. Her favorite thing to do was to stack her**

money into bigger and bigger stacks. Then she would eat two roasted Beijing ducks while looking at her stacks of money. She didn't eat fermented vegetables.

"Unfortunately, we can't confirm whether or not we can issue a new passport unless you relinquish your current identity."

"But what happens then if I can't get a new one?"

...sitting on the handrail of the terrace overlooking the Forbidden City, with their arms wrapped around their boyfriends' necks and tight-denim legs wrapped around their boyfriends' waists, whispering something, then laughing, then licking their boyfriends' ears; people in bulletproof uniforms standing on the sidewalk with shotguns as people put money into ATMs from armored vehicles; there are people...

长 *chun* 街站到了

We are arriving at Chang 椿 *jie Station*

WHERES YOUR NAME HELLO WHAT ARE YOU FROM SIR

Wallet *ludicrous*

iPhone

622.0 RMB

kinetic

Antibiotics

You wake up at midnight sweating. Your dreams all happened in a stuffy office with ceiling fans and sliding wooden doors. Men were discussing your stomach ***Passport***. You feel weak and can't remember where the bathroom is. A slippery, bubbly **<u>mystical</u>** fermented cabbage squish is coating your tongue and gums and teeth and rising sourly and caustically from your throat and into your nostrils. You shouldn't have had that café latte, but you wanted to talk to someone before coming back to this room alone. You pointed to the smallest cup. The woman at the *mystical* counter, frowning, gave you the largest one and no change for your light-green 50 RMB bill. You said xièxie but she didn't reply. You walked out with the paper cup, sucking the hot milky coffee through the hole in the plastic lid. On the sidewalk people flowed around you. Now the vegetables and latte are writhing and bubbling **<u>kinetically</u>** in your stomach.

The man had no money. Every day he sat in the park and cried. It was <u>ludicrously</u> cold. It was so cold that his tears froze as soon as they came out of his eyes. He took his frozen tears and stacked them into bigger and bigger stacks. All he could do was stare at his big stacks of tears and cry.

nebulous

"It is true that your identity may become temporarily **<u>nebulous</u>**. Shall we commence the disintegration?"

"What will happen to me?"

...wearing white gauze masks, black masks, blue masks, plaid masks, fox masks, panda masks, cat masks, heavy duty industrial 3M masks with special filtered valves; people waving metal-detector wands around crotches; people buying things with paper; people stacking frozen tears; people digesting fermented cabbage; people puking; people shitting; there are people...

Fuxingmen 站到了

We are arriving at 复兴门 Station

SIR WHERES YOUR NAME HELLO WHATFROMARE YOU

Passport

Wallet

iPhone

antibiotics

<u>oblivious proverbial</u>

345.2 RMB

The vomit leaps out of you angrily. You lean over your small trashcan, puking undigested meat and white foam over the empty water bottle and single ticket stub from the Temple of Heaven. There are four crashing vomit waves. You are sweating.

You sit up.

"Please place your passport into this machine. It will first be shredded and then pulverized...

Then one day, there was a big change in the oblivious world. After that, everyone saw that proverbial money was only paper with nice pictures and writing on it.

qualmish

You lay back down again. You stand up. You fall down in your bed. The curtains are drawn against the **qualmish** Beijing winter afternoon. You are trembling and you pull wool socks over your sweaty feet. You pull your fleece hat over your **residual** eyes. The men in your dreams speak to you for a moment and then a pocket of air moves in you. There are six distinct exhalations from your anus, filling the room with a **sophisticated** putrid smell. You need to get to class. You have to get your story to Lǎoshī.

residual

...then liquefied. The liquid will be dried at a high temperature until it is reduced to a fine blue powder which will be scattered..."

"Please wait."

sophisticated

...pushing past people getting on and off the subway; people walking past people; people stopping in front of people; people walking towards people; people walking around people; people looking at people; people looking through people, people being peopled; people peopling people; people with no names; there are people...

LOARE 到 FRNAMESIR 门 *arriving*WHEOMREHEL

We YOU *are at Fu* 成 *Station*

Of course you can not use paper to buy things.

阜 *chengmen* 站 WHATYOUR 了

Antibiotics

Twenty minutes later you limp to the bathroom and realize that each of those six anal exhalations contained an opaque squirt of tan liquid that has soaked into your underwear.

You take these from around your feet as diarrhea dribbles from you into the toilet below.

You wipe, then stand to wash the underwear, but you are too weak.

Transient

Many people had no food. Many people had no water.

Uncertain

"Yes. Thank you, **uncertainly** sir. You may stack your **transient** frozen tears over here. Now, just place your

passport

story into the spinning shredder blades."

violent

xenoglossia

You are trembling **violently** again. You splash your underwear with cold water, then hide them under a mop that sits in the corner of the bathroom. Your pajamas also stink, but they are mostly dry.

wistful

The woman was very thirsty and alone in her big wistful house

You stuff a handful of toilet paper between your butt cheeks the pull on your pajamas. then walk down the hallway with its erratic flickering **xenoglossia** light.

You have to get your **Passport** to Lǎoshī.

"I don't know my name."

Your tears are melting.

You have to get home.

...who have food; people who have water: people who want to rip everything apart, until they make a little rip and see themselves,

in a puke-stained

threadbare tweed

sport coat and

shit-soaked
lime-green
sweatpants,
lying
unconscious
on the sidewalk
under the
Number 2
Ring
Road
overpass
in the
orange
haze
of
a
freez
ing
Bei
jing
w
i
n
t
e
r
.
.
.

北京站到了

We are arriving at Beijing Railway Station

HELLO SIR WHAT ARE YOU FROM WHERES YOUR NAME

Passport
Wallet
iPhone
15.2 RMB
Textbook

youthful
Zealous

After three days, and a full course of antibiotics, you stop sleeping with the trashcan next to your bed. The dreams fade and the trembling subsides. You still stuff toilet paper in between your butt cheeks. Your stomach gurgles and chirps and bubbles with volatile gasses and liquids. You skip the morning classes and eat a piece of dry white toast. You still don't dare fart on the crowded subway. The school looks unfamiliar after a three-day absence. Misty puts her breasts on the counter and says she was worried about you, but you know she wasn't by the way she laughs. You give your story to Lǎoshī. You could ask her to scan your WeChat QR code, but you know that you will never see her again. After you have said zàijiàn, you are shitting in the toilet. Hot liquid is spilling out of you and filthy cold water is splashing back up. You hear Lǎoshī call your name. You wipe quickly, stuff toilet paper in your butt cheeks and rush to see her. She asks you to sign the attendance sheet. There are three open spaces for the classes you missed. You sign the last open square at the bottom of the grid. You say zàijiàn again and walk out of the school with toilet paper clenched in your ass, knowing you can never return.

When the <u>youthful</u> Beijing spring came, the man's tears began to slowly melt. They melted into clear and delicious water. The man took his tears and found the <u>zealous</u> woman in her house. Together, they drank the clear and delicious water.

"Passport."
"Nǐhǎo."
"OK. Next!"
"Xièxie."

...dying; people being born; people stamping passports; people falling in love, out of love, back in love; people arriving at the airport; people hugging; people writing stories on parchment paper; people ripping the stories apart, scattering them on the floor, shitting, spitting, puking, and pissing on them. And there are people collecting the pieces of parchment paper, drying and bleaching each fragment in the sun, layering and pasting the pieces back together. With careful brushstrokes, there are people writing stories.

November

$100 for 100 Words Contest Finalist

Jodee Stanley

I didn't mean to have this conversation again: about why the heat is on and the window open. Why sometimes my mouth bleeds for no reason. Why I bought that hat but never wear it. November's just like that. One day you look outside and the sidewalks are empty. You find yourself walking on the gray edge of everything, shoulders hunched up around your ears to block the wind. You talk and then you stop talking. Listen. Our bones are trying to tell us something.

Ernest Seton Thompson, Malcolm X and Me. A Sort-of Book Review.

Guinotte Wise

A few books have cut through the bumps and clutter of my gray matter, made changes up there, negotiated the neural mazes and worn paths of their own. Ernest Seton Thompson's *Wild Animals I Have Known* is one of the earliest. It taught me to regard animals as what they are, not Bambi creatures with happy Disney/Pixar endings. Our fellow passengers on this deteriorating mothership, wild animals, are the most admirable of creatures—they put their lives on the line every single day. Root, hog, or die. Birds that are wounded beyond flight join the food chain pretty quickly. Old coyotes grown feeble have no assisted living or Medicaid safety net.

I learned crow calls from that book. I could call crows from across a pasture with a "Come look at this!" three rapid caws repeated. Instead of all the crows flying over to take a gander, they'd send one recon bird (if the call was good enough). That crow would scope out the source of the call, determine it was a human, fly back and communicate that fact to the others. They would either ignore any future calls or fly away.

I cannot find my boyhood crow call so will have to order another online and try my hand and lips at it again. I imagine it will be expensive, having bowed to inflation exponentially. I just looked them up and, good God, they have electronic ones! What would be the fun or accomplishment in that? The breath-driven models look about the same as my old one and can be had for ten bucks up. I'll check Ebay.

I have two books by Ernest Seton-Thompson. One is by Ernest Thompson Seton, (?) titled *Rolf in the Woods*. I don't remember anything about that one except its ornate cover and great plate art. Both are quite old. Rolf has an inscription, *Cyril & Mick, 1918.* They are my dad and my aunt. In 1918 they'd have been quite young, three or four. That book has a 1911 copyright.

Wild Animals has a barely legible pencil inscription of August 1918 from Jules (a great-uncle of mine) also to Cyril & Karleen (my aunt Mickey), then it is over-inscribed to me from Aunt May, Dec. 25th, 1950. Its copyright is 1898. I would have been twelve that Christmas, and at the age where books were probably quite a disappointment as gifts. Why not a Benjamin air rifle? A Hornet model airplane engine? A rocket-making set? But this Scribner's book, this collection of animal wisdom, with its gold leaf and embossed cover, its beautiful illustration plates (also by Ernest) is the single most reverberative book of my lifetime, echoing and reechoing down through the years.

Oh, other books of my youth, *Giant, The Great Gatsby, Catcher in the Rye*, the Mickey Spillanes and the Raymond Chandlers, the lurid-covered pocket books, the good, the great, the bad, the prurient, all had their effects. The beat books. Burroughs, Ginsberg, Ferlinghetti, Kerouac. The books of the protest era and Vietnam. Too many to mention. But surely cumulative in my love of words connected and placed with one another to form new chains of thoughts, awe at the writers' ways of using them. Later years brought the pleasures of Didion, McGuane, Barry Hannah, Anne Beattie, Annie Proulx, Cormac McCarthy, many more. Pure word wizardry.

But the tectonic upheaval years offered me books that I read to try and understand the world and my small place in it. Books like Marshall McCluhan's *The Medium is the Message* and Viktor Frankl's *Man's Search for Meaning.* Napoleon Hill's *Think and Grow Rich*, Maxwell Maltz's *Psycho-cybernetics.* Mind-expanding books with deep value and application to more than the moment.

The assassination years (how awful to be able to say that) of JFK, RFK, MLK, Malcolm X brought books and more books. I read them then and I read them now. We had murderous men in government bureaus then. Sociopaths who felt they could right the ship of state just by jettisoning cargo, killing the "dangerous ones." Even our own government admitted that, yes, there was "probably a conspiracy" involved in the death of JFK. Coverup books like the spurious volumes of The Warren Commission really do speak volumes about that. One must read between the holes, the Arlen Specters and the magic bullets, the suspension of physics and logic, and counter it with the damning evidence of the Zapruder film, the threatening of witnesses, the coloration of testimony. These books are among the worst ever published. The above few words will be the only review I give that set of horrors, as it galled me to look through them. Out of this scarification of the truth and justice came a book I cannot recommend strongly enough: Sylvia Meagher's evenhanded *Accessories After the Fact: The Warren Commission, the Authorities & the Report on the JFK Assassination.* She fine-sifted through the 26 volumes, and completely destroyed any credibility the report claimed to have. Her book today remains one of the best of the JFK case, standing the test of time and mountains of new information. It's no rush to judgement or a rubber stamp to conspiracy theories. It stands alone.

I related to all the assassinated leaders, except for Malcolm X. He had angered me after Kennedy's death with his famous statement that chickens had come home to roost. He'd missed the point, I felt. He'd muddied the waters. I wanted to know more about him; what was his game.

It turned out he had no game. He was quite real. After his own assassination, I read his autobiography which was really a collaboration between him and Alex Haley. I had read conflicting things about this man, but no one denied his powerfully charismatic presence, his magnetism and dedication to cause. It's why they killed him in the end; they couldn't stand his heat, his visceral authenticity. As Maya Angelou said after meeting him, "His aura was too bright...a hot storm eddied around him...making my skin contract, and my pores slam shut."

I picked up the autobiography with some trepidation; I didn't want to read about myself as some over-privileged White Devil, and it wasn't about that. I wanted to know more about why he'd distanced himself from the Black Muslims and why anyone would want him out of the way. I knew why they wanted JFK and MLK gone—they were powerful, they were loved, they were now martyred. RFK would meet the same fate in 1968. Che Guevara was martyred for no real reason that I could see. He wasn't quite what he claimed to be, yet ended up as a t-shirt symbol for self-styled revolutionaries. I recall an overalled farmer spitting Red Man and saying, "Any preacher with more than two suits is a hypocrite." The same could go for a closet full of berets and Rolex watches. We're all poseurs to some extent; Che was just one of the more successful. Maybe he deserves the t-shirt, the logofication. The deification. Probably as much as Father Junipero Serra deserved sainthood and statues, but that's a whole 'nother complicated essay, with sepia-tinted Jesuits in my own family album, eyes glowing like coals.

I keep veering away, prefacing, ambling and preambling. I want to get this right. How I feel, and how I felt before and after reading his autobiography. I don't want to preach, or absolve, or misrepresent. The first feeling that comes to me now when I think of, or am reminded of, Malcolm X is admiration. I have saved a magazine picture of him from the sixties; it is a side view, head shot. He is wearing a fedora, short snap-brimmed hat in the style of the times. He looks like an adman or an FBI agent. Many of us did back then, dark suits, skinny ties, fedoras before we cast off that uniform in favor of others.

I have dug through my books to try and find the 1965 Grove version of the autobiography, but like so many other important books, I may have lent it out or otherwise misplaced it. This is unfortunate because that early edition had an epilogue that said a lot. It had my margin notes of the time, my buts and question marks, which subsided after I was about a quarter of the way into it; I was reading rapt, in thrall, side notes be damned. What could I say in the margins or in a notebook about this man?

Black Americans who read this book, back then and more recently, say it changed their lives. It rocked them high up on some African-American Richter scale of kickass. Lemn Sissay says so. Spike Lee says so. This is a club that doesn't admit me, but I don't require admittance. The book changed my life, too, in that it skewed me to a slightly different reading, as a compass needle might be changed by the introduction of a ferrous metal, or a Geiger counter sounds at a more excited pitch. I don't pretend to understand Malcolm X on the level that blacks do, but I cannot be stopped from admiring the man he became at his zenith, or marveling at his resilience and journey from virulent racist to a more tolerant tone. But only tolerant to tolerance, not oppression. And god knows he was oppressed, as was his family.

The book itself was missing some chapters which only recently have come to light in a sad case involving Rosa Parks and her lawyer Gregory Reed. It appears that Reed may have sold many Parks artifacts and memorabilia, valuable items that should have been earmarked for African American history museums. History lost forever. But that's an ongoing story that unfolds daily. Why it's mentioned here is Reed bought those Haley/Malcolm X chapters from the Haley estate in 1992 for more than $100,000. In those days, Reed was known as a "prominent attorney" and his client list, which included Motown greats, was impressive. The chapters were considered too explosive for publication and they were locked away in Reed's safe. When he declared bankruptcy, the chapters were sold at auction to New York Public Library's Schomburg Center for Research in Black Culture.

Fortunately, the pages didn't suffer the same fate as many Rosa Parks ephemera and books, and are deemed an extremely important find. They possibly show, more graphically, why Alex Haley changed his co-authorship to "as told to." He didn't agree with Malcolm X on certain points. And the original publisher, Doubleday (who had advanced $30,000 on the project) canceled when Malcolm X was assassinated, citing fear for the safety of its employees. This has reportedly been regarded as one of the most disastrous, perhaps *the* most disastrous publishing decision ever made. Grove Press picked it up and, eventually, six million copies of the book sold by 1977. Plays, movies and other publicity enhancing events and news items returned it to the best seller lists, and the book sales increased by 300% by 1989.

Max Elbaum wrote in *Revolution in the Air: Sixties Radicals Turn to Lenin, Mao and Che* (2002) "*The Autobiography of Malcolm X* was without question the single most widely read and influential book among young people of all racial backgrounds who went to their first demonstration sometime between 1965 and 1968."

I was hardly a Sixties radical, though I was one of those "young people of all racial backgrounds" who read the book. When I finished it, I was changed. Few books have done that to or for me. I regarded Malcolm X as a stalwart, a man from whom to learn tenets of dignity, perseverance, belief in one's worth. A man to emulate in many ways. To me, he's never been a myth, though some say the book made him one. I disagree. The book showed him in conflicting beliefs, very disappointed in the Nation of Islam's leader, and having to forge ahead with the painful knowledge that the mentor in whom he'd invested so much was not at all who he'd seemed or purported to be. And, as far as desegregation and integration, Malcolm X has been described as "lukewarm." If I was black, I wouldn't care so much about integration as I would rights. Civil rights. Equal rights. *Human* rights. I think that's what he was after.

His words, "The white liberal differs from the white conservative only in one way: the liberal is more deceitful than the conservative," were not designed to endear him to either group, and to be real frank, he didn't give a rat's ass, and neither do I. We put such foolish and pompous store into "speaking truth to power." Well, he was one who *actually* practiced it daily. Minute by minute. He was a rare man. He didn't spit when he talked or yell curse words to egg himself on.

When he was wiretapped, it's ironic that some of the listeners were reported to surmise that Malcolm X wasn't a firebrand nut, but a rather levelheaded leader who just didn't brook a lot of bullshit. (My words, to describe what I read about their feelings.)

When I was about seventeen, I worked in a filling station, and a nearby carwash, with a black kid my age. One day when he was running late, he missed the streetcar to take him home, and he asked me if I would drive him, beat the streetcar, to a stop where he could still catch it. We were hauling ass in my old Ford, a cop magnet on its own due to loud pipes and lowering blocks, when we were pulled over by a motorcycle cop.

He asked me some questions, checked the interior, then said, "Well, it just looked funny, you know, a white and a Negra, driving together." And we were free to go after I explained we were looking to catch his streetcar. I didn't know what to say to the kid but I could feel the heat in my face. If it made me angry, what did *he* feel? Not much, it turned out. He was used to it. He would have to sit in the rear of that streetcar once we'd caught it.

I hope he read *The Autobiography of Malcolm X.*

ZAPPED BY ELECTRICITY

$100 FOR 100 WORDS CONTEST FINALIST

JUDITH RALSTON ELLISON

William Faulkner's words were my hell at fourteen. My father, professor of American Literature at an Ivy League . . . okay, Harvard, made me make a poster with Faulkner's words: *Gratitude is a quality similar to electricity: it must be produced and discharged and used up in order to exist at all*. . .. I didn't study at Harvard but became fascinated by the mystery of electricity. I am a happy man, a hands-on electrician. I own my own company and my dad works part-time for me cutting lumber and selling nails. The poster hangs in the shop.

Other People's Land

Pushcart Prize Nominee

Claudine Jacques

Translated by Patricia Worth

Originally published in French in
Le cri de l'acacia (Au vent des Îles, 2008)

And then, one day, you latch onto
a cause greater than you.
Marylin At-Chee

The noises were coming towards her, strangely distinct, a feverish clamour, screams guttural or piercing, all of them harsh, from deep down, engines over-revving, authoritative commands, dull explosions of teargas grenades, whistling, scuffling and more coarse, raspy shouting and insults.

She was tempted to get closer to them, to join in, disappear into the tumult.

But held back.

Clung to the first tree she came to.

A kind of calm fury rose within her. She couldn't define this new feeling that had nothing to do with anger, its rashness, its blindness. There was this fire inside her, pulsating in her belly, this ice paralysing her brain.

Nothing was as strange as this.

"Get out of here," ordered one of the aunties. "Quick. The men are angry. They're fighting down there. Some of them are injured, a lot of damage."

Yet, haltingly, she went back into the house, denying any haste that would have made her a suspect in her own eyes. Everything was ready. The briefcase containing the official papers and the origins of the conflict. Her bag, a few personal things.

Before stepping out the door, she turned round.

This place was a stopover where she was not leaving much that was tangible. Yet infinitely more. Namely hope, friendship, brotherhood and trust. Farewell to long evenings chatting over a tea or a milk coffee with a few sticks of fried cassava or a bowl of hot rice; gone were the possibility of a fight, dreams of victory and certainly her own utopian ideas.

"The beginning of exile," she mused.

She adjusted her sunglasses, pushed an unruly strand of hair behind her ear and headed for the car that lay idle under the oleander hedge. She opened the door regretfully, knocking herself on the branches, and sighed as she sat behind the wheel. She turned the key over and over to get the old Peugeot 305 to start and was surprised to see her hands shaking.

When she left the clan, it was midday.

The sun was beating down in murky waves of silvery heat onto the tar, an astonishing colour of burnt liquorice.

She drove past some police vans with window grilles, full of mobile gendarmes; one of them gave her a friendly wave. He was young and red as a newborn.

"If he knew who I was," she thought, not smiling, "he wouldn't wave at me like that. He mustn't read the papers!"

In the press they spoke of her as a woman to bring down. For once, the idiom was protecting her; a woman to beat up, rather, is what she had read between the lines, a woman to stone like in Afghanistan. The "Taliban" journalist, paid or manipulated to humiliate her, had not dared go that far in his commentary, but it's what his whole article screamed. For some weeks, indeed months, rumour had it that she was the face of a movement, the militant devotee of land claims, the clan powerbroker, what else?

She couldn't remember.

The punching bag, more like it! The troublemaker!

You'd think she made decisions alone.

But they knew little about her family, her big brothers and her uncles. What she had going for her, because she had an education, was a fluency in French and a good sense of epistolary retort. It was this that had determined her function in the heart of the clan, nothing more. The position was vacant, deserted by her father. Because, her father, well, he had long ago chosen the camp of the powerful.

Of course, she had put herself in danger!

They had photographed her in a mission dress, mouth open, wide-eyed, intentionally fierce, standing before banners written in big black letters, *Give us back our land ... Attack on the dignity of the first people ...* before trucks blocking the roads, before aggravated men.

She was not the only one venting her anger but she was different, more visible, almost white, unusual. In close-up. That was the photo they selected, the worst one. The best way to make her seem antagonistic.

No, even if he had seen this picture of her, the red young man would not have recognised her.

Driving under the Païta bridge, she was still asking herself: How can it be done differently? Not betraying, not hating? How can we progress?

Thanks to those she was leaving today, she had found a hunger in her soul and had satisfied it.

She had gone to them, torn, not by suffering, but torn like a piece of paper, from one end to the other. There was the white culture part of her on one half, the strange and foreign part on the other. One part had been written, the other was blank.

They welcomed her, recognised her.

So she stayed there.

Tried as best she could to bring the two edges of the paper together, even if time had badly damaged them.

And then she taped up the sheet of paper without much care; her only desire was to be one, whole, indivisible.

It was there beneath the adhesive strip in its deceptive brilliance that hundreds of small wounds were produced with every alteration of the paper. Because it's not about juxtaposing one's identities, one must also blend them, make of them a new thing, brand new.

But this was something she had only just come to understand.

She arrived at a small courtyard where she swapped the 305 for a Fiat in even worse shape, and dirty as well; she transferred her things, her spirits low. Tried to cover the stained seat with a sarong, tying it behind the headrest. Gathered up into a plastic bag the empty cans, greasy papers and various fruit peelings lying on the floor, and not knowing where to put them, locked them in the boot.

So where were her comforts? Her air-conditioned car? Her cosy apartment? The friends she used to have? And the man she had loved so much?

"Come on, this is just a bad spell you have to get through," she muttered to boost her courage, "be brave!"

But enthusiasm was most definitely lacking.

She started the car. Checked the fuel level. Fortunately, the tank had been filled, she wouldn't have to go to one of the local service stations where she could be recognised.

She took to the road immediately and headed for Noumea.

Where better to hide than in the city? Among its population who were now her enemies.

The radio tuned to Radio Djiido was broadcasting *Kaneka* music but she was hardly listening.

Lost in thought.

Besides, she preferred Vivaldi, or Chopin, or Bach, depending on the day...or her emotions.

Through her teenage years she lived with a certain amount of pride as a Westerner, moulded by white thought, protected by her barely tan complexion, her Chinese eyes, her education, her impeccable French, her ambiguous, exotic beauty and her clothing in the latest fashion. She was young, carefree, in love. She didn't have time to look around; she had to structure her life, earn a living, taste life and enjoy it.

Days and nights too short, ideas too immediate, confused, no perspective.

And then, of course, on a clearer morning everything took shape.

Curiously, the image of the *Disembarkation of the Thousand* led by Garibaldi thrust itself upon her. Who knows why? The red shirts of the Italians of 1860 were confused with the red scarves of the Kanaks of 1960. Or was it the other way round?

What had happened in her country since then?

The slow rebellion against the colonial State, the land claims, the events of 1984 and their bloody drama, the promise of rebalancing, peace accords signed, nickel-dusted handshakes.

And then the natural consequence of promises not kept, of restitution forgotten.

Her clan, suddenly a pariah, excluded, dispossessed of its rights, had become an undesirable tenant on other people's land. Other people's land!

How could they accept this spoliation?

Without raging, without yelling, without fighting?

So, she immersed herself in the claim, made it her own.

Admittedly, she understood the economic stake for the developers who bought these properties beside the lagoon, wanting to make a housing estate for rich people; it was her white side, that of reason. But also disgust.

She especially felt the suffering of her people who were seeing the land of their ancestors taken from them, and were rebelling; it was her black side, that of the belly. It was in this choice that everything had shifted: she had favoured the belly.

Yet she so wished she could propose something else!

A different path that leads everyone towards peace.

She had tried.

Now loneliness was flirting with her.

Her man, with his hugs and promises for the future, took off at the first ill wind. He didn't want to hear her new, woeful voice, or accept the entire, complete, total sense of her commitment.

He was afraid. He kept saying: "You upset things, you're putting us at risk, I've got a job and clients. I know people. I can't be involved in this."

One day, he didn't come home.

She experienced the empty bed, the unanswered phone calls.

"He's just in a bad mood," she thought with a shudder, "one of those moments when you ask yourself questions, when you have doubts."

But soon the bailiff was at her door, a divorce procedure in his hands.

The meeting was arranged. At the media library at Rivière Salée she would leave the vehicle beside the transformer in the car park, someone would be there, over near the laundrette, waiting for her but not openly acknowledging her, who would bring her back a bit later.

Then, without a signal, she would go up the street to the graffitied wall, as on the day when they scouted for a location.

Behind a wild hedge of false pepper trees she would find a small tarnished gate in an outdated blue, a key hidden under a flat stone, a door, a place to stay.

She entered the musty house, put her bags on the kitchen table, noticed the presence of the mobile phone, its charger and Liberty recharge cards, and checked it was working.

Then she hastened to slide the glass door of the living room open a fraction, just enough to let the air circulate.

A surprised lorikeet flew away.

The sarong curtains fluttered and diffused the harsh midday light. She took a careful look outside to admire the vegetation in the tiny enclosed garden, then decided to go out onto the shaded patio.

From where she was, she could hear the jumbled commotion of the two neighbouring houses, the end of a meal, the clatter of dishes and laughter of children, but the view was partly obstructed by a wooden fence visible here and there through red cordylines and yellow lianas. A Hawaiian hibiscus flower had opened, white with an orange heart, the size of a saucer; a jasmine vine perfumed the air, and in a corner a young flower-laden mango tree was abuzz with bees.

"A year for cyclones," she murmured.

She went upstairs, looked into the two bedrooms, chose by reflex the one she would sleep in because of the key in the door, and went back down.

She was hungry.

She opened the cupboards one by one: soups, cans of meat, crispbread, Sao biscuits, coffee and tea, soy sauce, salted butter in the fridge, a few slices of pink ham in a plastic pack, some bottles of water, a hand of bananas on the kitchen dresser with a huge barely ripe pawpaw, good, good, for now she would be fine.

They had spoilt her.

She put some water on to boil in the aluminium kettle sitting proudly on the gas stove that was armoured with foil, and, with her teeth, tore open a packet of prawn soup and sat down.

Render therefore unto Caesar the things which are—

She stopped, pen mid-air, and shook her head. Culture, her culture, straightaway quoted what was familiar. She was tempted to cross out the phrase, then resisted; those receiving this letter would be sensitive to the cliché.

...which are Caesar's. No, we will not buy our crabs and our yams at the Sunday market, no, we will not cultivate the very small plots of land that will be granted to us ... no, we will not be tenants in our own country ... These lands are ours, the lands of our chiefdom ... we reclaim them.

With each mention of her land, she choked with emotion. Her land, her dead buried there, all those from whom she had been born.

The disquiet she felt was the same as when her clan chief had led her along dusty tracks in white light down to the mangroves, to the small cemetery knocked about over time! He had defined for her the boundaries of their home, from the foamy reef scattered with islands, to the craggy bare ridges; from the peak where the sun rises to the bay where it sets. Then he had told her the age-old myths to which only the initiated should listen; feet in the sand, eyes in the distance, he had guided her heart on a long, still journey beside the fire.

It was only afterwards that he had spoken to her of the *indigénat* ...[1]

"I'm one of the last pillars of the clans of the sea," he had said to her with the kind of solemnity that gives weight to evidence, "never forget my words...."

That day she became the inheritor of her story, of History, enlightened about her blood. She stored it all away: what had been said, like what would be kept quiet.

The phone rang. The number displayed was not one she knew.

"Hello, it's Ginette. Hello, can you hear me?" The voice was jerky, strangely hoarse.

"What's happening?"

"I'm calling you from the phone box outside the hospital. The Old Lady, the Old Lady's in Emergency."

"What?"

"Yeah, the Old Man tried to take the excavator to scare off the mobile gendarmes. The Old Lady tried to stop him, I think she got between him and them. He didn't see her. She fell, he ran over her leg."

"Is it serious?"

"Yeah, very serious. She's lost a lot of blood. The doctors don't think they'll be able to save the leg. And then after the accident our brothers were arrested. Almost all of them. I wanted to warn you."

"Thanks. Call me again as soon as you hear anything new. Doesn't matter what time it is. Promise me!"

"Hey, OK, I promise. Poor us."

Without realising it she had slipped down the wall and was sitting on the floor, head bent down onto her chest.

She could not contain the feeble groaning coming from her mouth, a throbbing lament, dull and deep, that she had never cried before, that had something animal about it.

---

[1] French colonial status subjecting the Kanak people to reserves.

Tomorrow, she would give herself up.

Tomorrow, they would put her in police custody.

Tomorrow, she had no doubt at all, they would put her in prison to await trial.

At the announcement of the verdict, her anger was spontaneous, a ball of fire in her head, like she had been punched in the stomach, an urge to shout injustice at the top of her lungs!

And, at once, her exasperation was countered by the gross and grotesque insignificance of the sentence, given like punishment to an unreasonable brat, amid a pitiful stirring of the crowd, their jerky movements, their stunned faces.

Two years in prison, one without parole. That's what the State, the righter of wrongs, demanded of her for having disturbed its certainties.

Suspended sentence for the others.

She was paying for everything, for everyone. And dearly!

Apparently, she was the danger. She and she alone ... the half-White!

A year, a year of non-parole in prison for having been the mouthpiece for her clan's land claim!

She softly uttered:

"The past was the time of colonisation. The present is the time of sharing.... The future, that of the common destiny. Spoliation, appropriation, lies .... There's a long way between what's promised and what's accomplished."

And the fear that she had trampled down for months rose up out of the very ground beneath her. She could feel it, a liana sly and fetid, worming its way up into the soles of her feet, paralysing her ankles, climbing the length of her calves, tickling the back of her knees, scaling her thighs, filling her belly. Her legs began to shake. She staggered briefly then regained her composure, and to save her strength she forced herself to think this was a bad dream or a Sunday telemovie, one of those appalling films you forget the minute it's over.

But the delusion was beyond belief: she was imagining her own drama in it.

Then with her whole being she stepped back to better examine the scene and engrave it on her memory.

She would never forget that moment!

In a short while, tomorrow and every other day, there would be the prison, the cubicle of three square metres where she would isolate her dreams; her body cramped, abandoned to despair.

She, alone.

She, locked away.

She, covered in opprobrium and venom.

She, sobbing.

While waiting, she needed to smile. Smile and lift her head. The final provocation.

She had to smile.

Ginette threw her arms round her, held her tightly and whispered:

"Look, our brothers have shaved their heads."

"Why?"

"To be with you."

Tears burst forth, bottled up for too long; she didn't try to wipe them away.

When she left the courtroom in a stunned silence, a police officer on either side, she walked tall.

And more noble, or more dignified.

The Quadrangle

Peter Coe Verbica

Callas dragged her hand in the water.
It was the Mediterranean, so not too cold.

Pearly razorfish, thorn-backed rays
and parrot fish swam silently
over the seashells beneath her.

"Aristo," as she called him, like to show
that he could sail even a small dingy.

It brought him back
to when he was a boy,

before the yachts,
the windfall of tobacco trades
and arguments with Rainier
over control of casinos.

To the days of
his mother's wood block
of phyllo dough, chopped nuts
and cinnamon.

And the regaling
of his grandmother's silence
as she wrapped sticky rice
with grape leaves.

Before his aunts and uncles
were burned alive in a church.

And, though his parents lost
everything to the Turks,
he was still
the son of Socrates.

And there was comfort in that.

The press liked the triangle:
Jackie, with her odd manner of speech,
and the two glittering Greeks.

But, on the level, it was really a quadrangle
because of Caroline Lee,
the sister time tries to forget—
though she outlives them all.

In the middle of this geometric shape,
the ghost of the Black Jack
eats a sandwich on a card table.

The man with a big heart,
a series of bad bets and a love
for whiskey.

Years later,
with John and Robert gone,
the widow with the fish eye sun glasses
was free to roam.

In a Swiss hospital,
she had the tattoo of poverty removed
from her forehead
by the finest doctor she could find.

No doubt the muscle of money
helped both Bouviers ignore
the stink of fat cigars and too-tight swim trunks.

Meanwhile, the public mourned for
Maria's supernatural voice,
the one which punched holes
in the acoustic ceilings of music halls

and pounded finishing nails
into the Twentieth Century
like a powerful hammer.

Part of me wonders
if when it was reduced to a whisper,
that the woman who loved horses
snuck by the convalescing singer
and into the Tycoon's arms.

Of course, he had been plotting all along.

What else could a man do
who had access to everything.

All of this was auctioned off
in 1998 and 2017, and I was there,
observing.

The Cartier watch, the childlike painting
of Stas and Chuck,
the famous speeches, black veil,
and engraved toothbrushes.

To each conspiring photographer
who caught it all,
even the picture with the Pope,

should we thank you
for the artful and poignant illusions

or just bust you in the chops.

Callin' Mary

LD Sledge

When the wind was right you could hear him singin' just as plain. His voice was deep and sad and the air would somehow carry it so you could hear it real clear, and then it'd fade and you couldn't hardly hear it at all. It was a mournful, scary sound that'd come and go on the wind.

He'd sit on his porch and rock and sing in the evenin' just as the sun went down. It sounded sometimes like hollerin' at the top of his voice. But when he started callin' for Mary the hair'd stand right up on the back of my neck.

I was ten and Miz Mary Bogan had been dead just about all of my life.

His house was way off out in the middle of a ol' field and you could see a patch of his rusty ol' tin roof from our front porch. It set right smack dab in the middle of a bunch of great big old sycamores that must have been there forever. I remember him raisin' corn in that field when I was real little, but for a long time there wasn't nothin' raisin' in it 'cept weeds and briars.

One July evenin', me and Bobby, he was my best friend that lived down the hill, we decided we'd find out what ol' man Bogan was doin'. We'd been hearin' him holler at sundown so long we just had to see him do it up clost.

When the sun dropped behind the treetops we run through the field and snuck up on his house. We come up behind his henhouse. The chickens had done gone to roost and when we passed, they started makin' a fuss so we scooted on by in a hurry. His old hound come up and started beatin' us with his tail and whinin', so we had to pet him to shut him up.

The whole yard around his house was hard-packed dirt without a blade of grass. What the chickens didn't pick clean he scraped with a hoe and swept a broom made out of brush tops tied together. He didn't want no lawn or nothin' like it. Didn't have no lawn mower. Wasn't no sense in cuttin' no yard grass after workin' hard at the mill all day.

His house set up about three foot off'n the ground on stacks of bricks. His dog and chickens stayed under there when it rained. The house hadn't been painted ever, I don't reckon, cause the old boards was gray and stained, and the old screens had holes all over. Bugs could get in if they wanted to.

The evenin' settled in real quiet-like. A Whippoorwill whistled out in the field. Daddy once told me a Whippoorwill was sayin' "Chip fell out of the Whiteoak." Ol' bird wouldn't really say that but daddy told me that's what he said, and that's what his daddy told him. I knowed better. He was just whistlin'.

We ducked the overhalls and the long-john underwear hangin' on the line and waddled under the house like ducks. We got to where we could see him through some knot holes in the porch floor and we squatted there head to head tryin' to get a good look.

Old man Bogan had onct been a giant of a man and had worked in the loggin' woods cuttin' logs for the sawmill. It was told he could take a crosscut saw and cut a pine four foot across all by hisself. Then he'd chop all of the limbs off with a single bit axe so that big pine would look like a phone pole in less than30 minutes.

Onct he chunked a baseball from home plate all the way over the fence at center field, but he could tap dance and was as light on his feet as one of them fancy dancers—big as he was. They said Miz Bogan used to have flowers growin' everywhere around that old house. He was a hard man, but mama said his favorite was daffodils and Miz Mary growed a yard full of 'em just for him every spring.

He set in his rocker with his baldhead down between his old knotty fingers 'a cryin'. His heavin' sobs shook the whole porch. He'd moan and hit the arms of the chair and then beat his chest.

"Oohh, my sweet Lord. Come get me. Come take me now. Maaayreee. Where are you? I miss you so much, my sweet baby. Ohhh, pleeeze come back. Maayyreee."

When he started callin' for Miz Mary, me'n Bobby got real clost and looked all aroun' like she might jus' come a bustin' right up out of the ground somewhere any minute. We was scared enough to take off like scalded dawgs, but then he tuned up and start hummin' a little louder.

It was a deep rumblin' at first, like comin' out of a cave or somethin'. And then he bust out singin' so deep I thought things was gonna start vibratin'.

"Rock of Ages, cleft for me. Let me hide myself in thee." He got louder and louder and finally it was like hollerin.'

When Rock of Ages played out he went straight into Amazin' Grace. He leaned his head back and opened his mouth so wide you could see his pink gums where his teeth was onct at.

He would call out Maayree ever now and then.

He went on for a long time and then he sort of burnt hisself out and set there without rockin' or movin'—just lookin' out in front of him. I knowed he wasn't lookin' at nothin'.

He unhitched the galluses on his overhalls and let 'em fall down. He helt on to the chair arm and stood up unsteady-like and walked through the front door.

Me'n Bobby slipped out from under the porch and looked over the wore-out boards. He pulled open the screen door to the livin' room and went to the mantel over the fireplace where there was a bunch of old pictures in fancy little frames.

He squinted at each of 'em and finally took one down and come back out on the porch where there was yet some daylight. He trembled and sniffed a long sniff, lookin' at that picture. We could see it good from where we was, peepin' over the boards. He was too overcome to notice us just a few feet away.

The picture was of a lady of a pretty good size with a fancy lace collar standin' alongside of a tall big man in a suit and tie. He looked at it in the fadin' light and run the tips of his fingers over the glass.

He put the picture back and stood there, just lookin' blank at the mantel, with his ol' galluses hangin' to the floor, fore and aft.

After a little he sucked in a deep breath and sighed. He looked real tired and pale and like he had done emptied hisself out, kind of. He shuffled to the bedroom on the front corner, next to the porch. The windows was long and come all the way down to the floor and they was all open.

He took his overhalls off and dropped' em on a chair. Old man Bogan had on a full set of long 'hannel underwear with a baggy trap door in the back. He sat down in the middle of that saggin' old bed I thought it was gonna bust cause it squeaked somethin' fierce.In the almost dark he laid there a 'lookin' up at the ceilin'. His lips was a movin' but I couldn't make out what he was sayin'.

He closed his eyes and in a minute was snorin' loud enough to keep the skeeters off.

Me and Bobby run through the field under a early full moon. When we got to the trail down the hill to Bobby's house, we caught our breath and stood there for a moment and just looked at one another. There just wasn't nothin' to say. He turned and run to his house.

The singin' and hollerin' an' callin'went on through the rest of the summer 'til late fall when it started gettin'cool. Then it stopped.

One Sunday Miss Vitae Mae Wiggens from the Church stopped by his house to bring him a hot lunch. She found him settin' in his rocker on the porch, stiff as a poker, wearin' a suit and tie.

He was just a' settin' there, holdin' that little picture, the one with the fat lady and the man in the suit. He had a bunch of flowers in his other hand.

Miss Wiggens said he had on the happiest smile, and a look on his face like he was a' talkin' to somebody that he was really glad to see. That was true, 'cause I had to go to the funeral and pass by the coffin, and I seen that for myself. The undertaker couldn't have got that smile off if he'd tried. Even dead, old man Bogan looked happier'n when me'n Bobby seen him through that knothole.

We had done had a couple of good frosts by then, and the funny thing was, them flowers was daffodils, and they just grow in the spring. Them he was holdin' was fresh picked.

Plow in the Sky

$100 for 100 Words Contest Finalist

Jesse Sensibar

I looked up from my tractor and saw the plow in the sky turning white furrows, miles wide in a blue earth stretching across the northern horizon.

He didn't say a word, just kept working that plow in the sky, sowing thorns of hell, seeds of heaven.

RUNNING ON MOONTIME

EDITOR'S PRIZE RECIPIENT

KERRY MUIR

Characters:

Maeve Age 16. Eight and a half months pregnant. Any race, as long as it is believable that she *could* be Missy's daughter. Not necessarily gorgeous, but full of hope—which is gorgeous in and of itself.

Missy Age 32. Beautiful bordering on gorgeous. Any race.

A. Age 41. Caucasian, reddish-blond hair. Around 5'9". Resembles vanished-from-the-spotlight rocker (at the time) Axl Rose. Maybe a little out of shape, slight gut coming on.

Place:

Lancaster, Winnetka, Reseda—places near Hollywood, but not of it.

Time:

February, 2003, except where indicated in flashback.

Notes:

Direction can be somewhat expressionistic. There should be a dream-like quality present throughout the play that is not unrealistic. Most scenes take place in the kitchen of Missy and A's house, so—a table, a few chairs. A microwave. A sewing machine on the kitchen table, where Missy is piecing together handmade lingerie, nightgowns. To one side of the stage, a bed in shadows, indicating Missy and A's bedroom. Homemade curtains hang from a makeshift window—outside, a view of the moon. The moon can be photo-real, or crudely expressionist—a child's cut-out drawing of the moon, for example, dangling from a string.

"They told me not to leave, but I left anyway."
Axl Rose, on leaving his hometown of Lafayette, IN, in a 1989 interview with Del James for *Rolling Stone*

Spotlight on Maeve in the dark, who speaks to the audience.

Maeve:
—and straight ahead of me the full-moon, right above the road. So low in the sky it almost touched the divider line—and it was huge. That moon looked wider than the road itself, that's how full it was. And suddenly the moon was not a moon at all, but this big, round, shiny magnet pulling me, and this fierce thought just, like, *ripped* across my head—*Now! Go! Run and grab it—that road, that moon, that whole new shiny life ahead!* And I was about to do it. But then I thought—*What if I never see Sinclair and Aaron and Francess again?* I mean, you know, *What if?* 'Cause I bitched about going to Bible and all, but the three of them? Were like—All I had. In the *world*. I mean, those three gave me *everything*. But then I was, like, *That moon—! (stops herself)* And then I remembered something kind of weird, and I spoke it to myself out loud to make sure I heard it—I said, *Maeve*—cause I was speaking to myself, so—I was all, like, *Maeve, you might not remember this, but it was Sinclair who mentioned to you all about moon-time in the first place. And it was Francess, who confirmed it. And Aaron who backed her up after that, even when you still had your doubts*—it was those three at Bible who were the ones to tell me: how moon-time is different from time on earth. How time on the moon dilates... whereas time on earth? Is *compressed*. That's the words Sinclair used when he explained it to me—"*dilated*" and "*compressed.*" He said *A clock running on the moon will run slower than a clock on earth. And yet— they both are telling the truth. Chew on that a while, Maeve.* And this is a fact. Sinclair showed me on the internet, so—there you go. Scientists have proved it: There is no Reality. *(beat)* Or, better—there are many. *One's not truer than another, Maeve. They're all relative,* Sinclair said.

And I took those words to heart, and I ran and ran and ran.

Later, though, when I had time to think, I got afraid of God. Because God would not be thrilled for me to of run like that. Also, it occurred to me: God never mentioned moon-time in the Bible—I mean, not once. But then I thought, *Why would God put me in Bible study with Sinclair and Aaron and Francess if He didn't want me to learn about moon-time? After all, it was God who threw all of us in together like that.* And anyway—I sure as hell wasn't there for Bible, so—it must of been for the moon. God *must* of wanted me to know—at least, that's how I thought.

And then I was gone. No more looking back. 'Cause once you break the rules, they watch you like an eagle—you lose your privileges and bla-bla-bla, but—more than that? Looking back would've been a betrayal of everything they stood for—Sinclair, Francess and Aaron. A betrayal of the precious idea they gave to me. I had to follow through, if not for myself, then for them. And if not for them, then for the moon, and for the moon alone.

Sound of a heart beating low and steady and reverberating. Lights fade on Maeve.

8 p.m.—home of Missy and A. The sound of the heartbeat fades into the sound of rain on the roof. Missy at the kitchen table, sewing. A knock at the door. Missy opens it, revealing Maeve. Pause.

Maeve:

Hi, I'm here for Axl...?

Missy:

Axl? *(confused)* There's no Axl here.

Maeve:

Axl Rose?

Missy:

(beat) Is this a joke?

Maeve:

Um, no?

Missy:

(beat) Okay, is this? This is, like—a goof? Like a spoof for Youtube—? Where's the camera? I mean—come on! I'm not an idiot!

Maeve:

Um. I'm seriously here for Axl. So don't be all, like, you don't know.
Pause.

Missy:

Axl Rose doesn't live here.

Maeve:

Did he move?

Pause.

Missy:

Um. Honey? Do you think Axl Rose would live in a two-bedroom tract home in Reseda? If Axl Rose is anywhere he's in Malibu or Paris, France—he sure as hell ain't here. *Missy starts to close the door.*

Maeve:

God fucking dammit! God! Fucking damn fucking piece of shit!

Missy reopens the door.

Maeve *(cont'd)*:

He's such a liar! Such a liar! Lying sack of—oh, my God, I hate him!

Missy watches Maeve melt down. After a bit –

Missy:

Are you...? *(beat)* Do you...? *(beat)* Is everything...?

Pause. Maeve slumps to the ground, defeated.

Missy:

Look. It's raining. Would you like some. I dunno. Some tea or something?

Pause. Maeve remains inert.

Missy *(cont'd)*:

It'll be. It'll be all right. I think you. I think you might need to eat. Am I right? You need to eat? Look, just—come on now. Come on, come in, come in. *Missy helps Maeve off the ground. Escorts her inside the house.*

Missy *(cont'd)*:

When I was pregnant, I. Had um. I had this craving. I craved spaghetti and meatballs all the time. With little chunks of onions. I wanted to gnash those chunks between my teeth and split the flavor wide open. *(beat)* That and chocolate. I wanted chocolate all the time.

Missy and Maeve enter kitchen.

Missy *(cont'd)*:

I don't have that but—I've got lasagna. Cheddar cheese, zucchini. The little chunks of onion. You need a lot of vegetables—I hope you know that? I hope you've been eating lots of veggies all along? *(beat)* Have you? *(beat)* I'll bet you have. You're gonna be just fine. *Puts leftover lasagna in microwave.*

Missy *(cont'd)*:

Hot tea? I know—a glass of milk. Milk builds bones. Bones need calcium. So, milk, milk, milk, milk, milk. *(beat)* Milk.

Awkward, interminable silence. Finally, microwave bell dings.

Missy *(cont'd)*:

So. You're. Um.

Missy serves the lasagna to Maeve at the kitchen table. Maeve scarfs it down, ravenous.

Missy *(cont'd)*:

...looking for...Axl Rose?

Maeve nods.

Missy *(cont'd)*:

In Reseda?

Maeve nods again, mouth too full to talk.

Missy *(cont'd)*:

In this house?

Maeve nods once more.

Missy *(cont'd)*:

Huh. That's. That's strange... We've. Lived here almost two years now....

Maeve:
You and Axl?

Missy:
No. Me and— my boyfriend.

Maeve:
Blond-ish red hair, graying at the edges?

Missy:
Yeah, he—

Maeve:
Gravelly voice?

Missy:
Uh, I guess—

Pause.

Maeve:
Piercing green eyes?

Missy:
Uh...yes...

Maeve:
Any kids?

Missy:
One. But—she's. All grown now. More or less.

Maeve:
You had her before you and Axl met?

Missy:
I never *met* Axl! *(beat)* Do you? Want me to—to call someone?

Maeve:
I have someone. I have Axl. So, no, you don't need to call. *Maeve studies Missy's sewing machine next to her on the table.*

Missy:

Look—I can assure you, no one's sheltering any aging rock stars here! The sooner you get a grip on that—

Maeve:

(re: sewing machine) What are you making there?

Missy:

It's um. Lingerie. Of sorts. I—I want to. Start a line. *(distracted)* A long, long... line.

Maeve:

Cute. *(touches fabric)* A little *Frederick's of Hollywood,* but—cute. Overall.

Missy:

(caught off-guard) Thanks. *(beat)* I'm Missy.

Maeve:

Maeve.

Missy:

Maeve? That is so. Pretty. *(beat)* Maeve.

Maeve:

So he goes by 'A' now, huh? Sly dog.

Missy:

Would you come off of it! 'A' stands for *Anthony*! He owns pizza parlors in the valley! He can't sing for shit! He's as far from rock-stardom as you can possibly get!

Maeve:

That's what you think.

Sound of rain up. Blackout.

Midnight, same evening-Missy and A. in the kitchen. A. wears restaurant work-clothes. Missy sews away. Sound of rain continues from previous scene.

Missy:

Someone came by today, looking for—of all people!—Axl Rose? *(no reaction from A.)* Axl. Rose. *(beat)* Does that? Mean anything to you?

A:

Frontman for Guns N' Roses? I hear he's all washed up. Kurt Cobain and that whole Seattle scene bumped him out. Guy looked like some kinda douche after that.

Missy:

She was pregnant.

A:

Who?

Missy:

She ate like a fiend. Polished off your lasagna.

A:

You fed her?

Missy:

She was cold and wet—

A:

You invited some pregnant teenager into the house and fed her my lasagna?

Missy:

(beat) How do you know she was a teen?

A:

A girl, you said! Didn't you just say that? Some girl?

Missy:

She needed a bath pretty bad.

A:

Well, I'm surprised you didn't offer her use of our bathroom! Jeez, Miss!

Missy:

She was like eight months pregnant. She was all alone. She was looking for Axl Rose.

A:

And that didn't strike you as just the slightest bit loco? Unbelievable!

Missy:

She was totally alone!

A:

Okay—I get the gist. One minute you're a grown woman opening your front door. Next thing you know, you're staring at your reflection in the fun-house mirror. You had a bad trip. A flashback. You thought: *Do unto others as you wished others had done unto you.* And, babe—that was kind. Very, very kind. But the bottom line is: you don't know her. If she comes back here again, tell her to hit the road running. *(beat)* This is a weird world we live in! There's some whackadoodle-doozies out there! Just look at the goddam papers. Every day it's something! Every! Goddam! Day!

Missy:

A.? Can you lower your voice? *(indicates off-stage)* She's sleeping.

Pause.

A:

Are you shitting me?

Maeve enters from bedroom wearing one of Missy's nightgowns. It fits her funny. Long pause.

Missy:

Anthony, Maeve—Maeve, Anthony.

Maeve:

(beat) We've met.

Blackout. Sound of rain slowly fades, disappears.

Spotlight on Maeve. She talks to the audience.

Maeve:

He said his name was Axl Rose and I was all like, *Wow.* I mean. I know the music. I've heard him belt his lungs out. And I've belted my lungs out right along with him. *(sings) Where do we go now...? Where do we go-whoa...?* And then the *Ay-yi's* and you know, the whole rigamarole. I'm vaguely familiar but—the funny thing was? He didn't *look* like Axl Rose. I mean, I he's, like, *well*-past prime-time, but this guy had—I mean he had a *lot* of wear-and-tear on him, to put it mildly. And he was wearing sunglasses so—it was hard to tell. I mean, he *might* have changed over the years—I dunno. I thought, *Maybe he could be Axl Rose*—if he, like, had done a ton of drugs and gotten really sick and gone insane and bitter and crazy and gotten a whole lot of really bad plastic surgery—which, come to think of it, is, from all accounts, what really happened to the man—so. I thought, *It could be Axl, just older now.* I mean—you know? It could. *(beat)* So I told him about moon-time, right there, over spaghetti. And he, you know? He listened.

Lights up. Flashback to a few hours earlier, before A. came home. Maeve and Missy sit at the kitchen table. The lasagna dish is empty. Maybe they drink tea.

Missy:

Yeah but anyone can say, *I'm Axl fucking Rose!* But—how would you really know? I mean, any freak can saunter up to a pretty girl and say those three little words.

Maeve:

(counts on her fingers) That's four.

Missy:

(counts) Okay, whatever, four. But still—how can you be so sure?

Maeve:

I've heard him scream. That's how.

Rain continues, soft. Blackout on Missy and Maeve.

Heavy-metal music blasts—maybe something like the opening of 'Welcome to the Jungle.' Spotlight up on A.–he bops to the music, busts a few Axl-esque moves, lip-synchs in front of an imaginary mirror hanging on the fourth wall. Missy watches him for a while from the sidelines, then abruptly shuts the music off.

A.

(to mirror) Am I...? Am I Axl Rose? *(laughs, a few beats)* Are you really asking me that?

Missy:

Yes.

A. turns, looks at Missy as... lights shift. Sound of heartbeat up. A. turns from the fourth wall—takes a suitcase from under the bed and starts to pack in the background. Simultaneous spotlight up on Maeve, in the foreground. She talks to the audience.

Maeve:

—'cause you know the minute I started to run, it was like, *Oh my God,* it was just like, *Oh my God,* you know? Like the lid was just blown off the roof and the whole sky was pouring in. And you know—I could finally *breathe.* I could see *colors* again. And I was just like, *Wow.* I had close to three hundred from the Shake 'n Smoothie, so I was like, *Let's go.* And whereas usually things pass *me* by? Now it was *me* that was, like, passing everything—the Wind-chime hut and the *House of Gnomes* and *Tabitha's Thrift Shop.* And the police billboard over *Family Dollar,* offering rewards for snitching on dog-fighters, and the *Award-winning Menudo!*-place, and the *Ye Olde Gift Shoppe*—which they spell with two P's and an E—why? I don't have the slightest—and for once *I* was the one passing it all by! Leaving it in ye olde duste! Saying *Goodbye* to everything... *goodbye, goodbye, goodbye...* And all I could feel was, like—this joy—this pure and total and complete like, *joy*, at the thought of leaving.

Lights shift, come up on Missy and Maeve in the kitchen, in flashback.

Missy:

You're the same. Same age. Same—everything.

Pause.

Maeve:

(genuine) I don't mean to disappoint you, but I'm from Lancaster. Lancaster's not even close to Bakersfield. It's like, way south of there.

Missy:

I know Lancaster. High desert. Antelope Valley. Are there really antelopes?

Maeve:
There's a lion reserve. Tippi Hedron owns it. *(beat)* She was in *The Birds.*

Missy:
But when did you get there?

Maeve:
When did I get where?

Missy:
Lancaster.

Maeve:
I've been there all my life. *(beat)* Until now, I mean.

Sound of heartbeat fades. Lights shift bend and shift.

Spotlight up on A. He packs a suitcase, sings to himself—not just the vocals, but all the instruments: guitar riffs, percussion—everything.

A:
(growl-sings) Where do we go now...where do we go now...Bam-poom-pam-pam! Where do we go now...where do we go now...where do we go-whoa.... Bam-bam! Ay-yi-yi-yi-yi-yi-yi-yi-yi-yi-yi....WHERE DO WE GO-WHOOOOAAAHHHHH......? *(Pause, then sings last note of song)* ...whoa.

Light dim on A.

Wide, dilated spotlight up on Missy, who speaks to the audience.

Missy:
—and I ran and I ran and I ran, you know? After the white limousine! In Bakersfield. It was driving down the road, away from me. Under this huge full moon. And the limousine was the same exact color and shiny tone and texture as the moon—so much so that I remember having the distinct impression the limo was like, some rogue piece of it—some random, stray shard of moon that had wiggled loose and gotten away, and was now returning home to the sky, back to its origin. And I was like—*Hey! Wait! Don't leave me here! Come back and take me with you! (beat)* He was traveling incognito. And I was all like, *Rock stars in Bakersfield!*, you know? He'd come into the bar where I was working—no entourage, no nothing—and he'd sang one simple song—that song that ran on

continuous-loop in my head, after I had my kid? *Sweet Child.* Oh, man, right? I was in this weird, lost phase where I couldn't get a grip on much of—you know, much of anything. *(beat)* And like—*no* skills. I could tell you a lot about *Oh, Jesus saves* and *Jesus loves you* but they don't pay Sunday school teachers much. In fact—they don't pay them at all! So I stripped. Whatever—big deal. Lightning hasn't struck me down yet. Whatever, right? That's what *I* said! In Bakersfield. A friend of a friend of a friend of a friend had this bar. I did crunches for like two months, and I was set. *(beat)* The body bounces back real fast from childbirth when you're sixteen and a half. Whatever, right? Work nights. Baby, days. My family wrote me off and. Church wrote me off and. Well. I was. Pretty wiped. But there was this couple at my church. This, like, older couple. And when they heard there was this. Uhhhh... Baby. They were just like. *On me.* Like white-on-rice... White-on-rice... *(beat)* I wonder who made that up? White-on-rice... *white-on-rice.* Who came up with that...?

A:

(sings weirdly, under Missy) Where doooo we gooo nooow....?

Missy:

Anyway. Long story short: I gave her up. I was all out of gas you know? And. They were persistent. I mean, they had. Like, reserves of the stuff. Of persistence. *(beat)* I really hate them now—that's neither here nor there. But. I really— *(pause)* And that night after I relinquished her—that's the word they use—"*relinquish*"—I went to work. Mainly so I didn't have to think. Because the music there was so loud, and the crowd. And there was a bouncer, Major, who always had pot. So there I was at work, trying my best to numb out. And that's when he walked in. Rock stars do that, I guess. Every once in a while. They—I don't know—want to go, like, back in time, before the fame monster devoured them. Be anonymous in some roadside dive. Be *The Invisible Man.* He came in and sang. Just him, all-alone. In the corner of the bar. He was. Um. Barely lit. But you could see. It was him all right. *(beat)* It was him.

In another part of the stage, A. packs his suitcase and growl-sings quietly:

A:

(softly) Where do we go now...where do we go now.... Ay-yi-yi-yi-yi-yi-yi-yi....
Singing continues at low volume during the beginning of Missy's monologue.

Missy:

And after he sang, he got up and left without any fanfare. I don't think anyone even applauded, we were in so much shock. No *thank-you-very-much.* No *Elvis-has-left-the-building.* No *Thank-you-and-Good-night!*—one minute he was there, and then he was gone. Simple as that... And that's when it hit me: he is gone. And she is gone. And then, you know, suddenly *I* was going, going, gone... The walls of the club warped and bent right before my eyes... The walls I'd used to numb me out, suddenly—folded *in.* And all I heard was my own heart beating hard and slow and deep, like an LP on the wrong speed—one heartbeat, I'd thrown on my coat; the next, I stumbled outta the bar; the next, I ditched my high-heels and was running barefoot down the road... And the whole world went silent, except for this weighted, prolonged heartbeat that echoed off each passing second, like a ball hitting the backboard of a basketball hoop in slo-mo... each second like silly-putty, stretched-out and elastic... and as I neared the white limousine I saw him get inside it, and I heard the door closing, and the car pulled away on gravel... and I ran like holy hell after him all the way down the road...long after the tail lights disappeared into dark, completely...

A:

(sings) Where do we go-whoa....

Missy:

I mean—how fucked up is that? I mean— *(starts to laugh, then cracks)* Right? *(beat)* What a joke. I'm sorry. I'm just. Really. *(tries to pull it together, cracks again)* Man! Fuck this. *(beat)* Anyway—I saw him. *(beat)* And then—I ran and I ran and I ran.

Lights up on the kitchen. Maeve and Missy at the kitchen table.

Maeve:

But what would he be doing? In a dive like that? I mean, he was a big rock star. What was this, 1986?

Missy:

No! God, I'm not that old! It was more like.... *(counts, to herself)* It was more like. 1987.

Maeve:

Why would he bust out of his cooshy fame-bubble to visit some honky-tonk?

Missy:

Maybe he needed to get away.

Maeve:

From Hollywood?

Missy:

Why else does anyone ever want to get away? Leave themselves behind

Short pause.

Maeve:

I guess.

Blackout.

Spotlight up on Maeve, who speaks to the audience.

Maeve:

And I was having so much fun. I'd stop like, wherever and get soda and licorice. Sometimes, lottery tickets. More soda, more licorice... and then, for protein? A plate of spaghetti at this pizza place in Winnetka. But around the time of the spaghetti, all the wheels came off—that's when shit happens. When you get lonely over spaghetti. When the protein kicks in and all the sweets wear off.

Lights shift. Flashback to eight and a half months earlier. Maeve sits in front of an uneaten plate of spaghetti. A. enters, approaches her. Missy watches the scene between Maeve and A. play out.

Maeve:

Yeah, *right*!

A:

No really. I have I.D. *(beat)* Here, I'll show it to you. *(he does)*

Maeve:

(beat) It says you're Axl Rose.

A:

I'd love to see more of you.

Maeve:

You're seeing me right now.

A:

No, but. *(beat)* More.

Maeve turns to Missy, breaks out of the scene with A. for a moment.

Maeve:

(to Missy) And I was low on funds. And all I could think was, *How much more licorice and spaghetti was my money going to get?* You know? So when he offered me fifty bucks, I thought, *What can it hurt?*

Maeve turns back to A., reenters the scene with him. Missy watches.

Maeve *(cont'd)*:

(to A.) If you're really Axl Rose, then I want three hundred. *(turns to Missy)* I thought that was bold!

A. recedes into shadow. Spotlight up on Maeve alone, speaking to the audience.

Maeve *(cont'd)*:

But. Suddenly, I was stuck with him. With, you know. With Axl. I couldn't shake him. He had the edge on me. More money, for one. And for another, a car. And I just. Got stuck. *(beat)* I kept Axl company, for like— I don't know. Two months? Maybe more. He put me up at a motel. I watched a lot of TV. I must of seen a million episodes of goddam *Law and Order.* And in between homicides and murder trials, Axl visited me.

Pause. Maeve turns to Missy. Lights shift.

Maeve *(cont'd)*:

(to Missy, genuine) I'm sorry. This must be hard—

Missy:

Don't be.

Maeve:

No. Really. I'm really sorry.

Missy:

I'm not upset at all.

Maeve:

(genuine) Then. Why are you crying?

Low, reverberating sound of a heartbeat, in slow motion. In slow motion, to the sound of the rhythm of the heartbeat, Missy presses Maeve's palm to her cheek, her forehead, her mouth, her heart.

Missy:

Because I'm just. I'm so. Relieved. To have you with me, finally.

Lights down on the kitchen.

Spotlight up on Maeve. She talks to the audience.

Maeve:

In Bible we were talking about the moon. How time is different there. How a year on earth might only be a minute on the moon. So—there's no one Time that's correct. All times are accurate, only different. Which is to say there's no one Reality that's correct. Reality is relative, which is to say—there's no Reality at all. It doesn't exist. I mean—just look at me: in Lancaster I was an orphan. In Winnetka I was a prostitute. And here in Reseda? I'm a beloved daughter, with the most beautiful mother on earth.

Blackout.

Flash-forward. Lights up, revealing Maeve and A. in the kitchen.

Maeve:

I don't have anywhere *to* go.

A:

What do you want? Money? Huh? Is that why you're here? Because if it's money you're after, I'll gladly pay you off.

Maeve:

(re: Missy) I promised her I'd stay.

A:

I don't wanna have to hurt you—

Maeve:

I don't care if you do.

A:

What about your condition?

Standoff.

Maeve:

I don't care if you do.

Pause.

Maeve *(cont'd)*:

You told me yourself you were Axl Rose. How is it you *did* that?

A:

I think the real question here is: how is it you *believed* me?

Maeve:

But. Are you?

A:

(exploding) No, I'm not Axl Rose! Are you really that stupid? I was just having fun with a nice, little, *fresh-off-the-bus* kid-hooker. Isn't that what you whores are supposed to do? Play along with our fantasies? Isn't that what I paid you for? Yeah, I'm Axl Rose, baby—now go ahead and blow me!

Pause.

Maeve:

But what about the moon?

A:

What about it?

Blackout.

Dim spotlight. A. approaches it warily, steps into it, almost reluctantly, as if in slow-motion. He speaks to himself sometimes—other times, he relates to the audience.

A:

And Indiana, and my stepfather, and my father before that, and what else could I do? Sing, scream, go insane. Beat up anything that moved. Dream at night about running, fast. Dreams of running free. But the stepfather always appears and stops you in those dreams. Your mother hides out downstairs in a bomb shelter kind of thing. A bomb shelter of her own making so she doesn't have to hear. That's when the poetry hits the roof. Poetry and blasphemy, then it's off to church. Then back home to scream—screaming's kind of like throwing up, but with sound instead of food. Step-father bungles you, more screaming, more church. A family merry-go-round-and-round-and-round-and-round and before you know it you're in the front lines of a rock band and people pay to see you scream. Scream your fucking lungs out! You scream so loud, even mothers locked up in underground bomb shelters of their own making can hear you because—in truth—you want them to hear. You do.

Missy:

(sings softly, under A.'s monologue) Ay-ay-ay-ay-ay-ay-ay-ay...Where do we go now...?

A:

And the crowd screams back at you. They have their stuff, too—maybe not the same as yours, but—*something.* You read me? Or they wouldn't be there to hear you scream. I mean, am I right? Or what?

Missy:

(from the sidelines, listening) Sure.

A:

And finally you're on a Greyhound bus with thirty bucks wedged in your jock strap and still the perverts try to feel you up. They still try! Of course they do! Because they can smell the past all over you and you're now and forever this magnet and those fuckers are drawn to you like tides to the moon. And later they'll call you a rapist and an abuser and a bigot and a homophobe and a has-been and a monstrosity—but what else were the options? I mean—I could've stayed put in Indiana and worked in a pizza place or something—you know, some shit like that. But I didn't stay put. I didn't stay at all. I took my chance when I had it. *(beat)* And I ran and I ran and I ran.

Lights shift.

Missy and A., in kitchen.

Missy:
You know. Sometimes I don't think I know you.

A:
Sure ya do.

Missy:
No. Not really, I mean.

A:
How can you not know me? We've been together since around nine-eleven, so—

Missy:
I mean—I've never met any old friends of yours.

A:
—like, almost a year and a half—how can you say you don't know me?

Missy:
Or any family, even—

A:
I told you, I'm not on good terms—

Missy:
But—there's gotta be *somebody*—you can't have sprung out of a vacuum!

A:
Stop overthinking! Ever since your little protégé walked in the door, you're like suspicious or something! It's like we're in a freakin' detective movie all the time! Well, I'm sick of it! I'm Anthony, "A" for short! I got pizza parlors in Northridge, Winnetka, Pacoima and Reseda! With prospects in Santa Clarita! We're rich! We're fucking rolling in it! We don't want for food or clothing! You get a toothache, I take you to the dentist, first class all the way! You want your ass waxed, your nails shellacked, your highlights, whatever—no problem! You don't even have to work anymore! Fucking kick back, sew panties all day and read your horoscope! I mean—what the hell do you want?

Pause.

Missy:

Do you think we could have a kid?

Pause.

A.

Who, us?

Missy:

'Cause you know, it's not too late. I still got all my parts.

Lights dim.

Missy drifts to bedroom, sorts through her closet. Sorts through lingerie. In shadows, Missy selects lingerie, changes into it. Simultaneously, in the foreground—a flashback scene takes place between Maeve and A., eight and a half months earlier—

Maeve sits in pizza parlor, half-eaten plate of spaghetti in front of her. A. sits next to her at the counter, wearing sunglasses, mid-conversation.

Maeve:

But—you don't look anything like him.

A:

I've lived life pretty hard.

Maeve:

But—your face—you. You can't be him.

A:

That's the crazy thing. I am.

Blackout.

Flash-forward to the present— bedroom of Missy and A. A., eyes wide open, unable to sleep, lies in bed. Missy climbs into bed in lingerie, wraps herself around A. like a vine.

Missy:

You're you. And she's her.

A:

And you're you. Now go to sleep. *He stares up at the ceiling.*

Missy:

How did you know where to find me?

Pause. A. studies her a while.

A:

I went back to the bar in Bakersfield. And there you were. Still dancing, like an angel.

She swings one leg his torso, straddles him. Looks out the window at the moon.

Missy:

Full moon tonight.

A:

(beat) Full moon. *He pulls her towards him.*

Lights dim on Missy and A.

Spotlight up on Maeve. She appears exactly as she did in the opening scene. Same energy, same story—she's finishing what she started.

Maeve *(to audience)*:

And I didn't even realize it, but before the thoughts had even had a chance to crystalize in my head, my legs were already running on their own volition. Because my legs, they knew—long before my mind—what I was gonna do. So I found myself, suddenly, running—bound for the moon, bound for my new life, bound for the road that stretched out like an oily black ribbon coming undone, unraveling beneath that beautiful moon, and my feet slapped hard and flat against the pavement of that dark, bumpy road, and with every running step that went *slappity-slap-slap* I was thanking my friends, saying *Thank you, thank you, thank you,* under my breath to Francess and Sinclair and *Thank you!* to Aaron, for without them I wouldn't have known how time differs on the moon, I mean—I wouldn't have known at all! So I whispered *Thank you, thank you, thank you*, and my heart pumped and my legs sprinted, and my breath came in short, stabbing spurts that burned the back of my throat, and that's the way it went and the way it would go, me running like a crazyman full of wild abandonment until the moment would finally hit and my future would rain down into my lap like a river of quarters flowing from a lucky slot machine, or like a bolt of lightning zapping me in the head, or a block of cement crashing on me and shattering all my bones, or like dandelion seeds, all white and puffy and feather-duster-like, raining down on my head, clinging by all matter and means to my hair and eyebrows and eyelashes, the way dandelion seeds do when they're wayward and floating. That's how it went and how it would go until the future hit—all my thoughts zig-zagging in a million-and-one directions, me flying through the dark like an arrow released from the bow, soaring towards nothing less than the whole wide future before me, the whole wide world ahead—me, speeding towards my shiny new life, bright and full and surrounded by a soft white glow-y halo... and I fixed my gaze on that great big moon as if it were life itself, as if it were *my* life—my shiny, new life. *(beat)* And I ran, and I ran, and I ran.

Sound of heartbeat crescendos—then fades into sound of rain.

Lights out.

End of Play

To Russia with Love

Single Word Contest Winner

Morrow Dowdle

On any given night, the stories flow
like the filthy Volga in which the children
would wash themselves after eating supper
from the garbage heaps. It might be her friend,
wrapped in a carpet on an apartment roof,
doused with gasoline and set on fire
over and over until she died, slow-cooked.
Or how the prior tenant had been axed,
and she and her mother had to scrub blood
before they could move in. Or how
the elderly neighbors kept their brother
in the freezer, feeding off him piecemeal.
Or how soldiers and police would rape girls,
and girls would hook for spare change,
believing they lost less than they gained.
I marvel at how she can appear intact,
when the world was a rabid dog,
people its bared teeth and claws.
I can forgive, then, how she stroked
my husband from knee to thigh,
high as we were on wine. I can forgive
my husband for wanting to taste
the lips, the cunt that knew trespass
before it knew love, yet still
found its way to love. It tastes
as sweet as it ever did.

INTERVIEW WITH OPWONYA INNOCENT

ASSISTED BY COAUTHOR KEVIN MCLAUGHLIN

Opwonya Innocent was born in a time of great civil unrest in the northern portion of Uganda. Abducted at the age of ten, he was forced to become a child soldier in a rebel force known as the Lord's Resistance Army. His astonishing story of escape, and the long road back to a normal life, are chronicled in *Innocent: A Spirit of Resilience.*

Coauthor Kevin McLaughlin facilitated a conversation between *Sunspot* and Opwonya. In keeping with the journal's dedication to honoring all languages and making the pieces accessible to as many readers as possible, the interview is presented here in English, but can be found in the Luo language of Opwonya's people in Sunspot Literary Journal Volume 1, Issue #3.

SL: When you were kidnapped by the rebel soldiers, your father was killed. You thought a lot about your mother and siblings while you were held captive. How are the individual members of your family doing today?

OI: Thankfully, all of my family members are doing fine now. My elder sister has three beautiful daughters now. My younger sister is planning to complete university in one's year time, with a degree in Education. My mother is only growing younger and younger every day. My younger half siblings are yet another wonderful source of happiness in the family; they are funny, focused and full of energy.

SL: The traumas child soldiers endure are truly horrific. What would you recommend that people do when they face situations that seem insurmountable?

OI: Yes, the trauma is indeed life changing. My mum once told me that HOPE is the most valuable asset in life. Once you lose hope, you will have lost everything. No matter the situation you're faced with, my advice is to keep your hope alive; whether you can see it right now or not, you are tougher than the situation.

SL: When you were rescued and taken to a counseling center, what one thing helped you most as you struggled to return to the life you once knew?

OI: What helped me most at the counseling center was the constant reminder that I was loved no matter what I had done. It first made me feel so guilty at the beginning but slowly I learned to love myself and let go of the past.

SL: As you began to build a new life, a few people who said they would help let you down. How has this impacted the way you approach new people today?

OI: Through all the hardship I faced, I learned it was best to give people the benefit of the doubt, because everyone is different and faces challenges one is unable to see with the eye. Although I was disappointed many times in life, I knew there was never enough reason to stop trusting the people I cross paths with. More than anything, being let down rather caused me to be quite sure about a situation before making a promise, because I know how much it hurts when they go unfulfilled."

SL: A great deal of your life has been dedicated to obtaining a formal education and other types of experiences that can make your life better. What actions or steps would you recommend for teenagers who want to make the most of their lives?

OI: I would advise young people to practice self-love above anything else. If you love yourself enough, you will extend that love to another child or human in need, just like I was. Education is the only wealth that no thief can steal. Once acquired, it stays with you and paves the way to a more self-sustaining life. Let's join hands and support education of our youth. Keeping them busy is in itself reducing crime rates and opening doors to a better future.

SL: What would you say to people of any age who want to change their lives for the better?

OI: I would encourage all individuals to always look at the positive side of life. Sometimes it's the hardest thing to do when you are in the middle of sadness, trauma, loss of direction, and all sorts of negativity but that is exactly where a strong one rises. Everyone has that inner strength and we should always exploit it. Falling does not mean you are weak, provided you have the determination to rise again no matter how many times you fall down.

SL: What do you have planned next for your life?

OI: My biggest dream is to work hard and open an orphanage for children living on the streets in my home town and many others in dire need. Children are the future and the present. The future should not start tomorrow but rather now; this very minute and second.

CONTRIBUTORS

Kit Alloway is a mixed media artist living in Cleveland Heights, Ohio. In addition to making collages, she quilts, plays the piano, and has published three novels with St. Martin's Griffin. Her recent collages have appeared in *From Whispers to Roars* and in forthcoming editions of *805* and *Chaleur Magazine*. Her collages deal with globalism, juxtaposition, and (sometimes) absurdity. She has always been fascinated with the surreal, and her work is intended to transport viewers to an unsettling alternate future while raising questions about privilege, technology, and perception.

Kayo Chang Black, a librarian-turned-writer, is a Taiwanese Canadian who lived in Dubai, Bahrain, and finally decided to settle in Hong Kong. She has lived between the intersection of cultures and the clash of expectations. Currently, she is working on her first book, a collection of interconnected memoir-essays titled *In the Shadow of the Middle Kingdom.*

Timothy Boardman is predominantly a fine arts artist and printmaker with some design sensibilities. He's currently a student at UNCG in Greensboro, North Carolina.

Thomas Boos recently graduated from the University of Pittsburgh with a degree in creative writing. He is applying for MFA programs and submitting work for publication.

Max V. Carp is an award-winning filmmaker, short film festival director, and former coeditor of an international arts magazine. He resides in Los Angeles, where he is currently shopping his first novel.

Mallory Chesser has an MFA in fiction from Texas State University. She works for the University of Houston and serves as managing editor for *Story|Houston,* an online literary journal focused on short fiction and creative essays. Her work has appeared in *Electric Literature* and *Moon City Review.*

Zachariah Claypole White is a recent graduate of Oberlin College, where he majored in creative writing and minored in English literature. He is a member of the North Carolina Writers' Network and the North Carolina Poetry Society. His poetry has appeared in the *Albion Review, The Plum Creek Review, Scalawag,* and is forthcoming in *Thin Air.* He will be featured in *Be a Writer Like...* (forthcoming from Teaching That Makes Sense). His flash fiction also appears in Anchala Studios' recently published anthology, *The Collection: Flash Fiction for Flash Memory* and is forthcoming in *After the Pause.* Zachariah uses his lifelong struggle with mental illness (obsessive-compulsive disorder, anxiety, and depression) to fuel his writing and hopes that he can use his art to help others with similar disabilities. He currently lives in North Carolina and works at Flyleaf Books.

Peter Coe Verbica grew up on a commercial cattle ranch in Northern California. He obtained a BA and JD from Santa Clara University and an MS from the Massachusetts Institute of Technology. He is married and has four daughters.

AD Conner is a freelance writer and editor. She lives in a small Kentucky town along the Ohio River. When she's not in her nest, composed of books, lit mags, and lots of raggedy notebooks, she can be found wandering the woods or diving in the river, searching for new ideas.

Warren Decker's writing has appeared in *The Best American Poetry* 2018, *The New Ohio Review, Fifth Wednesday, Frogpond,* and elsewhere. He hopes to become a brilliant light wave of pure compassion, but for now he ripples dimly with good intentions in Osaka where he writes and teaches.

Morrow Dowdle's most recent publication credits include *River and South Review, Dandelion Review, Poetry South,* and *NonBinary Review.* She was a Pushcart Prize nominee in 2018. In addition to poetry, she writes graphic novels, most recently in collaboration with the North Carolina Museum of Natural Sciences. She previously attended Emerson College's MFA program in creative writing and currently works as a physician assistant in mental health.

Judith Ralston Ellison writes short stories and microfiction. She won two prizes for microfiction from Rochester Writers. Her fiction has appeared in *Third Wednesday,* a collection *Flash Fiction for Flash Memory,* and *The Mentor,* published by the Michigan State Bar. She writes four-hundred-word essays for *Art and Sole,* the inhouse publication of the Detroit Institute of Art. She retired from her position as an administrative law judge in 2009.

Epiphany Ferrell writes most of her fiction in Southern Illinois at Resurrection Mule Farm, so-named after a mule survived a lightning strike there. She received a Pushcart nomination in 2018, and her stories appear recently in *The Slag Review, New Flash Fiction Review* and *Pulp Literature,* and she blogs intermittently at Ghost Parachute. She is a reader for *Mojave River Review.*

Shaun Haugen is a writer and artist who enjoys paying attention to the details even though he is still very much influenced by the world of the abstract. Combining reality with what it is versus what it should be and what it could be, he hopes to encourage into light, expose, and tackle age-old social injustices such as poverty, abuse, addiction, mental health, personal/internal war, and incarceration, while emphasizing general tolerance and compassion. Relying heavily on poetic prose, the writing can get lost in the abstract and deep emotions, but bringing it back to the concrete is an enjoyable challenge. He hopes that through his literature, social issues that plague society's core and that have been pushed aside from mainstream concern will be addressed. Limiting political boundaries to left or right is not the goal. Revealing how society leaves part of the moral psyche ignored is the focus.

Although **Mary-Chris Hines** recently concentrated primarily on fine arts, she has played with writing poetry since she was a wee tot. The poem in this edition comes from raising a son who was very different than she was. He is far beyond his teenage years now, and somehow, they have come to be more alike than before. She is grateful.

Wynne Hungerford's work has appeared in *Epoch, Blackbird, The Normal School, The Boiler, Okey-Panky,* and *SmokeLong Quarterly,* among other places. She received her MFA from the University of Florida.

Opwonya Innocent is the author of *Innocent: A Spirit of Resilience.* The book reveals, in his own words, his struggle to heal from the trauma he experienced, a desire to help others, and his tireless effort to realize meaningful, positive change. Innocent's inspiring story embodies the triumph of hope and determination over pain, trauma and fear.

Claudine Jacques was born in France, moved to New Caledonia in her teens, and is now a much-published novelist and short story writer. Island life and her cattle station are rich sources of inspiration for her writing. She is a founding member of l'Association des Écrivains de la Nouvelle Calédonie (Association of New Caledonian Writers).

David Joseph is a graduate of Hobart College and the University of Southern California's Graduate Writing Program, where he was awarded the Kerr Fellowship. His writing has been published in *The London Magazine, Wall Street Journal, LA Times, Doubletake Magazine,* and *Rattle.* A recipient of the John Henry Hobart Fellowship for Ethics and Social Justice, he spent the past two decades as an educator and nonprofit executive in Los Angeles. He has taught at Pepperdine University and Harvard University, where he was a recipient of the Derek Bok Award. He lives in San Roque, Spain with his wife Karen and sons Jackson and Cassius.

Roeethyll Lunn is a retired educator, grandmother of three, and experimental writer. She has a BFA in Broadcast Media from Morris College, Sumter, South Carolina, and an MFA in English and Writing from Long Island University, Southampton College.

Kevin McLaughlin, coauthor of *Innocent: A Spirit of Resilience,* has a background in policy and communications work at the local, state and federal government levels. He currently resides in Durham, North Carolina, where he works with local government, nonprofit agencies, local businesses and religious institutions to address issues surrounding social justice, inclusivity, and community development. He earned a Bachelor of Arts from Miami University in public administration and American studies, and a Master of Public Administration from the University of North Carolina at Chapel Hill.

Sharmin Mirman is a writer/artist/musician who sings and plays tenor sax.

Kerry Muir has obsessions that crop up with staggering regularity in jer screenplays, stage plays, short films and literary nonfiction. These include: the surprise element of beauty within the grotesque. The surreal. The drunk and disorderly yearning for love, even for love gone bad. She's prone to write characters who live on the margins, in severe isolation, who simply don't belong.

Tiffany Promise has been published in *Black Clock, Blanket Sea, High Shelf,* and *Gingerbread House.* She received an MFA from CalArts a few years ago, and is currently figuring out how to juggle motherhood and writing. She just completed her first novel.

Ron Pullins is a fiction writer, playwright, and poet working in Tucson, Arizona. His works have been published in numerous journals, and his plays have been produced across the country. He sees his work as an adventure in thought and language. His fiction has been published in numerous journals including *Shenandoah, Kansas Quarterly, Sunspot, Southwest Review, Dark Ink, Steel Toe Review,* and others. More can be found at pullins.com.

Claudia Reed spent seventeen years as a news writer, during which she won an award for investigative journalism. Many of her reports covered actual or potential environmental damage and related health problems. She now facilitates memoir workshops and devotes her time to short fiction and a memoir. A short epistolary memoir was published in *The Letters Page* project at the University of Nottingham. Two short stories took awards in the 2009 Prose Contest sponsored by the California Writers Club's Redwood branch, and "Damnation" received honorable mention in the 2005 EM Koeppel contest.

Christina Robertson has an MA in Clinical Counseling and devoted years to the professional examination of Nature's terrible beauty as it exists within people. Now she writes about it. Her work has appeared in *The Bellevue Literary Review, Anastamos, Midwestern Gothic, Ponder Review,* and in the anthology *Eclectically Heroic* (Inklings Publishing), among others.

Steven B. Rosenfeld is a retired New York lawyer, a graduate of Columbia College and Columbia Law School, who began writing short stories in 2015. Since then, his stories have been published or are forthcoming in *The City Key, Inigo Online,* JewishFiction.net, *Reflex Fiction, Good Works Review, Flatbush Review, The Rush* and *Magnolia Review.* His story "Separation" was a finalist for the 2018 Short Story America Prize, and will be published in the 2019 Short Story America anthology. His flash piece "For the Rest of Our Lives" won the 2018 Writer Advice contest. He has participated in fiction workshops at The Writer's Voice at the West Side Y in New York and at One Story. He is a member of the Columbia Fiction Foundry.

Lory Saiz is an Italian artist, a writer, and a sword-owner particularly interested in LGBT+ media, transformative works, and their intersection with politics and tech.

Janette Schafer is a freelance writer, nature photographer, part-time rocker, and fulltime banker living in Pittsburgh, Pennsylvania. Her play *Mad Virginia* was the winner of the 2018 Pittsburgh Original Short Play Series. Recent and upcoming publications of her writing and photographs include: *Watershed Journal; Yes Ma'am Zine; Feckless Cunt Anthology; Nasty Women & Bad Hombres Anthology;* and *Unlikely Stories V.* She is pursuing her MFA in Creative Writing at Chatham University.

Piero Schiavo-Campo has a degree in physics. After five years in scientific research, he moved on to software. Currently he teaches Theory and Techniques of New Media (the internet and its media-related services) at Università degli Studi, Milano Bicocca. As a sci-fi writer, he has authored various novels and short stories. Schiavo Campo has won the prestigious Urania Award twice for *L'uomo a un grado kelvin* (2013) and *Il sigillo del serpente piumato* (2017) as well as the Robot Award for short stories with "Rotta ai margini del tempo" (2017).

Jesse Sensibar's work has appeared in *The Tishman Review, Stoneboat Journal, Waxwing,* and others. His short fiction was shortlisted for the Bath Flash Fiction Award and the Wilda Hearne Flash Fiction Prize. His first book, *Blood in the Asphalt: Prayers from the Highway* was published in 2018 by Tolsun Press and was shortlisted for the Eric Hoffer Book Award. You can find him at jessesensibar.com.

LD Sledge is a professional author and ghostwriter. He is eighty-four and has accumulated many books, articles, blogs, poems and short stories over those years. He lives in Clearwater, Florida.

Jodee Stanley's work has appeared in the *Mississippi Review, 580 Split, Hobart, Crab Orchard Review, Electric Velocipede, Queen Mob's Teahouse,* and elsewhere. She is the editor of *Ninth Letter,* the literary journal published by the creative writing program at the University of Illinois, Urbana-Champaign.

Pamela Sumners is a constitutional and civil rights attorney from Alabama. Her work was published or recognized by thirty journals and publishing houses in 2018 and 2019. She was selected for inclusion in 2018's *64 Best Poets* and had been nominated for 2019's *50 Best Poets.* She was nominated for a Pushcart prize in 2018. She now lives in St. Louis with her wife, son, and three rescue dogs.

Bob Thurber is the author of *Paperboy: A Dysfunctional Novel* and two collections of short stories. Over the years his work has received a long list of awards and honors, appeared in *Esquire* and other notable publications, and been included in over sixty anthologies. Selections have been utilized as teaching tools in schools and universities worldwide. *Paperboy's* second edition was released in 2016. Bob resides in Massachusetts. BobThurber.net.

Katherine Todd has a B.A. in English from Kansas State University, where she hopes to return to get a Master's Degree in Creative Writing. She has only been published a handful of times. Katherine also has a YouTube channel called "Plots and Whatnots."

Born in Celaya, Guanajuato, Mexico, **Jose Trejo-Maya** spent his childhood in the rural pueblo of Tarimoró until he immigrated in 1988. His inspirations include Netzahualcoyotl, Humberto Ak'abal, Ray A. Young Bear, and James Welch. His work has been published in literary outlets in the UK, US, Spain, India, Australia, Argentina, and Germany. After being nominated for the Pushcart Prize in 2015, he placed in the El Centro Canario Estudios Caribeños–El Atlántico–2016 poetry contest. He was a *New Rivers Press* Many Voices finalist in 2018. While in ceremony with Chololo medicine men in the Tule River Reservation, he dreamt the prophecy written in his poem.

Born in London to British parents and raised bilingual in Italy**, Sarah Jane Webb** grew up in a house full of books and developed a passion for reading and writing. In 2006, she moved with her partner and cats to a hilltop hamlet in sunny Liguria. Inspired by her tranquil surroundings, she translates narrative (mainly speculative fiction) from Italian into English. Her work has appeared in several Anglophone publications, including *The Sunday Times' Crime Club;* Akashic Books' *Fri-SciFi*; the webazine *Speculative Fiction in Translation; Trafika Europe;* and *Words Without Borders.*

Randall Weber-Levine holds a JD from Columbia Law School, a Certificate in International Law from SciencesPo and the Sorbonne, and a BA in philosophy and economics from Colgate University. He is an aspiring writer who has been published in the *Burningword Literary Journal* and the *Morningside Monocle.*

Nina Wilson has published a novel called *Surrender Language.* Other credits include poetry, photography, essays, and short fiction in *Adelaide Magazine, Rascal, Dark River Review, Fishfood Magazine, Coe Review,* and many others. She enjoys photography, hiking, reading horror novels, and fishing. The poem in this edition is the cento form as she loves reading poetry, collecting lines and verses, and connecting them to make something new.

Melinda Winograd studied poetry at the University of North Texas, and currently studies fiction writing at Southern New Hampshire University. Her work has been featured in the *Tulane Review* and High Shelf Press.

Guinotte Wise writes and welds steel sculpture on a farm in Resume Speed, Kansas. His short story collection *Night Train, Cold Beer* won publication by a university press and enough money to fix the soffits. Five more books since. A five-time Pushcart nominee, his fiction and poetry have been published in numerous literary journals including *Atticus, The MacGuffin, Southern Humanities Review, Rattle,* and *The American Journal of Poetry*. His wife has an honest job in the city and drives a hundred miles a day to keep it. Some work is at http://www.wisesculpture.com.

Writing a New World

Sunspot Literary Journal believes in the power of the written word. Fiction, nonfiction, poetry and art can speak truth to power with the power inherent in all human beings. Our mission is to amplify every voice.

Four digital quarterly editions will be produced per year. For the first year (2019), *Sunspot* will product one print volume. Barring solar flares, the number of print editions will increase in 2020.

At times, *Sunspot* will produce special editions. These might be digital only, print only, or both. All will be filled with the same quality content being created by today's unique voices.

Support *Sunspot Lit*

Today more than ever, literary journals are forces of change in the world. *Sunspot Lit* is funded entirely through private means. Every donation, even ones as small as a dollar, makes a difference.

A PayPal link on the website (SunspotLit.com/Support) makes it easy to send a tip, donate enough to publish the next digital edition, or go supernova and fund the next print edition. A tip jar on Submittable allows for donations in preset amounts ranging from $5 to $50.

Advertise in *Sunspot*

Classified ads are available in quarterly digital editions and special editions. Spread the word about your writing and arts contests, residency programs, awards, workshops, and more. All classified ads are also posted on the website's classified page. Ad rate: $150 for up to 25 words; $5 for each additional word.

Print ads are available for the annual edition. All ads are black and white. A full page is $850, a half page is $450, and a quarter page is $295. Buy two ads of the same size for the same issue or for two sequential issues to receive a 10% discount. Set up three or more ads and receive a 15% discount.

Sunspot's groovy graphic designer can set up your ad to your specifications. Flat rate of $325, and the design is yours to use multiple times in *Sunspot* or any other magazine.

SUNSPOT LITERARY JOURNAL
WRITING A NEW WORLD

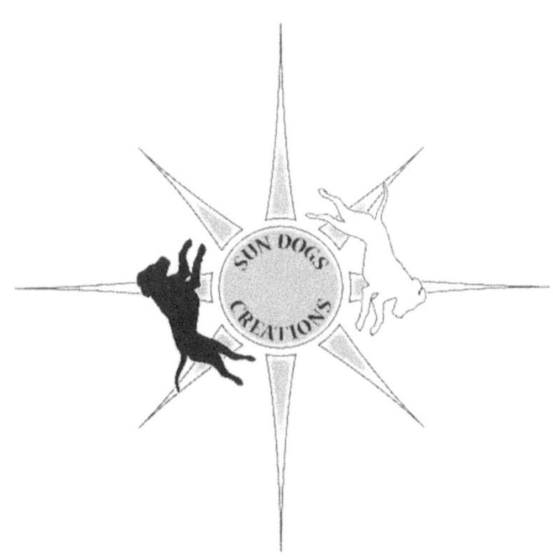

SUN DOGS CREATIONS
CHANGING THE WORLD ONE BOOK AT A TIME

www.ingramcontent.com/pod-product-compliance
Lightning Source LLC
Chambersburg PA
CBHW071152180726
48291CB00007B/2425

* 9 7 8 1 9 5 1 3 8 9 0 0 0 *